AF775813

Ecosystemic Counselling with Children and Young People

Ecosystemic Counselling with Children and Young People

Claire Harrison-Breed
Elisa Gusmini
Ferdinando Salamino
Matt Schofield
Rick Murphy

WILEY

This edition first published 2026
© 2026 John Wiley & Sons Ltd

All rights reserved, including rights for text and data mining and training of artificial intelligence technologies or similar technologies. No part of this publication may be reproduced, stored in a retrieval system, or transmitted, in any form or by any means, electronic, mechanical, photocopying, recording or otherwise, except as permitted by law. Advice on how to obtain permission to reuse material from this title is available at http://www.wiley.com/go/permissions.

The right of author names Claire Harrison-Breed, Elisa Gusmini, Ferdinando Salamino, Matt Schofield, and Rick Murphy to be identified as the authors of this work/the editorial material in this work has been asserted in accordance with law.

Registered Offices

John Wiley & Sons, Inc., 111 River Street, Hoboken, NJ 07030, USA
John Wiley & Sons Ltd, New Era House, 8 Oldlands Way, Bognor Regis, West Sussex, PO22 9NQ, UK

For details of our global editorial offices, customer services, and more information about Wiley products visit us at www.wiley.com.

The manufacturer's authorized representative according to the EU General Product Safety Regulation is Wiley-VCH GmbH, Boschstr. 12, 69469 Weinheim, Germany, e-mail: Product_Safety@wiley.com.

Wiley also publishes its books in a variety of electronic formats and by print-on-demand. Some content that appears in standard print versions of this book may not be available in other formats.

Trademarks: Wiley and the Wiley logo are trademarks or registered trademarks of John Wiley & Sons, Inc. and/or its affiliates in the United States and other countries and may not be used without written permission. All other trademarks are the property of their respective owners. John Wiley & Sons, Inc. is not associated with any product or vendor mentioned in this book.

Limit of Liability/Disclaimer of Warranty: The contents of this work are intended to further general scientific research, understanding, and discussion only and are not intended and should not be relied upon as recommending or promoting scientific method, diagnosis, or treatment by physicians for any particular patient. In view of ongoing research, equipment modifications, changes in governmental regulations, and the constant flow of information relating to the use of medicines, equipment, and devices, the reader is urged to review and evaluate the information provided in the package insert or instructions for each medicine, equipment, or device for, among other things, any changes in the instructions or indication of usage and for added warnings and precautions.While the publisher and the authors have used their best efforts in preparing this work, including a review of the content of the work, neither the publisher nor the authors make any representations or warranties with respect to the accuracy or completeness of the contents of this work and specifically disclaim all warranties, including without limitation any implied warranties of merchantability or fitness for a particular purpose. No warranty may be created or extended by sales representatives, written sales materials or promotional statements for this work. The fact that an organization, website, or product is referred to in this work as a citation and/or potential source of further information does not mean that the publisher and authors endorse the information or services the organization, website, or product may provide or recommendations it may make. This work is sold with the understanding that the publisher is not engaged in rendering professional services. The advice and strategies contained herein may not be suitable for your situation. You should consult with a specialist where appropriate. Further, readers should be aware that websites listed in this work may have changed or disappeared between when this work was written and when it is read. Neither the publisher nor authors shall be liable for any loss of profit or any other commercial damages, including but not limited to special, incidental, consequential, or other damages.

Library of Congress Cataloging-in-Publication Data has been applied for:

Paperback: 9781394381654
oBook: 9781394381685
ePub: 9781394381661
ePdf: 9781394381678

Cover Design: Wiley
Cover Image: annaspoka/stock.adobe.com

Set in 11.5/14pt STIXTwoText by Lumina Datamatics

Printed and bound by CPI Group (UK) Ltd, Croydon, CR0 4YY

C9781394381654_290726

Table of Contents

Preface

Children's counsellors train in tens, if not hundreds, of complicated ideas. We find that therapists in training grow confused by the variety on our university bookshelves, not knowing which ideas will help transform them into confident practitioners. It is for this reason we wrote this book. We want to simplify the main ways of counselling children. As Barry Mason said, we want to make complexity accessible. For years, we have taught integrative counselling in a stepladder-like way: person-centred counselling followed by cognitive-behavioural therapy, psychodynamic theory followed by systemic. While this collection of theories is profoundly life-changing for clients, we have realised that it's possible to combine their main ideas into a single way of working.

This book is a model of counselling that combines the most common children and young people's therapies. We melt cognitive behavioural therapy, Gestalt, person-centred therapy, and other models down to their basic principles, and we remould them into an accessible but rich approach. We call the model ecosystemic counselling with children and young people, and this is because we view the ideas in psychotherapy as originating from four basic levels – all of which explore the child's ecosystem or wider network. The model teaches you to think of counselling as a layered approach, with the child's internal world first, then the family, then society, and then their development. We researched the most effective counselling and psychotherapy modalities and translated their ideas into this four-tiered system – the inner world, the family system, the outer system, and the time system. Our aim in this book is to show students, graduates, and experienced counsellors a new way to think about working with childhood and adolescent wellbeing.

There is a political dimension to our book. Much of the counselling world has treated children as isolated from their family and social contexts. Child psychotherapy is largely based on the child's unconscious and inner self. We are in full agreement with the wider literature on the importance of a child's inner life, but we have found that by emphasising the thoughts, feelings, and behaviours that children carry, we sometimes miss their social context. Racism, ableism, classism, and other forms of social disadvantage take hold of childhood experiences. Children aren't always thinking their thoughts; they're thinking their family's thoughts or their culture's thoughts. Any emotional experience a young person plays out in therapy has a history that stretches back before they were born and is coloured, intensified – if not entirely determined – by how their identity fits or clashes with society's unobtainable standards.

Ecosystemic counselling emerges from the belief that social contexts are not background to the child's emotional life. They are active in every child's self-doubt, worried thought, and crushing feeling. Just as a plant cannot be understood separately from the soil, light, and climate that sustain it, neither can a young person be understood apart from the relationships and environments that shape them. This book is written for counsellors, therapists, trainees, and practitioners who want to work with children in a way that explores their individuality and their context. Our aim is not to replace existing models of therapy but to offer a framework that brings them into conversation with one another. The ecosystemic approach is less a new technique than a way of thinking – a way of asking questions about what is happening in a child's life and why. If there is a single message, we hope readers will carry forward that no child is a problem to be solved. Each child is a developing person embedded in relationships and histories, navigating the challenges of growing up as best they can. We invite you, therefore, to read this book as a practical framework for thinking and working effectively with children and young people. We hope it encourages you to look widely, listen deeply, and work creatively with the children and young people who trust you to help them.

Claire, Elisa, Ferdinando, Matt, and Rick

Chapter 1
Why an Ecosystemic Approach to Counselling Children and Young People?

Imagine a goldfish in a bowl. The fish glides in circles, its world bounded by glass. We add decorations ... a plastic castle, a few bright-green fronds of imitation seaweed, even a toy chest to suggest mystery and adventure. Then, with the best of intentions, we feed it. And feed it again. The fish appears content, darting eagerly at each pinch of flakes. Yet slowly, the water clouds, the surface dulls, and the bowl begins to sour. All the while, our attention remains on the fish, never the medium in which it swims. Only when illness sets in do we notice the neglected system, the invisible water on which life depends.

Counselling children is not unlike this. Too often, our focus narrows to the child-as-individual, as though problems float in isolation, sealed from their surroundings. In therapy rooms across the world, we hear colleagues insist that bringing in families or wider contexts risks diluting the child's voice. And, of course, the child's voice is sacred: it deserves protection and its own space. But to hear the child without hearing the system is to tend lovingly to the goldfish while ignoring the dirtying bowl. Safety, growth, and healing arise not simply from what is inside the child but from the quality of the environment that holds them. This is the starting point for an ecosystemic approach to counselling young people. In this book, we will introduce you to its theory and practice, guiding you through its four interconnected layers.

Let's imagine that a counsellor has sat down to read a new referral that was placed on her desk. In hurried handwriting, it briefly describes a British Pakistani girl of 12, Aisha, in her second year of secondary school. The referral reads that her mother requested support after she had grown worried about Aisha's frequent outbursts and long silences at home. One section noted her teacher's observations, "bright but gets distracted recently," and recorded a pattern of withdrawing from her peer group. Another teacher documented Aisha's own words, just four of them: "I don't like school." Beneath, the pastoral worker had simply jotted that Aisha "does not understand why." Counselling was arranged by the school to begin next week.

The notes offered little else. On paper, Aisha appeared as a set of symptoms. Changes in behaviour that, whilst worrying, made little sense of the meaning of her difficulties or the wider world in which she lives. Yet, it is from this kind of starting point that many therapists first begin their work with children and young people and where an ecosystemic approach begins to ask questions. In this chapter, we will introduce the five fundamental questions in ecosystemic therapy: How does the child experience their world? What does family life contribute or take away from the problem? Which social systems like friendships, school, and societal norms help us make sense of the difficulties? Why is this happening now rather than at some other time?

When we return to Aisha in the pages ahead, we will see that her story is more complex and that her behaviour is more coherent than the referral suggests. Behind words like "outburst" and "withdrawal" lies a living network of feelings, relationships, and contexts. It is in those wider patterns that her world, and the possibilities for change, begin to take shape.

Ecosystemic Counselling: The Key Ideas

When we think about Aisha's world, we might imagine a phone buzzing with unanswered messages, exercise books left untouched at the bottom of her bag, a crumpled note from school about another disagreement with peers, or the bedroom door pulled shut. But a child's world is not just a set of objects; it is a system of living processes. As ecosystemic counsellors, we see the child's feelings, thoughts, relationships, and environments as woven together in constant interaction. Many therapy models find it helpful to separate the child's world into smaller pieces, with emotions and behaviours here, family life there, schooling in another area, and social identity aside from all that. And these divisions are convenient for making complexity accessible, but they fragment the child's reality and blind us to them as a whole person.

Similarly, the systems around the child can often provide a limited picture of their difficulties, as seen in referrals like Aisha's that rarely go beyond describing challenging behaviours and symptoms. Counselling, when it is truly alive to systems, invites us to see a child not as a problem to be solved but as a participant in overlapping biological, cognitive, behavioural, cultural, and ecological networks. What looks like "anger" may be better understood as a loop between body tension, family stress, and school pressure. What seems like "shyness" might be a finely tuned adaptation to group dynamics, a way of staying safe in peer relationships. To think systemically is to see beyond the symptom, to notice the patterns that maintain it, and to imagine the wider possibilities for change.

In this book we will explore the four layers of a child's ecosystem through the different systems that shape their growth. We will begin at the most intimate level, which is the inner world of feelings, thoughts, and bodily signals. From there, we will move outward to the family system, where patterns of communication and belonging shape identity in profound ways. Beyond the family lies the peer group, classroom, and culture that form the child's larger social climate. Finally, we will trace the role of time, that great unseen system, in shaping growth, transition, and change.

These four layers are not separate compartments but nested worlds. Each contains and influences the others, like ripples in a pond. A disturbance in one reverberates through the rest. A child whose nervous system is perpetually on edge may struggle at school; difficulties at school may ripple back into family tensions; family tensions may amplify the child's inner unease. Conversely, an attuned ecosystemic counsellor can help support the system, softening family stress and helping the child's body to relax.

Within each section of the book, you will find simple tools, including maps, drawings, and exercises, that help children and families make sense of their own systems. These tools invite children to picture their feelings, map their relationships, and discover resources that already exist around them. The act of mapping is itself therapeutic. To draw one's inner world or family pattern is to step back, observe, and realise: I am part of a system, and systems can change. In what follows, then, we will journey layer by layer through the child's ecosystem, guided by a curiosity about patterns and possibilities. We will begin with the child's inner world, exploring thoughts, feelings, and how relationships live within us.

Part 1: The Child's Internal World – Thoughts, Feelings, and the Body

Consider the situation where Aisha sits on the edge of her bed, pulling her school jumper over her knees. In half an hour she's supposed to leave for the bus, but her stomach is tight again, like a knot she can't untie. She tells herself, "If I stay very quiet, maybe no one will notice me today," yet she longs for a teacher to ask how she is. The image of her father's last cancelled visit flickers across her mind: "Maybe he forgot because I'm not important." Her eyes sting, but she blinks hard, and crying makes her mother worry. She hears her younger brothers shouting downstairs and feels protective but slightly resentful.

Aisha strokes the sleeve of her jumper in slow circles, a habit that calms her racing thoughts. She imagines herself in one of her fantasy stories, invisible under a magic cloak. Her heart thumps; she can almost hear the bus engine in the distance. She wonders if she should tell the school nurse about the stomach-ache but worries she'll be told to "just get on with it." Aisha's morning routine gives us a window into a child's inner world. In the few moments before school, she is already holding multiple experiences at once: a tight stomach, private thoughts about being forgotten, a wish for someone to notice, and a fear of what might happen if anyone did. In therapy, we rarely meet these experiences as directly as described. Instead, they emerge in indirect ways: a child's posture or tone of voice, the feeling left in the therapist at the end of the session, drawings, metaphors, or the stories they tell. Learning to listen to these channels is one of the core skills of counselling children and young people.

This "inner world" is not just a collection of thoughts and emotions; it is a whole system of expectations, memories, and bodily states built up through the child's relationships. Relational experiences guide the child's expectations over time: the often-unspoken beliefs about self ("I'm not important"), about others ("adults may not notice me"), and about the world ("school is unsafe") that shape how a child anticipates and interprets new experiences. When we meet a child like Aisha, we notice that the surface behaviours point to a rich and complex inner world. Beneath a stomach-ache, an outburst, or a quiet withdrawal lies an interwoven matrix of thoughts, feelings, memories, and beliefs.

The focus for the first section of this book is to explore the child's inner world. Describing how therapists can help children and young people to tune into their experiences, particularly the thoughts, feelings, and bodily sensations that lie out of awareness. It invites therapists to ask questions like "What story might the body be telling?" "What meaning might the child be making of what's happening?" "How might past experiences be echoing in the present moment?" and "What does the child hope for when they hide or show their feelings?" When we slow down and notice these signals, we begin to meet the child not just as a set of behaviours to be managed but as a person whose inner world can be felt, understood, and held. As Aisha's story shows, every child brings a unique inner world, shaped by their history, culture, individual development, and current context. This inner dimension lies at the core of ecosystemic work: therapy begins with seeing and feeling alongside the child, the subjective, moment-to-moment experience of thoughts, feelings, sensations, and meanings. The therapist pays attention to their bodily signals, honouring their unspoken thoughts and feelings, and offering a safe relationship.

Practically, this calls for questioning and listening tools that prioritise presence, curiosity, and careful pacing. We draw on techniques such as active listening, which is not merely repeating what the child says but tuning into the emotional and embodied resonance of their words. Active listening involves paraphrasing, gentle summarising, and empathic reflections that help the child feel heard and understood on a deep level. We will also introduce techniques like phenomenological inquiry, which is about asking questions that open up experience without interpreting or judging it. For instance, "Aisha, what's it like for you when you're in class?" or "Where do you feel that in your body?" These questions invite the child to explore, rather than explain, their world.

By creating space for the child's experience to emerge organically, we allow patterns of experience to become visible from the inside out. Here, we are not guiding the child towards our truth; we're walking beside them as they find their own. And we will find that there are limits to centring on the child's inner world.

However deeply we listen to the child's experience, we will find that their family life frequently comes into view. Knowing how to navigate between the inner world and the family is one of the cornerstones of ecosystemic counselling.

Part 2: The Family System – Relationships at Home

The second section of the book explores how family life impacts the child's referral concerns. Returning to Aisha helps us see how her worries, emotions, and ways of making sense of herself are connected to patterns of interaction at home.

Imagine that we can hear the clatter of pans downstairs as Aisha's mother gets breakfast ready for her younger brothers. The house feels smaller in the mornings, full of movement and noise. Since her stepfather moved in last year, the routine has changed: stricter rules, more chores, and a louder atmosphere. Aisha often ends up helping to find the boys' school shoes or pack their lunch boxes before she can finish her homework. She loves them but sometimes dislikes the way their needs seem to take priority.

Her mother, who has recently increased her working hours at the local cafe, is usually tired, and Aisha tries not to add to her worries. She rarely talks to her stepfather except when being told what to do; he expects respect and obedience but seldom asks about her day. Her biological father just moved to another city with his new partner and calls irregularly. Each time he cancels a visit, Aisha feels a sting of disappointment mixed with anger, but she hides her feelings to avoid upsetting others.

Aisha's morning scene hints at her family world: a mother rushing to get everyone ready, younger brothers demanding attention, a stepfather whose rules have changed the household rhythm, and a father whose visits come and go. Even before she reaches school, Aisha is already navigating shifting loyalties, hidden feelings, and unspoken expectations. This illustrates why understanding the family system is such an important part of therapeutic work with children and young people like her. Family life shows how a child's inner world is constantly shaped by the relationships, rules, and stories that surround them. Counselling referrals often come through parents or carers and, therefore, reflect the family's hopes, fears, and expectations. Ecosystemic therapists approach families from a position of curiosity, allowing us to enter a family system we do not yet fully know. We aren't trying to diagnose or correct them, only to explore how the everyday household norms influence a child's experience of self and others.

Holding this attitude also helps us step back from our own assumptions. Many psychological ideas about "family" have grown out of Western, heteronormative models; without awareness, these can colour how we interpret what we see. A curious, respectful approach acknowledges that families organise themselves in many ways and that these arrangements have their own meanings and histories but also their effects. From this position, we can start to notice how a household is structured and how roles and responsibilities shift with time; how relationships between members form alliances or tensions; how stories circulate, which ones dominate, and which are silenced; how the family relates to the world outside; how emotions are expressed or contained; and how help is offered or accepted. Exploring these interconnected aspects does not mean imposing "better" patterns but opening space for the child and family to see themselves differently.

In Aisha's case, family exploration might reveal how her self-soothing, her silence, and her anger are not just individual reactions but expressions of the family system in which she grows. Exploring these areas helps us understand the context in which her presenting difficulties arise. Tools such as genograms and ecomaps can provide a visual scaffold for these conversations, and we will explore these later in the book.

Families are not static but move through lifecycles and external changes, constantly adjusting their rules, relationships, and stories. By holding a stance of respectful curiosity about the whole system, we begin to see the child as a person embedded in a living network of relationships that shape, and are shaped by, their inner world. We will describe how and why an ecosystemic therapist explores:

Family Structure: the way boundaries, roles, and rules are negotiated over time, with different life stages in mind.
Family Dynamics: the way relationships develop, including attachment relationships, cooperation and competition between members, and alliances and coalitions.
Family Meaning Making: the way stories emerge in family conversations, what narratives are dominant and which ones are suppressed, untold, or unheard.

From an ecosystemic perspective, family exploration uses specific questioning approaches that make relational patterns more visible and, therefore, more open to change. We will introduce ways of talking with children about their family worlds that highlight roles, expectations, loyalties, and unspoken rules – not to assign blame but to increase understanding. As these patterns come into view, difficulties that once seemed to belong solely to the child can be recognised as part of wider relational processes. This shift often brings relief because the problem is no longer who the child is but how the system has learned to operate. By helping children notice these patterns, we open possibilities for new positions, new responses, and new stories about themselves within their families. But, like centring on the inner world, seeing from a family lens also has its blind spots. Where do families get their beliefs from? What pressures or expectations are families navigating? Questions such as these lead us to add another layer to the ecosystemic model, which is the impact of the wider social context.

Part 3: The Outer System – School, Friends, Culture

Now let's follow Aisha as she walks quickly through the crowded corridor of the school, her bag clutched tight. Since starting Year 7, she has begun wearing the hijab most days, a choice that feels important to her but also makes her feel more exposed. Some classmates have asked clumsy questions about "why she covers her hair" or joked that she "must be hot under there." Teachers tell her not to take it personally, but she finds the comments confusing and isolating. At lunchtime, she often slips into the library, where it's quieter, and she can read or write stories about characters that live between two worlds.

Her closest friend from primary school still talks to her but sits with a different group now. Aisha enjoys Qur'an class at the mosque twice a week, where she feels part of a familiar rhythm, but she rarely talks about it at school. In her notebook she draws bridges and hidden doorways, pictures of movement between places that only she understands.

Though a referral may present Aisha as self-contained, and her presenting issues in therapy may intuitively feel self-located, they are always afloat in a sea of family and social relationships. As we discussed in the previous section, the child's emotions or outbursts do not drift in empty space. They are born from millions of emotion-laden interactions with their family members, and this section, this outer world layer, adds in the social context of teachers, classmates, neighbours, institutions, cultural stories, and social symbols. The child's struggles and their successes, often presented to a counsellor as though they were self-generated from a fixed personality, are understandable as dependent on vast social systems.

Thinking systemically is about resisting the fiction that children are solitary. We are tempted, in a culture of individualism, to locate problems inside a person, as if anxiety were a private possession or resilience a personal medal. But anxiety in children like Aisha is a layered signal of cultural alienation and isolation. Resilience arises not as a personal trait but as a distributed resource, spanning teachers, friends, uncles, cousins, coaches, and safe adults who together absorb life's shocks. This third ecosystemic layer focuses on the outer system: the circle of school, friends, and culture that shapes the family and the child's developing self.

Ecosystemic counselling says that the wider environment is not background noise; it is the defining medium in which presenting and family issues take form. Just as a fish cannot be understood apart from its water, a child cannot be understood apart from their school, peers, and culture. School is perhaps the single most consistent ecosystem of childhood outside the family, and it is not merely a place for academic tasks. It's a place for figuring out what emotions are socially acceptable, experimenting with gender identity, practising religious beliefs, learning age-appropriate behaviours, and solidifying the self-image. A child who thrives in a small, nurturing classroom may wither in a busy secondary school with shifting teachers and large peer groups. A religious child's curiosity can be strengthened or silenced depending on whether their beliefs are framed as acceptable or unusual. Emotional outbursts might signal a concerning change in the social environment.

We take the view that society and peers are the social mirror by which children evaluate themselves. If Aisha's peers respond sensitively to her, she becomes more self-confident. But if her beliefs or quietness are responded to with hostility or rejection, then it is rarely just the cruelty of one child towards another. It's often more of a systemic storm, sustained by silent-but-mocking bystanders and institutional blind spots. A culture that discriminates against shyness and religiosity, for example, will create harsher school environments for some children and families. For counsellors, listening to stories of friendship and discrimination is as important as listening to emotions and fears. Each story reveals the psychological climate in which the child must survive.

As such, children are not blank slates. Shy and confident behaviour is possible because children inherit culture. Their race, ability, language, religion, and social class are fundamental parts of their experience. The social context advantages and disadvantages different children, and their behaviour communicates this loudly. A child who sees their culture reflected positively in school life feels valued and secure. One who never hears their language spoken, or who endures stereotyping, absorbs corrosive messages about their worth. We think that counselling that ignores culture risks colluding with discrimination. An ecosystemic approach encourages a widening of the lens, acknowledging that each child's struggle is entangled with histories and structures larger than themselves. For children navigating marginalisation, due to race, neurodivergence, gender identity, or language, these tools can be profoundly validating.

Overall, the third layer of ecosystemic counselling puts forward the following perspective: effective counselling is not just an internal or a family journey; it's an ecosystemic intervention, one that helps children thrive in the wider world. The ecosystemic model encourages counsellors to look within and around the child but also beyond them, towards the broader social, educational, and cultural structures that shape who they are and what they can become. In this book, we describe how the therapeutic task is not always to go deeper but sometimes to widen the field, making room for the full complexity of a child's world.

Part 4: The Time System – A Child's Growth over Time

Over the past two years, Aisha has been growing quickly. She has shot up in height, her voice is lower and steadier, and she is noticing mood changes she cannot always explain. Puberty has brought a new awareness of privacy and self-consciousness that sometimes surprises her family. While her younger brothers still play noisily in the living room, Aisha now prefers to close her door and write or draw. She is starting to think more abstractly about the future, imagining careers, weighing up her beliefs, and questioning rules she once accepted.

At the same time her family is in its own period of transition. Her mother is working more hours, her stepfather's work shifts are unpredictable, and her father's visits have become less frequent. Extended relatives are also moving through lifecycle changes: a grandmother's illness, an aunt's new baby. These events subtly alter the patterns of attention, care, and expectation around Aisha. She senses that the adults are busier and sometimes less available, just as her need for guidance is changing. At the same time, she is often conflicted between reaching out to her parents for a hug and a cuddle and the desire to distance herself from them, with their strict rules and their old-fashioned principles.

As Aisha's story shows, change is inevitable. Children develop physically and emotionally; families adjust to new jobs, new members, losses, separations and migrations; communities shift in values and resources. Each of these movements can either unsettle or support a child, depending on how it is experienced and held. The development of the family across time provides scaffolding for the child's own growth. As boundaries, roles, and expectations are renegotiated, children test out autonomy and belonging within that framework. When adults manage change with some predictability and openness, children are more likely to feel secure enough to explore and develop. In Aisha's vignette, understanding changes in this interplay of individual and family life helps us see her worries and self-soothing not as isolated "symptoms" but as ways of negotiating continuity and connection in a moving system.

In ecosystemic counselling, we see children face the task of making sense of life's transitions. In this respect, adjusting to new dynamics and roles may at times feel like trying to merge onto a very busy motorway. Some parts of the drive are smooth, others are bumpy, and there is limited time to complete the trip. To complicate matters, the sat-nav occasionally loses signal and sends you completely the wrong way! The fourth ecosystemic layer will take this idea further, inviting you to think about how children and families sometimes find themselves "lost" on their journey together and need to pause, reroute, or simply take stock. It will look at how growth often arises in moments of honest communication, identifying resources and sharing experience. Over time, families create new traditions and experience moments of healing that mark how far they have travelled.

We know from the research that how an individual, family, or culture navigates change can be extremely influential in contributing to their wellbeing. Ranging from common events such as a birth or a couple moving in together, to life-changing crises such as the loss of a child or major degenerative illness of one member, families are requested to prepare emotionally and practically to deal with responsibilities and developmental tasks that come with change and transition. In our example, Aisha and her family try to navigate a transition involving a progressively detached biological father, a new birth coming, and an elderly member losing their health. This is all while they also try to make sense of the child's bodily and personality changes in the household. Her mum is redefining her identity as a working mother, her stepdad is struggling to adjust to a new family with different rules and roles, and he's navigating ways to build a relationship with someone else's daughter. At the same time, the world around them continues to shift, marked by new cultural tensions and changing expectations around gender.

In the ecosystemic model, it is important to explore transitions without judgement so that every unique way of facing transformations is valued. Children grow within temporal rhythms: losses, seasons, school years, and anniversaries. The past is alive in the present; the future is often a source of anxiety or hope. We apply tools such as timelines about key moments, changes, and developmental shifts related to their presenting difficulty. This is not only to process past events but to help them construct a coherent narrative of who they are becoming. This includes the use of therapeutic rituals around endings, goodbyes, and milestones. The counselling session and journey are deconstructed into a timeline for us to consider how we use time as a healer to empower each child. These rituals respect the temporal depth of experience and offer a way for children to integrate change rather than merely endure it.

Part 5: Applying the Ecosystemic Model to Children's Presenting Difficulties

Children and young people do not usually arrive in therapy speaking the language of systems. Like Aisha, they come described in the language of concern: "anxious," "depressed," "angry," "obsessive," "out of control." Parents, teachers, and sometimes children themselves use these words to make sense of struggle. In the wider culture, these labels are often medicalised, linked to ideas of "disorder" or "symptom." As ecosystemic counsellors, we do not dismiss these terms; they can be a useful shorthand and, for families, sometimes a relief to name what has felt overwhelming. But our role is not to treat a diagnostic category. Our role is to understand the child-in-context and to respond to the particular loops of experience that have given rise to distress.

The fifth and final section of the book describes how to use the ecosystemic model practically in your role as a counsellor. We describe how an ecosystemic counsellor might, for example, work with anxiety across the four ecosystems. We might listen to an overactive nervous system, validate a parent's fearfulness, and draw a classroom atmosphere of performance pressure. "Anxiety" is not a thing located inside the child; it is a pattern sustained by body, relationship, and social values. Similarly, what might be called "depression" may be seen as the weight of accumulated losses, moves between foster homes, ruptured friendships, or cultural dislocation that have settled in the child's body and sense of self. Even behaviours described as "OCD" can be reframed as cunning, if exhausting, attempts to restore a sense of order in a chaotic system. Ecosystemic work does not ask the counsellor to ignore diagnostic or problem language, nor to argue against it with families or schools. Instead, it invites therapists to hold labels lightly, as one description among many. The tools we will teach in the final section of the book will help the child move from problem descriptions of themselves towards more empowering ways of seeing themselves, helping them join the dots between their feelings, family, social world, and change.

This work calls for attunement on multiple levels and, with it, an array of tools that are themselves deep yet systemic in orientation: techniques that invite connection, reflection, mapping, and movement. In this section, we explore the practical application of the model, with a focus on techniques and modes of inquiry appropriate to each domain of the child's ecosystem. The application of the ecosystemic model is not a step-by-step formula but a way of attending, a shift from intervention to relationship, from problem-solving to system-seeing. It draws on tools that bring clarity and that seek connection. It recognises the child not as a unit of suffering but as a being-in-context, always embedded, always becoming themselves.

Throughout the chapters which follow, you will see how the ecosystemic model can be applied to real-life presentations. Each part of the child's system – inner world, family, social environment, and development over time – offers specific entry points for understanding and supporting children. An anxious child may benefit from learning body-based regulation (inner world) but also from shifts in family reassurance cycles (family system), classroom expectations (outer system), and support during a transition (time system). What looks like one "problem" becomes many possible routes for change.

For trainees beginning their practice, this stance can be freeing but challenging. It is freeing because you are not required to become an expert in every counselling modality or diagnosis. It is challenging because it resists the comfort of fixed categories like cognitive-behavioural therapy or person-centred therapy, instead inviting you to think in patterns, relationships, and processes. Chapters 10–12 will model this way of thinking, offering case examples and tools that bring ecosystemic insight to the everyday struggles with which children and young people present. By the end of the book, our hope is that you will feel equipped to meet whatever label or difficulty a child brings, not with a treatment protocol but with a present and caring ecosystemic perspective. In doing so, you can honour both the individuality of the child and the wider networks that shape their growth.

Bibliography

Bateson, G. (1972). *Steps to an Ecology of Mind: Collected Essays in Anthropology, Psychiatry, Evolution, and Epistemology*. San Francisco, CA: Chandler Publishing.

Beck, A.T. (1976). *Cognitive Therapy and the Emotional Disorders*. New York, NY: International Universities Press.

Bowen, M. (1978). *Family Therapy in Clinical Practice*. New York, NY: Jason Aronson.

Bowlby, J. (1988). *A Secure Base: Parent–child Attachment and Healthy Human Development*. London, England: Routledge.

Byng-Hall, J. (1985). The family script: a useful bridge between theory and practice. *Journal of Family Therapy* 7 (3): 301–305.

Byng-Hall, J. (1995). *Rewriting Family Scripts: Improvisation and Systems Change*. New York, NY: Guilford Press.

Carter, B. and McGoldrick, M. (1999). *The expanded Family Life Cycle: Individual, Family, and Social Perspectives*, 3e. Boston, MA: Allyn & Bacon.

Dallos, R. and Draper, R. (2010). *An Introduction to Family Therapy: Systemic Theory and Practice*, 3e. Maidenhead, England: Open University Press.

Dallos, R. and Vetere, A. (2009). *Systemic Therapy and Attachment Narratives: Applications in a Range of Clinical Settings*. London, England: Routledge.

Egan, G. (2014). The Skilled Helper: A Problem-management and Opportunity-development approach to Helping, 10c. Belmont, CA: Brooks/Cole.

Erikson, E.H. (1963). *Childhood and Society*, 2e. New York, NY: Norton.

Freud, S. (1923). *The Ego and the Id*. London, England: Hogarth Press.

Gendlin, E.T. (1978). *Focusing*. New York, NY: Everest House.

Lambert, M.J. (1992). Psychotherapy outcome research: implications for integrative and eclectic therapists. In: *Handbook of Psychotherapy Integration* (ed. J.C. Norcross and M.R. Goldfried), 94–129. New York, NY: Basic Books.

Lambert, M.J. (1999). Are common factors the central issue in psychotherapy research? A review of research and a critique of methodology. In: *The Heart and Soul of Change: What Works in Therapy* (ed. M.A. Hubble, B.L. Duncan, and S.D. Miller), 33–55. Washington, DC: American Psychological Association.

Lambert, M.J. and Barley, D.E. (2001). Research summary on the therapeutic relationship and psychotherapy outcome. *Psychotherapy: Theory, Research, Practice, Training* 38 (4): 357–361.

McGoldrick, M., Gerson, R., and Petry, S. (2008). *Genograms: Assessment and Intervention*, 3e. New York, NY: Norton.

Minuchin, S. (1974). *Families and Family Therapy*. Cambridge, MA: Harvard University Press.

Norcross, J.C. and Lambert, M.J. (2011). Psychotherapy relationships that work II. *Psychotherapy* 48 (1): 4–8.

Patterson, J. and Fisher, C. (2002). *Clinical Applications of Bowen Family Systems Theory*. New York, NY: Haworth.

Rogers, C.R. (1951). *Client-centered Therapy: Its Current Practice, Implications, and Theory*. Boston, MA: Houghton Mifflin.

Satir, V. (1983). *Conjoint Family Therapy*, 3e. Palo Alto, CA: Science and Behavior Books.

Stern, D.N. (1985). *The Interpersonal World of the Infant: A View from Psychoanalysis and Developmental Psychology*. New York, NY: Basic Books.

Wampold, B.E. and Imel, Z.E. (2015). *The Great Psychotherapy Debate: The Evidence for What makes Psychotherapy Work*, 2e. New York, NY: Routledge.

Winnicott, D.W. (1965). *The Maturational Processes and the Facilitating Environment*. London, England: Hogarth Press.

Yalom, I.D. (2002). *The Gift of Therapy: An Open Letter to a New Generation of Therapists and their Patients*. London, England: Piatkus.

Chapter 2
Understanding the Child's Inner World

The clock read 1:30 pm. It was time for Jordan's session, and sure enough he announced his arrival at the therapy room with a loud roar, leaping round the door to surprise the counsellor. He looked expectantly for signs of shock. They were easy to see; the counsellor had jumped out of her skin. "You got me that time!" she said playfully. A smile spread across his face before he abruptly ordered his teaching assistant to "go away," shutting the door firmly behind them. Next, Jordan turned to his shoes. "Come on then. I'm going to win!" he shouted, furiously pulling at his shoes whilst gesturing for the counsellor to do the same. "This is the way you want us to begin today," she reflected with animation, as they performed what had now become a weekly ritual. With shoes off, Jordan grabbed the monster puppet and began running around the room, erupting into further roars. Their work had already begun.

Jordan often played with monsters in his sessions. Monsters that would attack the counsellor, put her down, or beat her at games. Monsters that were powerful, invulnerable, and dominant. Jordan's play revealed an inner world full of terrible creatures, and the counsellor couldn't help but recall the social worker's account of his life history. A story of domestic violence, a father in prison, and a mother and grandmother who were unable to care for him. A home that bore the scars of uncontained aggression and a move to residential care, many hours from home. The monsters of his imagination spoke to his monstrous past: experiences seeped in fear, rage, and violence. The monsters encountered in therapy were rich metaphors for environments that had rarely felt safe. But Jordan's monsters weren't only echoes of the past; they were invitations in the present. Each roar, each attack, each effort to take control tested how the counsellor would respond, whether she could be bullied, pushed away, or provoked into becoming a monster too. His play represented part of a living feedback loop, shaped by what he had already learned from adults and alert to what might happen next.

As Jordan's imagination shows, children and young people bring powerful communications of their inner world to therapy, giving therapists a visceral sense of what it might be like to live in their minds and bodies. Playing with monsters is one manifestation of this internal landscape, but children reveal aspects of themselves in many forms, through drawing, poetry, music, posture, patterns of engagement, and even in how they dress. A rich body of counselling theory helps us understand the language of symbol, metaphor, drama, and visual image – and how it opens doors to children and young people's inner lives. Yet this literature has historically been less attuned to the ways in which these inner worlds act not only as repositories of past experiences but as a set of responses that maintain and shape relationships in the present. This chapter examines how the world of imagination, beliefs, bodily states, and behavioural responses develops, what functions they serve, and why they remain essential for the ecosystemic therapist to hold in mind in their work.

A Relational Blueprint

Children's inner worlds do not exist in isolation; they emerge within a relational field. Even genes related to a child's temperament are expressed and moderated through the environment in which the child develops. Humans are ultimately social creatures, and, unlike other mammals, we are born entirely dependent on the care of others to meet our needs. After all, a human baby is born with a brain only 25% of its adult size, meaning the bulk of neurodevelopment takes place postnatally, in the context of the social environment. The relational field, therefore, plays an outsized role in shaping the quality of a child's internal world. This field is coloured by the different familial, cultural, political, and developmental layers covered across this book, but the focus of this chapter is the role of the primary attachment relationship. As in all systems, this relationship is not one way. The child is influenced by, but also influences, the quality of their caregiving. For a child such as Jordan, his early experiences of relationships were monstrous. But in turn these experiences influence how he responds to adults in the present, increasing the likelihood of further patterns of relational rupture and disengagement. A closer look at the attachment relationship explains how this happens.

A child first learns about relationships through their primary caregivers. In some families this may be one person; in others care is shared amongst several people within the household or community. Even at the very first stages of development, the relationship between caregiver and infant is reciprocal. The baby's calls, gaze, and bodily movements communicate needs and wants, eliciting caregiver responses that in turn shape how the baby communicates. This has typically been called call and response but, from a systemic perspective, might be thought of as a continuous feedback loop. What begins as a dance of two individuals attuning to each other becomes the child's first sense of what kind of world they live in and what kind of self they need to be within it. Rather than a simple sequence of cause and effect, it is a self-organising dialogue through which patterns of expectation, regulation, and meaning gradually emerge. This iterative process allows the child to learn about others' trustworthiness, predictability, and sensitivity and to adjust to this environment accordingly.

The child's ability to adapt to their environment is one of the key insights from attachment theory. Mary Ainsworth noted that children's adaptations follow predictable patterns (attachment "styles") and are informed by unconscious expectations that she named internal working models. As the interactions between child and mother typically follow a pattern, like a dance, the child's internal systems adjust to the rhythm, pace, and tone of this dance. Or to put it another way, over time, the child's nervous system settles into patterns that best fit the caregiving environment and maintain a predictable to-and-fro. How the child thinks, believes, feels, acts, and experiences the world matters in keeping the dance synchronised.

Pause and Reflect

- What were the early rhythms between you and your caregiver/s?
- How has the back-and-forth of early relationships influenced you today?

Embodied Beginnings

The child's internal world begins in the body. Infants' first experiences are rooted in touch and sensation. They come to know comfort through the feel of the breast or bottle in their mouth, the secure hold of a caregiver's arms, or the gentle sound of being sung to sleep. These preverbal experiences cannot be put into words and are encoded in patterns of bodily sensation. The tone of the caregiving relationship is imprinted in the nervous system. When a baby cries and is gathered up quickly, their body learns that distress leads to soothing. The heartbeat slows, breath deepens, muscles release. Long before words, safety is remembered as a bodily shift from tension to calm.

The baby's body offers few options for self-regulation in the first months of life. It is the caregiver who must act as an external regulator, attending to the baby's need for feeding, warmth, cleanliness, and comfort. Without this support, the baby is vulnerable to both physical and emotional overwhelm. Imagine a baby who is distressed and alone. Without external comfort and soothing from their caregiver, the baby quickly becomes overwhelmed, moving through stages of alertness and then distress, dysregulation, and eventual psychological collapse, falling back on emergency resources such as withdrawal or dissociation.

Without a responsive caregiver, the child does not become familiar with their own body. Bodily cues are perceived by seeing them mirrored in the caregiver's facial expressions and timely, accurate responses. What we call mirroring gives meaning to what would otherwise remain frightening and unintegrated bodily sensations, making the child's emotional and physical needs both knowable and predictable. Without this mirroring, the child's sadness, hunger, tiredness, or pain remain split off from experience, as we often see with young people who cannot name or feel their own emotions.

Pause and Reflect

- When different emotions arise (tiredness, overwhelm, sadness, anxiety, calm), what are the first bodily signals you tend to notice? Is it your breath, muscles, posture, temperature, energy, or something else?
- How easy or difficult is it for you to recognise these bodily cues as they're happening, and what do you think shaped that ease or difficulty?

Emerging Patterns

Whilst the child's internal world emerges through the body, it is an ecosystem that evolves and becomes more complex with development. At around nine months, children's internal working models have typically settled into a coherent "style," reflecting the infant-caregiver pair's achievement of finding a familiar and consistent relational dance. As the child grows older, this style comes to shape not only bodily responses and behaviour towards their caregiver but the child's emotional sense of self and beliefs about the world. Their attachment style can be secure or insecure, and this depends on the caregiver's attunement. When a child learns to predict caregiver safety, they regulate emotions well and trust themselves to explore their environment. Secure parents only attune about 30% of the time, but "good enough" parental attunement rears children who are self-confident and emotionally resilient.

For children like Jordan, where caregiving environments were unpredictable, frightening, or dangerous, a range of protective attachment responses may be adopted in order to survive. Jordan alternated between controlling, frightening, and disarming behaviour to navigate unsafe interactions with adults. The insecure attachment style shows itself in Jordan's monstrous play. When he playfully attacks the counsellor, he physicalises his inner world. His message is that connecting with other people feels unsafe, and he must push people away. Acceptance from the counsellor provides enough safety for his inner world to explore itself. The temptation is to shut down insecure and aggressive play, especially when a child's aggression seems to take a worrying aim at the counsellor. John Bowlby said that nothing helps children more than being safely able to express hostile feelings. He said that one of the most valuable parental tasks is accepting a child's expressions of hate. Withstanding an emotional outburst shows children that we are not afraid of difficult feelings. This provides children with a tolerant environment that encourages self-growth. The ecosystemic counsellor sees through the monster play, confident that safety for horrible feelings will help the child to emotionally regulate.

Other insecurely attached children, rather than aiming hostility towards caregivers or counsellors, may learn that taking care of parents is the best way to survive. The lesson of attachment research and systemic thinking is that children's adaptations make sense in the context of their environments. The difficulties these strategies pose for the child often only emerge when children move into new environments like school, where these ways of relating are no longer helpful and where vigilance, mistrust, or control constrain rather than protect them. The parentified inner world shows up in different kinds of play. Themes of looking after others, subtle resentments about caregivers, and exaggeratedly polite play permeate the counselling room. An ecosystemic counsellor views both scenarios in a similar way, despite them looking opposite. They are both insecure attachment processes made visible by the child's feelings, behaviours, and play. We discover the inner world of attachment by reflecting on how each child responds to us, to the materials in the room, and to the counselling space itself.

Functions of the Inner World

Context helps us understand the form a child's inner world takes, but it also clarifies its function. As an interconnected set of systems, the inner world organises the child's ongoing efforts to stay safe, connected, and regulated within their relationships. It allows the child to anticipate others' responses, rehearse relational moves, and regulate feelings in their absence. In this way, the inner world supports the child to maintain continuity and predictability in environments that may be anything but. We could, therefore, think of the inner world as a relational workspace. It stores emotional learning, organises expectations, and allows children to rehearse relationship possibilities before enacting them in real interactions. When Jordan played at monsters, he was using this workspace to predict how the counsellor might behave and structure the interaction. His internal world kept him alert to threats, but it also gave him a way to approach her, provoke her, and check her reliability without exposing himself all at once.

All children, whatever their histories, rely on these internal systems. While the emotional tone of the inner world may differ from child to child, its functions remain the same. In the sections that follow, we will explore four roles the child's internal ecosystem holds in sustaining relational life.

A Regulating System

Emotional regulation is often thought about as children's ability to soothe themselves when feeling heightened emotions such as anxiety, anger, or upset. But it might be better conceptualised as a self-organising system that works continuously to keep the child in balance. The nervous system not only downregulates heightened emotion but upregulates vitality and engagement when the child is withdrawn or under-stimulated. When the body keeps emotional intensity within a tolerable range (the Goldilocks zone of "not too hot, not too cold"), the child's capacity for social connection comes online: eye contact, facial expression, tone of voice, and posture naturally signal safety and openness. If regulation is not possible, children can become stuck in states of too much or too little feeling, blunting their capacity to interact with others.

Regulation is never a purely individual achievement. The nervous system is tuned by the presence, tone, and responsiveness of others. A child who has had secure, consistent, and sensitive experiences of relationships will be more likely to have a nervous system that, at the baseline, allows them to feel safe in their bodies and the world around them, keeping stress and distress within tolerable limits. Early exposure to danger, rejection, or inconsistency, on the other hand, conditions the child's nervous system to anticipate threat, making regulation much more challenging. As a result, some children cling closely to key adults for regulation, while others learn to shut down or bury their feelings to survive.

The nervous system, therefore, colours children's experiences of their minds and bodies. When children come to therapy with some capacity to regulate their feelings, their internal worlds may be challenging but bearable places to be. For those who live with frequent dysregulation, however, their inner worlds may feel toxic and unpredictable. A central task of the ecosystemic therapist is to contain these states, helping the child tolerate intense feelings through the safety and co-regulation of the relationship. In doing so the child can begin to develop new regulatory capacities.

Sigmund Freud argued that emotional regulation was based on a dynamic interaction between biological needs and internal policing. In his psychodynamic model, the child's inner life is not calm by default but shaped by tensions between bodily impulses (the id), moral and relational expectations absorbed from caregivers and culture (the superego), and the child's effort to manage these forces in ways that preserve connection and safety. Regulation, from this perspective, is the child's way of keeping instinct, feeling, and relationship in workable balance. When this mediating function is sufficiently supported by reliable caregiving, the child develops an internal capacity to delay action, symbolise feeling, and find compromise solutions that maintain emotional expression and bonds. When early relationships are frightening, rejecting, or inconsistent, however, the child may rely on defensive strategies – such as avoidance, inhibition, or emotional flooding – that protect them from overwhelming anxiety but restrict growth. Freud's account reminds us that regulation is not simply calming down; it is the child's attempt to hold together bodily experience, inner conflict, and belonging within the limits of what feels safe.

Pause and Reflect

- What do you notice happens to your ability to reflect, communicate clearly, and connect with others when you feel overwhelmed?
- How do you tend to try to regain balance – do you seek help, shut down, distract yourself, become more controlling, withdraw, or push through?

An Organising System

When we observe a primary-aged child at play in therapy, we see different characters emerge and reemerge in the unfolding story of the work. Each seems to carry its own emotional tone: powerful or submissive, nurturing or destructive, heroic or villainous, relating to one another in shifting patterns of alliance and conflict. As children grow into adolescence, this internal drama doesn't disappear. Rather than imaginary figures, it shows itself in creative expression, shifting identities, and the contrasting ways young people behave across social contexts. A teenager may seem light-hearted with friends but withdrawn at home, or confident in the football team but uncertain in the classroom, each situation giving us a window into the underlying parts that constitute their inner world. A child with an insecure attachment might create monsters in their play, where an adolescent might create monsters out of their teachers. Their ages differ, but their inner world processes are similar – each revolving around insecure themes. A change in context means a change in how the child must relate, with some contexts triggering more attachment responses than others. Freud's psychodynamic model adds that the monster is a symbol that helps the child or young person to express and manage feelings that would otherwise feel too dangerous or overwhelming to face directly. In this sense, symbolic figures in play or imagination act as psychological organisers, giving form to inner conflicts and relational fears so they can be approached at a safer distance. What appears on the surface as a story about monsters or persecuting teachers is often the child's unconscious way of negotiating powerful emotions like anger, dependency, jealousy, or fear of loss. By locating these feelings in symbolic form, the child can explore them, gain some mastery over them, and gradually integrate them into a more coherent sense of self.

Psychotherapists have long observed patterns such as these, proposing that rather than being made up of a single, unified self, we are naturally multiple. That is, our internal world is a system of self-states that emerge in different relational and bodily contexts. Freud thought of these parts as voicing the competing demands of bodily impulses, moral or cultural influences, and the individual's efforts to mediate them. In everyday life, certain relational environments may fit more comfortably with a child's established attachment patterns. A social group might suit an insecure attachment style if it allows the young person to remain physically present but emotionally detached. By contrast, the emotional closeness of a counselling relationship may activate more vulnerable attachment responses. Insecure attachment can show itself through withdrawal from care, anxious clinging, or an uneasy oscillation between pushing others away and pulling them close. In this way, attachment processes become a key organiser of the child's relational world. The different parts of the self activate depending on what the situation demands.

The organised parts of the child's inner world allow them to function in their social environment. When experiences have been rejected or shaming, this system may prioritise protection over authenticity. An inner critical voice may police behaviour and emotion, silencing aspects of the self that feel risky. This is very common in children who have been bullied, where the aggressor's voice may "live on" inside the child's head, taunting them long after the bullying has stopped. In this way, the system organises parts into roles and relationships, much like a family or community, where protective parts may subdue frightened ones, compliant parts may override anger, and confident parts may mask need. Difficulties often emerge when parts are pushed out of awareness altogether, with their corresponding needs sacrificed to meet external demands.

Pause and Reflect

- How comfortable are you with the idea that children (and yourself) are not unified selves?
- Which parts of yourself tend to take the lead in helping roles? The organiser, the comforter, the problem-solver, the placater, the advocate? What might each of these parts hope to offer or gain in therapeutic work with children?

A Meaning-Making System

As well as organising the ongoing drama of the self, the inner world weaves together the relational messages the child has absorbed into an underlying script. This meaning-making system synthesises key experiences into a coherent whole for the child to understand themselves, others, and the wider world.

Scripts colour the child's emerging sense of identity and relationship and provide a logic for how to act with others, shaping what feels possible or expected in their environment. It is rare for children to express such meanings explicitly; instead, scripts are typically an invisible, unconscious force, quietly informing the difficulties that bring children to therapy.

For a securely attached child, their script might comprise a set of beliefs such as "I am lovable," "I can go to adults when I need help and they will respond to me," or "the world is a safe place to be." Cognitive-behavioural therapists call these "core beliefs." That is, they are inner-world beliefs that are core to the child's experience of relationships. For children who haven't experienced this security, scripts speak to the conditions they have learned are necessary for them to feel loved, safe, or seen. In therapy we are unlikely to hear this script directly, too, but the way children act, talk, or think points to underlying messages. Some common insecure scripts or core beliefs include:

- "I'm a disappointment to others. I must perform or be good to be loved. That way others will be pleased with me."
- "I must always make sure adults stay close to me, otherwise they might forget or leave me."
- "I must always be on the lookout with adults. They can't be trusted to keep me safe so it's better if I take charge."
- "I need to look after others, as their needs matter more than mine. There is no space for my feelings."
- "Being close to others is dangerous. It's better to keep my distance and manage on my own."

Scripts lead to emotional and behavioural coping strategies that, while necessary for survival in their original context, often create problems for children in later life. These internal rules operate largely outside awareness, shaping how children interpret events, anticipate danger, and organise their responses to stress. Because they were originally adaptive within a particular family or cultural context, they carry a compelling emotional logic, even when they lead to distress in new environments. From the child's perspective, the behaviour is not irrational or oppositional but a coherent attempt to preserve their safety.

If we imagine Nia, for example, a 12-year-old young person who came to therapy due to school refusal. On the surface, we see her classroom anxiety, nausea, and stomach aches, and the anger when mum tries to get her to the bus on time. But as she talks more in therapy an underlying script emerges, "I can't be apart from Mum. If I go to school, something bad might happen and she might not come when I need her. When I'm anxious or angry she stays close, so that's how I know she won't leave me."

When adults can't see the script behind the drama, children and young people's problems often appear confusing or become moralised as naughtiness or bad behaviour. Knowing that children are guided by internal scripts helps us to know that there is a logic to the problem. The problem is consistent with internal rules that have their origins in family and cultural systems.

Pause and Reflect

- What personal scripts or relational messages from your own development shape how you understand safety, closeness, and boundaries today?
- How do these scripts show up in small, everyday ways, that is, in how you explain things to yourself, interpret others' behaviour, or anticipate what might happen in relationships?

A Stability-seeking System

The final function we will explore is the inner world's tendency towards stability. Experiences, beliefs, and expectations are arranged into familiar patterns because predictability, however restrictive, feels safer than chaos. Humans favour emotional and relational coherence, even in the face of painful consequences. This stability-seeking process explains why children often repeat relationship patterns even when these may be self-destructive. Internal systems prioritise what is known over what is new: the critical voice that once guarded against shame becomes a trusted organiser; the expectation of rejection leads children to distance themselves first; vigilance feels more tolerable than uncertainty. In this sense, inner worlds are conservative systems, promoting continuity rather than disruption.

Stability is not the same as positive mental health. A child's scripts, regulatory strategies, and internal representations tend to organise themselves into a coherent inner system, one that feels familiar and predictable from the child's perspective. This internal organisation may be shaped around anxiety or conflict, yet still function to preserve a sense of safety and relational continuity. For this reason, children often behave in ways that seem illogical or self-defeating from the outside, while remaining internally consistent with the relationship templates they have learned about closeness and threat.

Take Zainab, a 17-year-old, referred for anxiety around exams. As she described her relationships at home, the coherence of her inner world became clear. A critical, emotionally distant mother and a distracted, unavailable father left her attuned to threat and wary of closeness. Over time, these dynamics crystallised internally. Her mother's voice lived on as perfectionism and self-attack, and her father's absence as an expectation of emotional aloneness. People-pleasing and self-censure maintained relational stability, while self-harm offered an outlet for unspoken feelings that would otherwise overwhelm her.

These patterns can look like symptoms of dysfunction, but ecosystemic counsellors see them as evidence of stability-seeking. Zainab preserved connection by adhering to the relationship rules she had grown up with: stay perfect, stay compliant, need little. The cost was high, but the logic was consistent, maintaining a coherent inner world in an environment where comfort felt conditional.

Pause and Reflect

- What patterns do you tend to recreate in your personal and professional relationships? Seeking approval, avoiding conflict, over-preparing, staying invisible?
- How might these patterns impact how you work with children and young people?

The Child's Experience of the Inner World

Ecosystemic therapy is concerned with the systemic patterns in which difficulties emerge. Yet children and young people often arrive at therapy more anxious about the lived experience of their inner world, particularly when it no longer feels bearable. We can see this in Alisha's story below. When she arrived in therapy, she did not talk in the language of systems or theory but of how she felt:

Alisha:	"Um ... I guess I've just been feeling kind of down recently. ... I haven't really talked to anyone about it."
Therapist:	"Mmm ... feeling down, and you've been mostly alone with it .... As you say that, I wonder where you notice that 'down' feeling most? In your body, or maybe in the space around you?"
A:	"... It's like a heaviness, here." [touches chest] "Like I'm carrying something."
T:	"Something weighty you've been carrying inside for a while."
A:	"Yeah. It makes me so tired. Sometimes I just want to sleep all day."
T:	"Part of you longs to rest, and another part keeps carrying this load. I wonder what it's like between those parts of you, how they get along."
A:	"... They don't. I just feel stuck."

Alisha's words reveal an internal system under strain. The heaviness she carries describes more than a feeling. It conveys the cost of containing unspoken emotion and the weight of trying to maintain balance when one part of the system (her social world) offers little space for release. Children often describe their internal states through bodily sensation, image, or metaphor, languages that express how their inner world of feeling and thought is responding to the wider emotional climate around them. We can imagine each child's inner world as an ecosystem or landscape with its own varying climate, terrain, and vitality. Some landscapes are rich, fertile, and safe, where thoughts and feelings move freely and support growth. Others are eroded by harsh conditions, where little grows, and energy is simply spent on survival. For some children, their inner landscapes provide refuge from an unpredictable external world. For others, the landscape is so inhospitable that constant distraction or activity is required to avoid it.

Not all children and young people who come to therapy will be able to easily describe this landscape. After all, the capacity to sense and symbolise internal experience emerges in repeated emotional exchanges between a child and a caregiver. When caregivers are harsh or rejecting, children learn to keep emotional information out of awareness to preserve connection. These children have limited access to, and vocabulary for, feelings that were unacceptable within caregiving contexts such as anger, sadness, or worry. An inner landscape left underdeveloped. When caregiving exchanges are anxious or inconsistent, the opposite pattern can emerge. The child's emotional signals become amplified to sustain proximity and care, while parts of reality that might calm the child are omitted. In therapy, these young people may struggle to self-soothe and understand that their emotional worlds are not reality. The inner landscape here is totalising.

For those for whom relationships have been dangerous, dissociation becomes the child's way of breaking the circuit altogether, temporarily isolating painful experience to maintain overall stability. Here children's inner landscapes may fragment into separate territories, divided by fault lines of fear and forgetting. When a child dissociates, they are unable to name or describe feelings. The more the counsellor invites, the less the child can give. It's an emotional seesawing effect. The inner world is locked for fear of intruders, yet the world can be visited by play, drawing, acting, and imagining, as long as the child's nervous system doesn't detect a threat. Dissociation is another insecure attachment response and one that ecosystemic counsellors know to name out loud and bring to awareness. We place great value on understanding the child's inner world, noticing how behaviours, emotions, and play express many parts of the child's inner life that remain outside their conscious awareness.

Pause and Reflect

- If you had to represent your inner world as a place, what kind of environment would best describe how it feels right now?
- Would it be open or closed, friendly or hostile, safe or dangerous, empty or crowded, bright or muted, predictable or unpredictable, easy to navigate or hard to find your way through?

Conclusion

Whether the child's inner world appears muted, overwhelming, or fragmented, it is never sealed off. It is continually shaped by, and in turn shapes, the emotional climates in which the child lives. The ecosystemic approach proposes that the inner world is a continuation of the interpersonal world. Internal experience is relationally formed and sustained. Working "inside," then, is not a retreat from systemic practice but one of its expressions. The child's feelings, beliefs, and parts of self are living traces of the systems that shaped them, and working with these internal experiences inevitably impacts the outcomes in counselling. Ecosystemic therapy makes space for the person as well as the pattern, for the child's private meanings, imagination, and agency. Attending to individuality within the system honours the child as more than a node in a network; it affirms them as an experiencing subject with a mind of their own.

Chapter 2: Summary

Key Ideas

- A child's inner world forms within a relational field. It is an internalised form of early caregiving systems, not a private, isolated realm.
- Inner experience is embodied, patterned, and systemic: nervous system regulation, internal parts, and relational scripts together create a self-organising internal ecosystem.
- The inner world functions as a social survival system, rehearsing relationships and preserving coherence and connection, even when this means constraining spontaneity or growth.

Practice Implications

- The child's ways of expressing themselves in therapy, whatever forms they take, communicate relational history and test how adults respond.
- Counselling problems often reflect adaptive strategies that once preserved connection or safety in a specific relational environment.
- Working "inside" (with feelings, beliefs, scripts, parts) is still systemic work. Shifts in the child's inner world can initiate change in family, school, and care relationships.

Reflective Prompts

- Where do you tend to individualise what is actually formed relationally?
- How might you listen differently to a child if their "symptoms" are understood as survival scripts?

Bibliography

Ainsworth, M.D.S., Blehar, M.C., Waters, E. et al. (2015). *Patterns of Attachment: A Psychological Study of the Strange Situation*. Psychology press.

Bowlby, J. (1969). *Attachment and Loss* (No. 79). Random House.

Bowlby, J. (2008). *A Secure Base: Parent-child Attachment and Healthy Human Development*. Basic books.

Crittenden, P. (2013). *Raising Parents: Attachment, Parenting and Child Safety*. Routledge.

Fonagy, P., Gergely, G., and Jurist, E.L. (2018). *Affect Regulation, Mentalization and the Development of the Self*. Routledge.

Porges, S.W. (2011). *The Polyvagal Theory: Neurophysiological Foundations of Emotions, Attachment, Communication, and Self-regulation (Norton Series on Interpersonal Neurobiology)*. WW Norton & Company.

Siegel, D.J. (2020). *The Developing Mind: How Relationships and the Brain Interact to Shape Who We are*. Guilford Publications.

Stern, D.N. (2018). *The Interpersonal World of the Infant: A View from Psychoanalysis and Developmental Psychology*. Routledge.

Trevarthen, C. (1998). The concept and foundations of infant intersubjectivity. In: *Intersubjective Communication and Emotion in Early Ontogeny* (ed. S. Bråten), 15–46. Cambridge University Press.

Von Sydow, K. (2002). Systemic attachment theory and therapeutic practice: a proposal. *Clinical Psychology & Psychotherapy* 9 (2): 77–90.

Weinberg, M.K. and Tronick, E.Z. (1996). Infant affective reactions to the resumption of maternal interaction after the still-face. *Child Development* 67 (3): 905–914.

Winnicott, D.W. (1962). The theory of the parent-infant relationship. *The International Journal of Psycho-analysis* 43: 238–239.

Chapter 3
Creating Safety and Change in the Therapy Room

Left alone, the child's inner world will continue to replay familiar patterns that have formed to navigate key social interactions. The teenager who has grown up in a volatile home environment expects to find hostility or danger in the relationships around them. The child who has had to care for their sick parent believes that others need attending to as well. In either case, the child's scripts promote behaviours that elicit the very responses that sustain their problems, even in relationships where the pattern did not originate. The conscientiousness and compliance of the young carer are rewarded with praise and gratitude from their teacher. The defiance of the aggressive teenager is met with disgust, punishment, and eventual expulsion from school.

Many counselling traditions have acknowledged that individuals, families, and organisations get stuck in these vicious and self-fulfilling cycles. The predictability that once ensured survival becomes a rigidity that now constrains growth. Therapists have long understood that the rules that govern these patterns change only through new feedback within a relationship, often through new relational experiences. This chapter focuses on a particular kind of relational experience: that which occurs within the therapeutic relationship. Firstly, it will look at the qualities and processes that research shows are effective in promoting safety and trust, supporting the child and therapist to work together, and addressing difficulties that occur in the work. We will then take a closer look at how change occurs both in the child's inner world and with the therapist in parallel. Lastly, we will reflect on the position of the therapist and how the stance that is taken impacts both the relationship and the inner work.

The Ecosystemic Relationship: Beginnings

The emphasis on relationship does not deny that interventions that focus on a child's behaviour and beliefs or use toys and creative work are unhelpful. The next chapter will show how important they are in engaging the child in reflective work. The ecosystemic approach simply recognises that all therapeutic work happens within a relational field and that even the most creative interventions are unlikely to be effective without a positive relationship between client and therapist. The relationship between counsellor and client begins before the child enters the therapy room. Help-seeking or being referred for therapy, for example, elicits a common sequence of cognitive, emotional, and behavioural responses – all of which are shaped by the child's relationship history. Equally, as the therapist reads the referral or speaks to a caregiver, they preemptively begin to form an image of the child. The child's expectations of adults and the therapist's assumptions about the child are, therefore, already preparing the emotional climate of the first meeting.

Many children and young people will arrive at the opening session with positive ideas about the therapist, trusting that they will receive timely and sensitive help, ready to share what is troubling them. For others, their expectations are coloured by feelings of mistrust, fear, or anxiety. Counsellors may represent another adult who will disappoint, abandon, or hurt them. In either case, the first encounter is the meeting of two relationship histories, each bringing patterns that will cocreate the interaction.

Our ability to explore the child's inner world is, therefore, inseparable from the relationship that forms between us. This is not a fixed bond but an ongoing process in which both therapist and child influence and adapt to each other. From the outset, the therapist attends to how safety and openness are being cocreated, noticing how the child tests, retreats, or reaches out. The early task is not simply to agree on what counselling is for but to begin shaping an environment of trust in which exploration of the inner world becomes possible. Without safety, the child's inner world shuts down.

Crucially, safety and trust are not the products of technique but emerge because of being with the child in ways which help them to feel understood and heard. Interactions that communicate acceptance, genuine presence, and empathic attunement signal to the child that the therapeutic relationship can be used to explore and express their inner world. These relational qualities regulate the child's internal systems, allowing new experiences to be encountered without threat. In our experience of assessing trainee therapists, their early counselling skills can feel mechanical. Before we enter a counselling interaction, the student is emotionally present and vivid. Once they focus on empathising and accepting another person's experience, however, the colour drains from their voice. One explanation for this is that treating counselling purely as a skill dehumanises people. This isn't the student's fault; they are having to unlearn their spontaneous and human responses, which often close down the negative parts of the inner world. When the counselling skill becomes second nature, the student seems reborn. Their natural empathy fuses with a therapeutic ability to tolerate deep emotions.

In the following sections we explore several of these interrelated skilful yet congruent processes, beginning with empathy, which lies at the heart of how therapist and child come to know and influence one another.

Empathy

Empathy has been acknowledged as a pivotal component of therapy. It has traditionally been understood as the therapist's ability to communicate the felt experience of the client, what Carl Rogers described as "entering the private perceptual world of the other and becoming thoroughly at home in it." Framed in this way, empathy is a quality of the therapist that helps the client feel heard and understood. The validation that empathy provides helps to bolster the client's sense of self and their confidence in the inherent trustworthiness of their experience.

An ecosystemic perspective extends this view of empathy, proposing that it is not simply a quality that exists in the therapist that, in turn, generates a felt experience in the client. Rather, empathy is a relational process that is cocreated through ongoing feedback between both partners. The therapist's sensitive attunement is shaped by the client's responses, and, in turn, this shapes how the client feels understood. Consider this interaction between a 14-year-old client and their therapist:

Young Person:	*fiddling with a pencil* "They're always on my case at school. Like I'm the bad one even when I'm not doing anything."
Therapist:	"It feels like people see you as trouble, even when you're just being you."
YP:	*half-smiles* "Not really trouble ... more like annoying."
T:	"Ah, annoying, like they get fed up even if you haven't done much."
YP:	"Yeah. They say I talk too much. I just want to explain."

T: "So you're trying to be understood, but it ends up making things worse."

YP: *nods quickly* "Exactly. Then they tell me to stop answering back."

T: "That must be hard. You're trying to fix it and it just proves their point."

YP: *softens* "Yeah ... that's it."

(brief pause)

T: "Sounds like that happens a lot, being misunderstood."

YP: "Mm-hmm ... I guess that fits."

T: *smiles* "Mmm, it sounds like I got it right there. I might've missed it if you hadn't corrected me earlier."

YP: *grins* "Yeah, well, I do talk a lot."

(both laugh lightly; atmosphere relaxes)

We can see that empathy emerges through a relational dance in which both participants are continually adjusting to one another. The therapist imaginatively enters the child's inner world, and the child responds by confirming or refining this attunement, offering new information that further shapes the therapist's understanding. In this way, empathy develops as a mutual, evolving process rather than a one-sided act of insight.

Empathy is connected to mirror neurons in the brain. They are thought to support our capacity to sense and respond to the emotional states of others. Yet, as this interaction illustrates, empathy is not simply a neurological reflex. It is a lived, relational process that unfolds through moment-to-moment contact. In ecosystemic counselling, empathy becomes one of the primary ways the child's inner world meets another mind without being overwhelmed or dismissed. Through repeated experiences of being felt, corrected, and understood, children develop a more coherent sense of their own experience and a growing trust that their emotions can be shared without loss of connection. In this way, empathy is one of the key mechanisms through which emotional regulation is strengthened, allowing the child's internal ecosystem to reorganise in the presence of another.

Acceptance

The aspects of children and young people's inner worlds that often need exploring the most are those which have been hidden, neglected, or forgotten. For example, the child whose depression masks anger about unmet needs. Or the young person whose self-doubt hides inner resources. Historically, these parts have not supported the child in adapting to the rules that govern attachment relationships around them. They can be shrouded in shame and guilt, which may provoke feelings of anxiety when efforts are made to explore them in therapy. For the child to feel safe to explore and give voice to these aspects of self, the therapist must foster a climate of permission, openness, and containment. For some young people, containment means experiencing the therapist as emotionally steady and psychologically spacious – something psychodynamic counsellors have described as the therapist's holding function. Within such a holding environment, aspects of the inner world that were previously disallowed can begin to show themselves without overwhelming the child's capacity to stay present. Acceptance in this sense signals that all internal experience can be thought about, even when it is painful or socially unacceptable.

From an inner-world perspective, many children organise parts of themselves into what might be called exiled or disowned self-states – feelings or vulnerabilities that could not be safely expressed in earlier attachments. These parts often carry shame or fear of rejection, and so are kept out of awareness. When the therapist responds with consistent acceptance, these self-states encounter a different relational response than the one that shaped them. Instead of being met with alarm or withdrawal, they are met with interest and steadiness. Over time, this therapeutic experience supports integration. Threatening feelings can be recognised as meaningful expressions of the child's inner world. In this way, acceptance repairs the split-off parts of the inner world, and they can help establish a securer sense of self.

Person-centred counselling, developed by Carl Rogers, has often used the language of unconditional positive regard or acceptance to convey the therapist's efforts here. In the ecosystemic model, we can think of this as the therapist's commitment to holding space for the entirety of the child's internal world (bodily, affective, cognitive, and behavioural), providing the secure message that is safe for these systems to integrate new information. This means tolerating and containing the full complexity of the child, including painful feelings that may leave us also feeling uncomfortable or wishing to rescue. Typically, a child in distress causes a caring adult to want to urgently soothe them. Accepting the distress is a healthier response in counselling; it allows the feeling to be known, understood, and metabolised rather than hurried away, giving the child's inner system time to reorganise around the experience that has been shared and survived. Within an accepting relationship, new stories emerge that enable shifts not only in how the child sees themselves but also in how others respond to them. The harder it is to accept a child is related to the degree of attachment insecurity they carry, as these children often express distress in ways shaped by troubling experiences. This can evoke powerful reactions in adults and make steady, non-defensive acceptance both more difficult and more essential for change.

Authenticity

The therapeutic relationship cannot be accepting or empathic if it is not genuine. Empathy, after all, captures the therapist's concern and resonance, which, if lacking in authenticity, is no empathy at all. Similarly, when a therapist communicates acceptance verbally while internally judging the child, the encounter fails to be therapeutic. Carl Rogers called this congruence – the therapist's willingness to be real in the relationship rather than hidden behind professional performance. Research has supported his observation that clients are acutely sensitive to emotional mismatch, and even children detect when words of care are not matched by tone, posture, or attention. When therapists try to "do" empathy or acceptance without being emotionally present, young people quickly withdraw, escalate, or become compliant in ways that preserve distance. By contrast, when the therapist's responses arise from genuine contact – when their voice, body, and attention are aligned – the child experiences the relationship as trustworthy. It is this felt authenticity, more than technique, that allows guarded parts of the inner world to emerge and risk being known.

In supervision, a newly qualified counsellor spoke about the strong maternal pull she felt towards a child who was expressing suicidal thoughts. Her instinct was to show how deeply she cared. At the same time, she worried that these feelings might lead her to step into a parental role, especially as the child was neglected at home. She tried to push the feelings down, fearing that expressing them would cross a boundary. The supervisor saw something else. The counsellor's concern was not a problem to remove but information about the depth of contact in the relationship. If she suppressed it entirely, her presence might become careful but distant. If she acted it out, the relationship could shift into rescue. Between these two lies congruence: the capacity to be aware of one's feelings, hold them, and communicate their meaning in a way that keeps the focus on the child. She might say, calmly, "I've been feeling quite concerned about you," not to soothe herself or take over but to let the child know their experience has reached another person. The question, then, is not whether the therapist has strong feelings but how those feelings can be used in the service of the child without displacing the child's own inner world.

Congruence is essential in all therapeutic relationships, but it takes on particular significance when working with children and young people, who are often quick to sense mismatches between an adult's words and their underlying feelings, or between personal presence and professional role. Ultimately, children are unlikely to share their inner world with us if they sense they are not in the presence of a real person. One of the therapist's tasks, therefore, is to bring the whole self into the therapeutic relationship while discerning which aspects to share with the client. For the relationship to be therapeutic, the child needs to experience us as a person, not a role. At the same time, our openness has limits: the child does not, and should not, have access to every part of our lives. What matters is that our responses, whether verbal or nonverbal, come from a genuine engagement with the child and with the relationship itself.

Relational Challenges

The therapist's efforts to foster a positive relationship, characterised by the child-centred qualities of empathy, acceptance, and authenticity, do not mean that the work will be without challenge. Young people may be persistently late for sessions, reluctant to open up, or mistrustful of efforts to establish safety, leaving the therapist addressing issues of process rather than hearing from the child. These relational difficulties may at first appear to be issues to be resolved in order that the "proper" work of exploring the child's inner world can happen. It is a miscalculation, however, to see a dichotomy between process and content, between inner work and problems in the relationship. Ecosystemic counselling understands that addressing relational difficulties *is* inner-world work. Freud developed the idea of countertransference, which is the therapist's feelings towards the client. He said that the counsellor's feeling of self-doubt or rejection is useful information about the child's inner world.

Countertransference suggests that the therapist's emotional responses, when noticed and reflected upon, can reveal how the child expects relationships to feel. A sense of being pushed away, ignored, or tested may mirror the child's own experience of closeness as unsafe or unreliable. What shows up between therapist and child is rarely accidental. The late arrival, the silence, the challenge, the charm – these are ways the child organises connection. When the therapist responds thoughtfully, the relationship becomes a place where these patterns can be experienced differently. The "process issues" are, therefore, not obstacles to the work; they are the work. In staying present with these moments, the therapist helps the child bring into awareness the relational expectations that shape their inner world and offers a new experience in which difficulty does not lead to rupture or rejection but to understanding and repair.

Consider the therapeutic relationship below as an example:

> Eight-year-old Leo entered the playroom with explosive energy, crashing cars, throwing Play-Doh at the walls, and eventually hitting the therapist with a foam sword. The child seemed out of control, a whirlwind wreaking havoc in its path, and the therapist struggled to keep up with the constant shifts in the child's stories and behaviour. It took weeks of limit-setting from the therapist before Leo's play took on a more coherent form, and he began to invite the therapist in.

It is tempting, particularly for those early in their practice, to focus on what isn't happening here. The absence of coherent play and the therapist's exclusion from it might be seen as signs that therapy is failing. Yet what feels like a lack of progress is often the child's way of showing how relationships have felt: unpredictable, fragmented, and unsafe. These opening exchanges *are* inner work. Chaotic play and aggressive behaviour are communications of the child's inner world and their experience of relationships. From this perspective, holding limits is not separate from inner work but one of its forms. We could imagine the implicit communication behind the boundary-setting articulated verbally like this:

Leo:	"I don't feel safe here. You're a stranger and might hurt me, so I'll take control first."
Therapist:	"You're showing me how hard it is to trust. I'm here to keep us both safe, and I won't let you get hurt or hurt me."
L:	"I'm not sure you mean that, so I'm going to keep testing."
Tt:	"That's okay. I'll keep showing you that I mean what I say."

Addressing difficulties in the relational process, what we refer to as counselling "ruptures," can be amongst the most transformative aspects of therapy. With Leo, inner work did not begin only once he could play like a "secure" child. It began the moment he entered the room, when his struggle to trust and the therapist's steady containment created the first possibilities for change.

How Change Happens

As we explored in Chapter 2, one of the functions of the child's internal world is to maintain stability and predictability within caregiving systems. The anxious vigilance of an adolescent who frets over every social interaction helps sustain connection in a family where high standards and control are key to belonging. Anxiety enables the young person to maintain closeness, with parental values privileged over their own wishes. Understanding this helps us to see why internal systems can struggle to change.

For the child's inner world to change, it must absorb new information, which Gregory Bateson called "the difference that makes a difference." Across this book we explore different types of information that can make this difference, but here we will examine what the therapeutic relationship can introduce. One of the aims of the therapeutic relationship is to offer an experience that confounds the child's expectations. In Leo's case, he anticipated that the therapist would be dangerous or unable to contain him. By offering calm, consistent limits, the therapist introduced new information to the child's system. Change is not immediate, but the experience begins to unsettle the stories, beliefs, and defences that sustain his current relational patterns.

Micro-Processes of Change

The potential for change in a single session or across a course of therapy exists within each moment that client and therapist share. Every interaction may promote small steps to shifting the client's beliefs about themselves and the world. For instance, the genuine expression of concern that a young person's disclosure of abuse prompts in the therapist may initiate a confounding of the deep belief in their badness and blame, which in turns lead to further openness. In this way, therapy is made up of hundreds of interactional loops. Each response from the therapist influences the child's next move, which in turn shapes the therapist's follow-up. Each moment or loop forms a relational rhythm. Sometimes this leads to new ways of connecting, and at other times it pulls back into old patterns.

A climate of empathy, acceptance, and authenticity promotes change, but the therapist's part in this feedback loop is greatly supported by other elements of what we named in Chapter 1 as active listening. The different elements of active listening can be seen in Table 3.1.

We could think of these elements as skills, and while they can be developed with practice, it is more helpful to think of them as ways of being with children and young people. When used together with empathy, acceptance, and authenticity, they help to set the tone of the relationship and invite connection. The following exchange between a therapist and a 17-year-old client, Amira, shows how elements in action (Table 3.2).

In this short interaction, we can see various forms of information passing between the therapist and the young person that offer differences. This information communicates messages about the young person, their inner world, and the relationship with the therapist. For the young person, this might be summed up as "someone can hear about my pain and still stay connected," a small but significant difference to what their internal system expects.

It is worth noting that a short interaction like this is unlikely to foster lasting shifts in the child's inner world or ways of relating with others. Some clients may initially be unable to accept the therapist's efforts to explore their inner world or take in empathy and acceptance. However, the exchange between Amira and her therapist illustrates how therapeutic change unfolds through countless micro-moments of relational difference. These small differences,

Table 3.1 Elements of Active Listening

Physical presence	Embodying a stance of "being with" the client through sensitive use of eye contact, posture, silence, and nonverbal encouragers (mmms, head nods, etc.).
Reflecting and paraphrasing	Mirroring the client's words, intentions, feelings, or body language to demonstrate understanding and attunement.
Summarising	Bringing together what the client has said to help clarify, draw out common themes, or manage pace.
Open questions (who, what, where, when, how, why)	Inviting open dialogue and exploring with curiosity.
Immediacy	Drawing attention to what is happening in the here and now by naming one's own emotions and bodily responses or observing what is taking place in the relationship.
Naming feelings	Paying attention to implicit communication, where client feelings are expressed nonverbally through body language, tone of voice, or in what is and isn't said.

repeated over time, accumulate to reshape the child or young person's internal world and in turn their outward behaviour.

The Therapist's Stance

Difference in therapy is introduced not only through the relational tone of the work but also through the position, or stance, the therapist adopts towards the child's inner world. Although the overall climate of safety and attunement may be similar across different approaches, the experience offered to the child can vary greatly. Some therapists will participate through a highly responsive, unstructured style, while others bring more form and direction. These contrasting positions rest on different ideas about how

Table 3.2 Micro-Change in Counselling

Therapist–Client Dialogue	Micro-Processes of Change
Therapist: You said you cut again last night. **Amira:** Yeah. Not that it matters. No one cares. **T:** *leans forward slightly* You sound really alone with it right now.	**Physical presence and naming feelings:** therapist's posture, tone, and empathy signal engagement and attunement, conveying that the client's experience can be held.
A: I'm not alone. It's fine, I don't need anyone anyway. **T:** It's important for you to feel you can cope by yourself. I'm wondering what it would it be like to need someone?	**Paraphrase + open question:** captures client meaning while inviting client to further clarify.
A: People just mess things up. Say they'll help and then disappear. **T:** So, when you're hurting, it's easier to go it alone than risk being let down again.	**Reflection:** therapist reflects the relational function of withdrawal, not just the content.
A: *nods* People think it's about dying but it's not. It's more like ... calming down. **T:** Cutting helps you find calm when everything inside feels too much. **A:** Yeah. It's the only thing that actually works.	**Naming feeling and communicating empathy:** gives language to the soothing function of self-harm, validating without condoning.
T: I can hear how powerful it feels. And how hard it must be to imagine something else working.	**Empathy and acceptance:** joins with the client's experience, while subtly holding space for possibility.
A: *glances up briefly* You don't seem freaked out by it. Most people do. **T:** You're checking how I'll react right now? **A:** Maybe.	**Immediacy:** brings the live relationship into focus, naming what's happening between them.
T: It makes sense you'd want to know if I can handle hearing it. You've had people disappear when it got too real before. **A:** *sighs* Yeah.	**Empathy:** acknowledging the client's anxiety in the context of their life history.
T: *quietly* It sounds like this has been something you've carried on your own for a long time.	**Summary:** succinct summary of the meaning of what has been shared.

change occurs and on what each child's system may need to take in something new.

A nondirective stance trusts that change arises from the child's inherent potential. The child's physical, emotional, cognitive, and meaning-making systems naturally move towards integration when held within a relational climate of safety and trust. Whether through play, creative expression, or talk, the therapist participates through responsive presence, communicating trust in the child's agency and capacity for growth. Child-centred models of therapy are based on nondirective stances. In ecosystemic counselling, we see nondirectiveness as one of many possible therapeutic positions. A directive stance, by contrast, recognises that the therapeutic relationship alone may not be sufficient for change. Some systems need a more deliberate introduction of difference, forms of experience that the relationship alone may not yet generate. Here the therapist participates more actively, offering structured activities, interpretations, or tasks designed to help the child encounter new ways of thinking, feeling, and relating.

Karl Tomm, a systemic psychotherapist and psychiatrist, described such differences in stance as *ethical postures*. These are ways the therapist positions themselves in relation to responsibility and influence. At times the therapist takes an ethic of care, prioritising protection, emotional holding, and responsiveness to vulnerability. At other times an ethic of justice is needed, where the therapist introduces challenge, structure, or limits in the service of fairness and growth. An ethic of curiosity invites exploration without assumption, while an ethic of respect guards the child's autonomy and perspective. No single posture is sufficient on its own. Effective therapy involves movement between them, guided by the child's needs and by the therapist's ongoing reflection on the impact of their participation. In this way, stance becomes part of the ecology of change: the therapist's position is just one of the active elements shaping what the child is able to experience and express.

These two positions have often been described as a matter of who leads and who follows. From an ecosystemic perspective, however, these distinctions miss the circular nature of influence.

In every exchange, therapist and child shape one another's responses. Each gesture, silence, or intervention reorganises the relationship and invites a corresponding movement from the other. What matters is not who acts first but how therapist and child begin to find new ways of being together that help the child's inner world to change. In this sense, the work is not simply child-centred, as though the therapist were arranged around a fixed core. Nor is it therapist-led. It is child-in-relationship-centred because the focus rests on the living system that forms between child and therapist. Change emerges within this shared field of influence, where the child's expressions alter the therapist's stance and the therapist's participation alters what the child can risk showing. Direction and responsiveness are not opposites but movements within the same relational circuit. The therapist listens and leads and follows and shapes, each action calibrated to what is happening between them. It is this ongoing mutual adjustment – this circular coordination – that creates the conditions for new experiences to take root and for the child's inner world to reorganise.

Deciding how directive to be is, therefore, less a technical choice than a sensitive attunement to what the relationship needs. We listen to what the child can tolerate and what is required for growth and adjust accordingly. Sometimes structure provides the difference that enables movement, at other times, allowing the process to unfold spontaneously is sufficient. Over time this becomes less about choosing a method and more about listening ecosystemically. The therapist notices what invites growth and what seems to inhibit it, whether this be containment, space, or challenge. One child may respond well to a nondirective course of play therapy, using their own initiative to make meaning through the toys. In the steady presence of the therapist, who tracks, names feelings, and sets gentle limits, the child experiences the freedom to express and integrate feelings of anxiety and jealousy about a new sibling, for example. Within this unstructured space, the relationship itself becomes the context in which emotional conflict is worked through.

By contrast, another young person might find the same level of openness overwhelming. In a nondirective setting following a recent bereavement, the lack of structure could feel uncertain and unsafe, leading to stuckness. What the child needs is greater direction and clarity from the therapist, a stance that offers more active guidance and transparency about the therapist's role. By introducing structure and shaping the conversation, the therapist reduces ambiguity, increasing safety and making it possible for the young person to explore their sadness and grief more freely.

Conclusion

Change becomes possible through the difference that the therapeutic relationship provides. The child's internal world shifts when sufficient safety and security allow new ways of seeing themselves, others, and the world to emerge. Both therapist and child cocreate the context within which this happens, but the therapist understands that their stance and ways of being shape the interactions that determine whether differences can be integrated. Each child responds differently to the person of the therapist, influenced by their history and expectations. The therapist's task is to notice how their responses impact the patterns of relating between them. Play, creative, and cognitive-behavioural approaches offer distinct opportunities to work with the child's inner world. It is to these ways of working that we turn in the next chapter.

Chapter 3: Summary

Key Ideas

- The therapeutic relationship functions as a new relational system in which the child's inner world becomes visible, tested, and gradually reorganised.
- Empathy, acceptance, and authenticity are relational processes cocreated through ongoing feedback, shaping safety and openness.

- Change arises through micro-moments of relational difference that gently disrupt rigid internal patterns and introduce new possibilities for regulation and connection.

Practice Implications

- The therapeutic relationship emerges because of the meeting of two relational histories. Therapists need to be aware of the influence of both themselves and the child on the relationship.
- Relational challenges are part of the work, revealing systemic histories and offering opportunities for feedback.
- The therapist's stance and ways of being in therapy shape the interactions that determine whether new information can be integrated by the child.

Reflective Prompts

- When relational difficulties arise, do you treat them as obstacles to get past or as communications to understand?
- What stance does this child need from you: more structure, more space, or a shift in your way of being?

Bibliography

Axline, V.M. (1969). *Play Therapy: The Inner Dynamics of Childhood.* Houghton Mifflin.
Bateson, G. (1972). *Steps to an Ecology of Mind.* Chandler.
Blake, P. (2021). *Child and Adolescent Psychotherapy: Making the Conscious Unconscious.* Routledge.
Bordin, E.S. (1979). The generalizability of the psychoanalytic concept of the working alliance. *Psychotherapy: Theory, Research & Practice* 16 (3): 252.
Clarkson, P. (2003). *The Therapeutic Relationship.* John Wiley & Sons.

Cochran, N.H., Nordling, W.J., and Cochran, J.L. (2010). *Child-centered Play Therapy: A Practical Guide to Developing Therapeutic Relationships with Children*. John Wiley & Sons.

Farber, B.A. and Metzger, J.A. (2009). The therapist as secure base. In: *Attachment Theory and Research in Clinical Work with Adults* (eds. J.H. Obegi and E. Berant), 46–70. The Guilford Press.

Gelso, C.J. and Hayes, J.A. (1998). *The Psychotherapy Relationship: Theory, Research, and Practice*. John Wiley & Sons Inc.

Gunner, A.L. (2006). Feedback loops in clinical practice: an integrative framework. *Australian and New Zealand Journal of Family Therapy* 27 (3): 143–152.

Holliday, C. (2014). The therapeutic relationship: building a working alliance with children and adolescents. In: *Therapy with Children and Young People* (eds. C. McLaughlin and C. Holliday), 88–100. SAGE Publications, Ltd. https://www.doi-org.ezproxy.northampton.ac.uk/10.4135/9781526402110.n7

Keeney, B.P. (1983). *Aesthetics of Change*. Guilford Press.

Landreth, G.L. (2023). *Play Therapy: The Art of the Relationship*. Routledge.

Norcross, J.C. (2010). The therapeutic relationship. In: *The Heart and Soul of Change: Delivering What Works in Therapy* (eds. B.L. Duncan, S.D. Miller, B.E. Wampold, et al.), 2e, 113–141. American Psychological Association. https://doi.org/10.1037/12075-004

Norcross, J.C. and Lambert, M.J. (eds.) (2019). *Psychotherapy Relationships that Work: Evidence-based Therapist Contributions*, 3e. Oxford University Press.

Norcross, J.C. and Wampold, B.E. (eds.) (2019). *Psychotherapy Relationships that Work: Evidence-based Therapist Responsiveness*, 3e. Oxford University Press.

O'Keeffe, S., Martin, P., and Midgley, N. (2020). When adolescents stop psychological therapy: rupture–repair in the therapeutic alliance and association with therapy ending. *Psychotherapy* 57 (4): 471.

Rogers, C.R. (1957). The necessary and sufficient conditions of therapeutic personality change. *Journal of Consulting Psychology* 21 (2): 95.

Rogers, C.R. (1995). *On Becoming a Person: A Therapist's View of Psychotherapy*. Houghton Mifflin Harcourt.

Safran, J.D. and Muran, J.C. (2000). *Negotiating the Therapeutic Alliance: A Relational Treatment Guide*. Guilford Press.

Shirk, S.R. and Karver, M. (2003). Prediction of treatment outcome from relationship variables in child and adolescent therapy: a meta-analytic review. *Journal of Consulting and Clinical Psychology* 71 (3): 452–464.

Winnicott, D.W. (2018). *The Maturational Processes and the Facilitating Environment: Studies in the Theory of Emotional Development*. Routledge.

Chapter 4
Approaches to Working with the Child's Inner World

In Chapter 3, we explored the therapeutic relationship as the context through which all therapeutic work takes place. This chapter turns to the modes by which this relationship engages the child's inner world. While talk is an important medium for connection, it is only one way inner experience can be accessed and organised in therapy. Much of children's emotional life is held and expressed beyond language, through bodily states and behaviour, symbolic play, images, and patterns of thinking. Different counselling approaches engage these forms in different ways, providing distinct pathways for therapeutic change.

Across the following sections, we will trace a map of practice, covering different entry points into the child's inner world. Although each is discussed with attention to developmental appropriateness, they should not be seen as hierarchical. Work may begin at any of these points, depending on what is most accessible or meaningful for the child and may remain there or move flexibly between them over the course of therapy. Children and young people will also bring their own preferences for how they wish to engage, requiring the therapist to adapt accordingly.

Working with the Body

Emotions are rooted in the body. When we feel anxious, our heart begins to pound, our palms become sweaty and our chest tightens. When we are ashamed, we avert our gaze, we make ourselves smaller, and we feel a sinking feeling in our stomachs. Our bodies record and communicate our experience in gestures and posture. When emotions aren't symbolised in language, they find expression in our bodies and our behaviour. This is particularly pertinent for feelings attached to experiences which are preverbal or overwhelming. As we saw in Chapter 2, such experiences are encoded in implicit memory, beyond awareness, and may find expression in sequences of movement and bodily sensation.

Utilising embodied ways of working offers children and young people several benefits, from establishing regulation and safety, to promoting expression and integration, and developing agency and comfort in the body. This work happens using movement, materials, and awareness rather than physical contact but welcomes the child's embodied expression of emotion and memory. Bessel van der Kolk proposes in *The Body Keeps the Score* that overwhelming experience is often stored as a bodily state. For children, particularly when experiences are preverbal or emotionally unmanageable, memory may be encoded as sensation and autonomic arousal rather than words. The child does not recall the event in narrative form; instead, the nervous system reactivates the state associated with it. Play and relationship reveal the body's story by sensitively observing its narrative themes.

The inner world is connected to Antonio Damasio's Somatic Marker Hypothesis, which suggests that experiences become linked to bodily feeling states that later guide unconscious perception and behaviour. These somatic markers are found in a child's withdrawal from the therapist or as embodied predictions about risk that show up in drawings or free play. Inner-world counselling attempts to safely activate embodied emotional memory rather than expect direct communication. A child who becomes suddenly withdrawn, restless, or highly reactive is likely inhabiting a physiological state shaped by earlier experience.

Embodied therapeutic work, therefore, meets the child in this primary language of sensation and movement. By supporting awareness and tolerance of bodily states through movement, materials, rhythm, and sensory experience, the counsellor helps the child develop the capacity to remain present without overwhelm. As regulation stabilises, experience that was once held only in the body may gradually become symbolised in play, image, and eventually words. Working with the body is thus a pathway into the child's inner world, where memory is packaged first inside feelings and sensations.

Safety and Regulation

Bodily work is particularly important for children and young people who struggle to regulate their emotions. For some, this may reflect a lack of secure attachment in relationships, where caregivers have struggled to respond to the child's feelings sensitively or consistently. For others, dysregulation speaks to challenges in sensory integration due to neurodevelopmental differences. In either case, children may negatively experience their bodies as overwhelming or chaotic.

Therapy begins by tuning into the child's bodily states and creating space for emotional sensations to be experienced safely in the presence of the therapist. This may involve noticing tension, restlessness, or urges to withdraw, and responding to these bodily cues as information about what the therapeutic process requires. Alongside this, children and young people may be offered simple psychoeducation about bodily responses, such as how breathing, muscle tension, or grounding strategies can influence arousal, supporting a shared language for what is happening in their bodies. The aim is not to remove difficult emotions but to establish a context in which bodily communication can be noticed, named, and worked with. In doing so the child will learn that regulation happens through the sharing of experience within a trust relationship.

This was evident with a 10-year-old client named Tommy. His body showed persistent signs of threat and hyperarousal in sessions. It was important to support his fight responses in ways that were both safe and relational. Aggressive impulses were contained within embodied play that had clear limits, redirecting Tommy to punch and kick a bean bag the therapist was holding, being emotionally present and non-retaliatory. The playroom also included other materials that invited bodily regulation and self-soothing, such as toys that could be squeezed, thrown, and hit safely, or materials that could be used to hide or defend. In one session, Tommy turned a cardboard box into a secret den, where he could control his distance from the counsellor, shutting the lid if they felt too close and his body needed to escape.

Regardless of the specific intervention used, the capacity to self-soothe develops through repeated experiences of co-regulation within a relationship. A central task for the therapist is, therefore, to pace the work in close attention to the child's bodily signals, supporting movement towards difficult or previously avoided experiences without tipping into overwhelm. As children begin to approach experiences that have previously been avoided or split off, their level of arousal often increases, particularly where there is trauma. This requires the therapist to adjust the intensity of the work in response. The therapist's own regulated presence, steady tone, grounded posture, and calm breathing function as both model and cue for the child's nervous system. As safety becomes established, the body can then serve not only as a site of regulation but as a medium through which unspoken experience begins to find expression.

Expression and Integration of Implicit Memory

Once bodily states can be tolerated within a relationship, embodied work can support a further developmental step: the integration of felt experience into symbolic and reflective forms. Some experiences that are held in the body as sensations, gestures, or actions have never been organised into a coherent meaning. At this stage, the therapeutic task is not primarily to regulate arousal but to support these bodily patterns to take shape in ways that can be represented and eventually reflected upon.

Giving words to bodily sensations draws inner-world experiences out into the open. Language gives the body and the child a means through which experience, once vague and without form, may be brought into shared awareness and held within the safety of a relationship. Unless the body is given a voice, the child unconsciously communicates through behaviour. As sensations begin to find words, what was previously experienced only as a physical feeling can come into the light of thought. The child is then less confined to simply reentering bodily states and more able to recognise them, to speak of them, and to place them within a growing understanding of self. In this way, embodied expression opens a path by which felt experience may enter reflection, so that the body may gradually be known and integrated into the child's sense of self.

Let's think about an example of an adolescent in counselling. Fifteen-year-old Tanya attended therapy following panic attacks and episodes of freezing during exams. She described "going blank" and being unable to think or speak when under pressure. During one session, she was drawn to a block of clay and began kneading it with sustained, repetitive pressure. The counsellor remained alongside her, noticing the pace and rhythm of her movements. As the clay was flattened and reshaped, Tanya's breathing slowed, and her shoulders dropped. After a pause, she said quietly, "It's like I can breathe again," shaping the clay into a smooth oval and resting both hands on it.

Here, bodily action provided a bridge between unformulated experience and emerging awareness. The sensations of pressure and release were organised into a form that could be observed from a distance. In our work, Tanya was able to link these bodily states to moments of pressure and fear in her everyday life, allowing experiences that had previously been enacted or avoided to become thinkable and sayable. Embodied work at this stage supports the movement from felt sensation to representation, enabling experience to be carried not only in the body but also in symbols, language, and reflection. It's important not to rush into language, however. The ecosystemic model sees shy play like the body's vocabulary, and we learn each child's unique way of communicating. Words are only important as a sign that the child's inner world is now conscious, spoken, and tolerable. Adding words too early usually shuts the client down. Counsellors who find themselves over-questioning children can pause, slow down the pace, and introduce a physical or symbolic activity (such as roleplay, sandtray, word, or drawing).

Developing Agency and Comfort in the Body

Beyond safety and communication, embodied work can also help children and young people to experience a greater sense of control and confidence. Dysregulation leaves children feeling at the mercy of their nervous systems or alienated from their bodies' natural responses. When a child pours sand over their hands in the sandtray, works the clay to form a sculpture, or feels the gentle rise and fall of their chest as they breathe with the therapist, they learn to control their body in new ways and see the effect that their body has on the world. For children who have experienced themselves as having little influence within the systems around them, it can be deeply empowering to recognise their capacity to effect change through their bodies.

Ryan was an eight-year-old boy whose body was often overtaken by anxiety, shaped by a historically fractured home life.

In therapy, he enacted lengthy fight scenes with puppets, repeatedly defeating imagined enemies through embodied sequences of attack and defence. These enactments were not only inner-world expressions of distress but early attempts to master conflict and uncertainty. As therapy progressed, Ryan's drive for mastery did not disappear but shifted in form. His body moved from conquering armies to mastering skills that support his burgeoning self-esteem. He showed more pride in his artistic abilities, especially in drawing and painting. The war talk was replaced with future talk about becoming an artist. In this way, his body transitioned from being organised primarily around conflict to becoming a site of competence and confidence. For children whose bodies have long been shaped by anxiety or control, reclaiming the body's skills and talents represents increased emotional regulation and a restored sense of self.

Working with Symbol, Metaphor, Image, and Play

Symbol, metaphor, image, and play provide powerful means through which children and young people express and organise their inner experience. In therapy, these processes can be enacted using creative activities such as role play, drawing, storytelling, puppet work, sculpting, and sand play, giving form to experiences that may be difficult to articulate in words. These media can be used in both non-directive and more structured ways, allowing the therapist to meet the child where they are developmentally and emotionally.

Working symbolically creates space for experiences to be approached indirectly, reducing pressure on the child while still allowing emotionally salient material to come into view. It also enables the therapist to engage with aspects of experience that are held beyond conscious awareness, including bodily sensations, implicit memories, and relational expectations. By privileging imagination over explanation, symbolic work creates conditions in which meaning can emerge gradually and safely. In doing so, it supports exploration, integration, and change without requiring children to think, speak, or feel in ways that may be beyond their current capacities.

Sigmund Freud proposed that the inner world is shaped by wishes, fears, and conflicts that often find expression not in direct speech but in symbolic form. Symbolic play can, therefore, be understood as a pathway through which unconscious meaning becomes representable, allowing what cannot yet be spoken to be communicated through image, metaphor, and enactment. In doing so, the counsellor supports exploration and change without requiring children to think or speak in ways that may be beyond their current capacities. Ecosystemic counsellors don't interpret the child's inner world as psychodynamic therapists might. Instead, we use child-centred active listening to safely help children make sense of their drawings, play, and behaviour.

Developmental Advantages

Adults working with younger children will notice that open, reflective questioning, whilst effective with many older adolescents, can be difficult to sustain, often met with silence, minimal responses or a change in subject. Play therapists propose that this is because talk is not children's primary language; rather, play is the medium through which children intuitively explore the world around them, interact with others, and work through emotionally salient experiences. Therapy that utilises play and creative mediums, therefore, meets the child at their level, in their world. It reduces expectations to communicate in adult ways by sitting still, listening, and conversing verbally.

While therapists can assume that older young people will be resistant to engaging in the same kinds of work, this is often misplaced. Anxiety about being evaluated on artistic performance can be a barrier to self-expression, but it is helpful for therapists to remain open minded about who can benefit from this way of working. Offering creative materials to older clients can address unmet developmental needs, including missed opportunities to play as a child. Research in art therapy and expressive therapies, including the work of Cathy Malchiodi, highlights that drawing and visual expression can help adolescents access emotional experience when verbal articulation is limited. Creative arts therapies with adolescents show measurable psychological benefits. Morison, Simonds, and Stewart found that creative arts-based interventions like visual art, drama, music, and expressive play were associated with significant reductions in low mood and anxiety amongst children and adolescents exposed to traumatic events. These interventions supported emotional expression and regulation in ways that conventional talking therapies often could not, demonstrating that symbolic and creative processes can be accessible and therapeutically effective for teenagers as well as for children.

Consider Kyle, a 17-year-old young person in residential care with a history of aggressive behaviour. While he could not tolerate open conversation about his difficulties, he was immediately drawn to a selection of puppets in the therapy room. Placing a devil and a wolf on his hands, he invited the counsellor to play the part of a small, vulnerable-looking duck. He intuitively began playing out interactions between his puppets and the counsellor's, bullying the duck and teasing it for being "weak." This continued over the course of several weeks before he was ready to begin talking directly. Seen symbolically, the play made visible an inner world that Kyle could not yet describe. The powerful, predatory figures he controlled may be understood as representing states of dominance or threat that he relied upon in relationships, while the duck embodied vulnerability or aspects of self that felt exposed or unsafe. By locating these dynamics in the puppets rather than in himself, Kyle could explore them at a tolerable distance. The therapy space allowed aggression and vulnerability to be expressed within the protective frame of imagination, where they could be observed and gradually thought about. In this way, play functioned as the medium through which the work became possible, communicating relational expectations and internal conflicts long before they could be spoken.

Promoting Safety

As Kyle's vignette shows, play and creative work also increase safety, allowing exploration of aspects of the inner world that might otherwise remain hidden. This safety is fostered in two ways: firstly, by creating distance between the child and their emotional material, and secondly, by introducing a third thing in the room that removes focus from the child, lessening intensity. To illustrate this, consider Ava, a nine-year-old child referred for social anxiety and difficulties making friends at school. In a free-play session, Ava drew a picture of an alien on a distant planet. When the counsellor asked about the story of her image, she described the alien as a strange creature, different from others in the galaxy, living alone and feeling very sad. The image was striking in its emptiness. Through this drawing, Ava was deeply capturing her lived experience of isolation.

Had Ava been asked to describe her experiences directly, her anxiety and limited reflective capacity would likely have restricted her ability to language her inner world. Through image and metaphor, however, her experiences found expression in a form that was simultaneously both hers and not hers. By focusing on the alien, she explored her inner world without making her the centre of attention, allowing safe talk about difficult experiences.

To maintain this safety, the therapist resists the urge to make things literal through interpretations. Stating that the alien reminded the counsellor of Ava may have increased insight but was equally likely to leave her feeling exposed or confused. By remaining within the metaphor, the child's inner world is more vivid and less defended. In Ava's case, this might involve asking questions that deepen our understanding of the problem, such as, "What helps the alien survive there?" "Has anyone ever tried to visit the aliens' planet? What happened?" "Does the alien want company, or does it feel safer alone?" To answer questions on behalf of the alien, Ava must draw on her own inner life – articulating her real emotions. The therapist might also interact directly with the image, inviting Ava to talk as the alien and creating a dialogue that allows her to communicate at a safe distance. By exploring the metaphor, feelings that have not yet been fully integrated can be expressed, witnessed, and gradually owned by the child, supporting emotional integration without overwhelming them.

Engaging the Unconscious

Therapists have long understood that play and creative work elicit projective responses. When children and young people make images, role-play, or write stories, they unconsciously project their inner world into the objects and stories. Because symbol and metaphor engage forms of experience held in implicit memory, they allow access to parts of the self that may not yet be accessible through language alone. In this sense, working with a child's creations is a direct engagement with how their experience is organised. Change can, therefore, occur within the symbolic process itself, without the need for immediate explanation or interpretation. A child who symbolically murders the therapist slowly begins to rescue them in later sessions. The child is rarely aware of the emotional transition, but they emerge from therapy with a safer and more hopeful experience of a relationship.

Many therapists find it helpful to understand this process through a parts-based lens, in which the self is not treated as a single unified whole but as a system of different positions, roles, and emotional states in relationship with one another. Children's play naturally gives form to this internal organisation. For example, ten-year-old Ella returned week after week to a play narrative involving a strict teacher who controlled the counsellor, criticised them for getting things wrong, punished them, and set increasingly demanding tasks. Within the play, the child's teacher figure held authority and control, while the counsellor was positioned as inadequate and perpetually failing.

The recurring narrative revealed an internal configuration that closely mirrored patterns in Ella's wider relational world: an experience of parental anxiety about performance and a feeling of desperation to please others. By taking on the role of the critical teacher, Ella was able to express a position she usually experienced from the outside. Playing this role gave her control over the criticism rather than leaving her to absorb it. Because Ella could play out harsh criticism without it leading to rupture or withdrawal in the relationship, the teacher character no longer needed to remain so rigid over time. As criticism softened within the play, other characters began to appear, including figures that were uncertain or in need of nurturance. In this way, embodying the critical role reduced its grip, allowing space for more vulnerable aspects of Ella's experience to emerge and be tolerated. In this way, Ella's play shows us how working with unconscious material can lead to a reorganisation of entrenched patterns without interpretation.

Working with Behaviour and Thinking

Behaviour is a common reason children and young people are referred for therapy. Because it is visible, sometimes disruptive, it often becomes the focus of adult concern and the target of systems such as education. The risk is that behaviour is treated in isolation, through the use of reward-and-sanction models that prioritise management over understanding. While such approaches can maintain order, they narrow curiosity about the meaning and function of children's actions. An ecosystemic approach makes space to be curious about why children do what they do.

As we explored in Chapter 2, behaviours cannot be separated from the beliefs that sustain them. Every action expresses an implicit assumption about how the world works, and every belief distils a history of actions. Thinking and behaviour, therefore, form a single feedback system, each part shaping and reinforcing the other: "If I stay quiet ⇄ I'll be safe"; "If I shout ⇄ someone will notice"; or "If I'm good ⇄ I won't be rejected." Ecosystemic work acknowledges this circularity and the relational context within which it has emerged. It helps children and young people recognise these patterns as adaptive responses to the demands of past and present relationships and makes space for new possibilities.

Mapping Patterns of Thought and Behaviour

While children may have an awareness of their behaviours (particularly those that are experienced by adults as destructive), many will have less understanding of why they do what they do or the thinking that is intertwined. For primary-aged children, reflective capacities are limited by their stage of development, with metacognition (the ability to think about thinking) only emerging fully by late teens. Even for older adolescents, the meaning of their behaviours can remain unclear while thoughts operate automatically and out of consciousness. Where reflective discussion is not possible, the creative methods discussed in the previous section offer alternative ways of exploring these aspects of the inner world.

One of the first tasks when working with thinking and behaviour then is to help children map the link between their inner world and their behaviours. Traditionally, therapists have found it helpful to do this in a structured way using thought diaries. Recording thought patterns between sessions helps strengthen self-reflection, developing an observer self that can notice inner events rather than being carried along by them. The result is a better sense of what the young person's patterns of thinking are, and a better contextual understanding of the behaviours that are connected.

The ecosystemic approach expands the scope of the thought diary to explore the role thoughts and behaviours play in sustaining helpful and unhelpful feedback loops. The young person is encouraged to consider the responses their actions elicit in others and how these responses in turn impact their inner world and future behaviour. From this perspective, the child's thoughts and actions are not seen as the cause of their difficulties but rather as responses to, and sustainers of, the relational contexts in which they arise. Figure 4.1 shows this cycle.

The relational context for thoughts and feelings may not always be immediately obvious. Take, for example, Amara, a 16-year-old who comes to therapy worried about failing her exams. As she talked about her internal experience of anxiety, her tight chest,

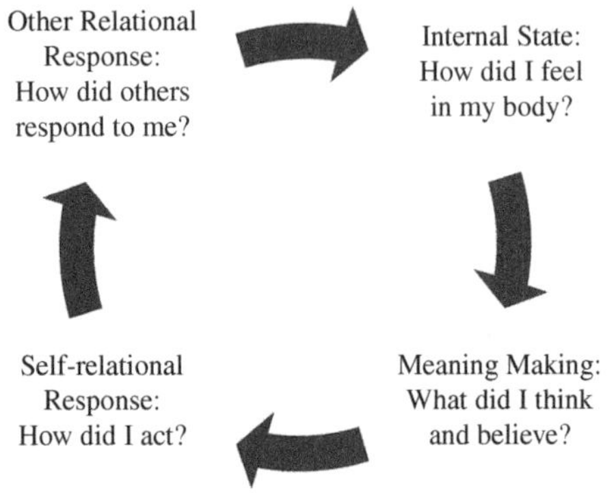

Figure 4.1 Behaviour and thought in context.

sweaty palms, and blank thoughts, it seemed isolated from her relationships with others, appearing as a demand she has placed upon herself. However, as Amara completed a diary of the thoughts and behaviours associated with her worries, a backdrop of interactions emerged. An excerpt from this diary can be seen in Table 4.1.

The intention of using diaries in ecosystemic counselling isn't to challenge "faulty thinking" or "unhelpful behaviour" but to create enough space to reflect on previously invisible, automatic processes. The therapist supports children and young people to understand that their thinking and behaviour have meaning and are communications of their place within relational systems. Mapping reveals how thoughts, behaviour, and social interactions are interconnected and how the child's internal world has evolved to navigate key relational contexts.

From Mapping to Meaning

Understanding form is only the first step in working with thoughts and behaviour. The next step is to create a space where it is safe enough to look at and begin experimenting with these patterns. The therapist does this by responding with curiosity rather than judgement, enabling young people to recognise that their responses are not personal failings but adaptations to context. Initially, the

Table 4.1 Amara's Thought and Behaviour Diary

When/where	What was happening	Bodily sensation/ feeling (rate out of 10)	Negative thought	What I did/what happened next	How others reacted/ what changed around me	What happened inside me next?
Monday evening, at home	Revising for exams alone in her room. Mum asked if I'd done enough revision.	Tight stomach, tense shoulders; anxious 8/10, restless 6/10	I'll fail. Everyone else has revised more than me.	Scrolled on my phone instead of revising.	Mum looked frustrated and said, "You need to focus more. Your sister had to work hard to get to Uni, remember?"	Felt judged and defensive; thought, "She doesn't get how stressed I am." Anxiety increased.
Tuesday morning, in school	Teacher handing out a practice paper. Reminded the class that it would "show who is on track" for final exams.	Heart pounding, sweaty hands; fear 9/10, nausea 7/10	I can't remember anything. I'm going to mess it all up.	Avoided looking at anyone, rushed answers to look busy.	Teacher paused briefly beside my desk, glanced at my paper, and then moved on to another student.	Felt exposed and inadequate. Thought, "They know I'm failing." Anxiety got worse, and concentration dropped further.
Thursday afternoon, in school	Results handed back in class; got a mark that was higher than most of my friends.	Brief relief in chest, then tension returned; relief 4/10, anxiety 6/10	I won't do this well next time; they don't know I'm not that clever.	Played down the result, avoided talking about it, and focused on the questions I got wrong.	Friends congratulated me. Teacher nodded and said, "If you keep this up, you'll do well in the real thing."	Felt pressure rather than pride; thought, "Now there's no excuse." Anxiety remained.

therapist uses mapped material to help the young person reflect on what their patterns have been doing for them. A belief such as "I'm a failure," for instance, is easier to approach when understood as an effort to prevent criticism or conflict rather than as a truth about the self. Similarly, behaviours like withdrawal or people-pleasing can be explored as strategies for managing relationship demands rather than character flaws. The counsellor invites reflection that situates the young person within their relationships, adopting a stance that is compassionate and collaborative, using questions such as:

- How did this belief help you in your family?
- What relationships or events have influenced these beliefs?
- What happens in your world when you act this way?

This contextualising enables the child or young person to distinguish between what once made sense and what continues to be necessary. Amara's diary reveals patterns of thinking and acting that help her to respond to others. These behaviours connect with family and school values, expectations about educational achievement, and social status. Amara's preoccupation with failure reflects her unconscious understanding that performance is required for belonging and reduced conflict. Behaviours around procrastination and disengagement, on the other hand, reduce exposure to her own feared inadequacy and preempt feelings of shame.

Behind the everyday thoughts Amara captures in her diary are core beliefs about who she is and her place in the world, such as "I am not good enough." Helping young people identify core beliefs can further support the meaning-making process, revealing the logic that accompanies the relationship loops. In counselling, children and young people express common core beliefs, and these are summarised in Table 4.2.

Exploring meaning with the young person offers opportunities for reframing thoughts and behaviours, from the kinds of pathologising narratives that are often dominant in their lives to preferred ways of thinking about their difficulties. This new story is

Table 4.2 Common Core Beliefs and Their Function

Core belief	Relational function (what it protects/organises)
"I am bad/defective."	Internalises blame to preserve attachment; keeps caregivers "good" so the relationship can continue.
"I am unlovable/not worth staying with."	Preempts emotional withdrawal to soften potential abandonment or rejection.
"My feelings are dangerous/ unacceptable."	Suppresses emotional expression to avoid overwhelming or triggering caregivers; maintains relational stability.
"I must be good/perfect to be safe."	Uses compliance or perfectionism to regulate adult responses and avoid criticism or conflict.
"Other people can't be trusted."	Maintains distance or hypervigilance to prevent further hurt, inconsistency, or unpredictability.
"People leave when you need them."	Organises clinging or avoidance patterns; reduces the shock of loss by anticipating it.
"I am responsible for others' feelings/safety."	Parentifies the child; stabilises a dysregulated system by making the child the regulator.
"I have to show how upset I am or people won't respond."	Amplifies distress to gain attention in systems where care is inconsistent.

co-constructed between client and therapist but may begin with the counsellor tentatively offering alternative ways of understanding beliefs and behaviour.

> "It makes sense that you learned to be perfect when mistakes led to tension at home. I'm curious whether that rule still fits who you are now?"

This expands the child's internal options without disputing or confronting their beliefs. The intention is not to replace one thought with another but to loosen rigid patterns and introduce new relational possibilities. The counsellor encourages psychological flexibility, a core process described within acceptance and commitment therapy by Steven Hayes. Psychological flexibility refers to the child's capacity to stay in contact with present experience and to respond in ways guided by values rather than by automatic, learned reactions. By shifting how the young person relates to thoughts and feelings, therapy reduces the grip of fixed behavioural rules and supports more adaptive responses in changing situations. Those who referred the young person for counselling will notice a positive change in behaviour, and the ecosystemic counsellor understands that change as a sign of a more flexible inner world.

Therapeutic Experimentation

Once meaning has been made of a young person's thoughts and behaviour, therapy can also act as a space to test new possibilities in action. Here, ecosystemic work uses relational experiments: small, therapist-supported attempts to challenge the expectations of old core beliefs, whether they relate to rejection, indifference, conflict, or some other fear. For a young person who believes emotions are dangerous, this might involve expressing a feeling in session and noticing that the relationship holds. For someone who anticipates disappointment, it might mean bringing a mistake to therapy and experiencing acceptance rather than criticism.

Ecosystemic work also looks beyond the therapist–client relationship. When the young person is ready, the therapist supports the child to think about their role in the relational feedback loops they are part of and where they might enact change. For the young person who has learned to please others, this may involve saying "no" for the first time. For the child who has learned to depend on others at the expense of their own sense of competence and autonomy, this may look like trying new things. Because feedback loops are maintained not only by the child but also by key others in the child's life, the counsellor may take an actively systemic role, supporting parents, carers, and teachers to understand the relational logic behind the young person's behaviour patterns. This might involve helping adults soften performance pressure, establish clearer boundaries, or respond to emotional expression differently. Such interventions can shift the relational contexts that sustain unhelpful loops, making it easier for new patterns to take root.

Working with thoughts and behaviour in the ecosystemic model is, therefore, neither an exercise in correcting cognition nor a simple reliance on relational safety. It is a way of supporting the child's implicit relational predictions to become visible and flexible. By mapping patterns, exploring their logic, and testing new relational possibilities, children and young people can gradually loosen the rules that keep them safe but constrain their development. Our view is that counselling the child's inner world, expressed symbolically or behaviourally, creates positive shifts in their experience. Being more able to hear, understand, and tolerate their feelings, the child becomes more comfortable in who they are.

Conclusion

This chapter has outlined three complementary ways of working with the inner world within an ecosystemic frame. Beginning with the body, we saw how safety, regulation, and implicit memory are held and expressed somatically, and how movement, rhythm, and sensory experience can provide both containment and a route to emotional integration. We then considered symbol, metaphor, image, and play as the child's natural languages of representation, allowing experiences that cannot yet be spoken to be approached at a safe distance, being held imaginatively before they are voiced more directly.

In turning to thinking and behaviour, the focus shifted to more explicit, surface-level expressions of the inner world. Here we explored how beliefs and actions form feedback loops with the systems around the child, and how mapping, reflection, and relational experimentation can loosen protective-but-constraining rules. Across all these modes, the task has been the same: to understand children's responses as meaningful adaptations within their relational and cultural contexts, rather than as isolated symptoms to be removed.

The chapter has also emphasised that no single pathway may be sufficient on its own. The therapist may need to move flexibly between bodily, symbolic, and reflective work, guided by the child's developmental level, preferences, and presenting needs. The relationship described in the previous chapter remains the constant context beneath these different modes of practice. Together, they offer a map for engaging with the complexity of children and young people's lives, and for supporting change that is both emotionally resonant and relationally grounded.

Chapter 4: Summary

Key Ideas

- Children's inner worlds are expressed through multiple channels beyond talk, including bodily states, symbolic play, images, thoughts, and behaviour.
- Different modes of working offer distinct but complementary entry points into experience.
- Therapeutic change emerges through understanding children's responses as meaningful adaptations within relational systems, rather than symptoms to be corrected.

Practice Implications

- Therapeutic modalities are held within and enacted through the therapeutic relationship rather than operating independently of it.
- Therapists may need to work across bodily, symbolic, and reflective modes, guided by developmental level, safety, and the child's preferences.
- Sustainable change often requires attention not only to the child but to the relational contexts that maintain existing patterns.

Reflective Prompts

- Which modes of working do you feel drawn to, and which do you feel more resistant to? How might this support and limit your therapeutic work?
- How do you recognise when a child is communicating through body, play, or behaviour rather than words?

Bibliography

Baron, S. (2015). *Play Therapy Interventions to Enhance Resilience* (ed. D.A. Crenshaw, R. Brooks, and S. Goldstein), 1e. The Guilford Press.

Carr, A. (2019). *Family Therapy: Concepts and Practice*, 4e. Wiley-Blackwell.

Dowling, E. and Vetere, A. (eds.) (2017). *Narrative Therapies with Children and their Families: A Practitioner's Guide to Concepts and Approaches*, 2e. Routledge: Taylor & Francis Group. https://doi.org/10.4324/9781315687063

Drewes, A.A. and Schaefer, C.E. (eds.) (2017). *Puppet Play Therapy: A Practical Guidebook*. Routledge.

Freeman, J.C., Epston, D., and Lobovits, D. (1997). *Playful Approaches to Serious Problems: Narrative Therapy with Children and their Families*. W. W. Norton & Company.

Freud, S. (1900). *The Interpretation of Dreams* (J. Strachey, Ed. & Trans.). Standard Edition of the Complete Psychological Works of Sigmund Freud (Vols. 4–5). Hogarth Press.

Fuggle, P., Curry, V., and Dunsmuir, S. (2012). *CBT with Children, Young People and Families*. Sage.

Hayes, S.C., Strosahl, K.D., and Wilson, K.G. (2012). *Acceptance and Commitment Therapy: The Process and Practice of Mindful Change*, 2e. Guilford Press.

Landreth, G.L. (2012). *Play Therapy: The Art of the Relationship*, 3e. Routledge.

Landreth, G.L. (2023). *Play Therapy: The Art of the Relationship*, 4e. Routledge.

Malchiodi, C.A. (ed.) (2015). *Creative Interventions with Traumatized Children*, 2e. The Guilford Press.

McCarthy, D. and Greene, R.K. (2007). *"If you Turned into a Monster": Transformation through Play: A Body-centered Approach to Play Therapy*, 1e. Jessica Kingsley.

McLaughlin, C. and Holliday, C. (2013). *Therapy with Children and Young People: Integrative Counselling in Schools and other Settings*, 1e. SAGE Publications Ltd.

Meersand, P., Gilmore, K.J., and American Psychiatric Association Publishing, issuing body. (2018). *Play Therapy: A Psychodynamic Primer for the Treatment of Young Children*, 1e. American Psychiatric Association Publishing.

Morison, L., Simonds, L., and Stewart, S.J. (2022). Effectiveness of creative arts-based interventions for treating children and adolescents exposed to traumatic events: a systematic review and meta-analysis. *Arts & Health* 14 (3): 237–262.

O'Connor, K.J., Schaefer, C.E., and Braverman, L.D. (eds.) (2016). *Handbook of Play Therapy*, 2e. Wiley.

Oaklander, V. (1988). *Windows to our Children: A Gestalt Therapy Approach to Children and Adolescents*, 2e. Gestalt Journal Press.

Oaklander, V. (2022). *Hidden Treasure: A Map to the Child's Inner Self.* Routledge.

Souter-Anderson, L. (2015). *Making Meaning: Clay Therapy with Children & Adolescents*. Hinton House Publishers.

Stallard, P. (2005). *A Clinician's Guide to Think Good-feel Good: Using CBT with Children and Young People*. John Wiley & Sons.

Treisman, K. (2016). *Working with Relational and Developmental Trauma in Children and Adolescents*. Routledge.

Treisman, K. (2017). *A Therapeutic Treasure Box for Working with Children and Adolescents with Developmental Trauma: Creative Techniques and Activities*. Jessica Kingsley Publishers.

Turner, B.A. (ed.) (2017). *The Routledge International Handbook of Sandplay Therapy*, 1e. Routledge, an imprint of Taylor and Francis.

Zhou, S., Li, H., Yang, Y. et al. (2025). Effects of art therapy on psychological outcomes among children and adolescents with serious health conditions: a systematic review. *BMC Complementary Medicine and Therapies* 25: 149.

Chapter 5
Making Sense of Family Patterns

In the previous section, we explored how a child's inner world is shaped within relational contexts rather than arising in isolation. This chapter builds directly on that foundation by narrowing the lens to one context in particular: the family, understood not simply as a set of relationships but as an organised system with its own structure, patterns, and rules.

Structural and dynamic counselling approaches to family life invite us to move beyond asking what a child feels or does, towards considering how these aspects of the internal world are shaped by family interactions. Families differ in how they balance closeness and separation, stability and change, and authority and autonomy. These differences impact the child's inner world, and they are maintained through repeated patterns of communication, role allocation, boundary-setting, and responses to stress and transition. From a systemic perspective, a child's presenting problem signals family pressure and contributes to family stability.

For ecosystemic counsellors, this way of thinking allows us to link a child's inner experience to the relational structures that give it meaning, without collapsing into either individual blame or detached contextual explanations. Understanding a family's structure helps to make sense of behaviours that may otherwise appear contradictory or confusing by situating them within the family's own logic. This chapter, therefore, focuses on understanding families as dynamic systems: how bonding, flexibility, communication, boundaries, and roles interact, and explores how these patterns can illuminate the lived experience of children and young people within counselling practice.

Towards a Structural View of Families and Children

It might come as a surprise that so many counselling and psychotherapeutic interventions with children tend to keep a narrow focus on the child, despite the consensus that family is an important factor in children's development. But ironic as this might sound, there are important reasons beneath the "disappearance" of families in the therapy room. On the one hand, early family interventions often prioritised verbal communication amongst adults, lacking specific tools and techniques to effectively engage children. On the other hand, family therapists have arguably forgotten their own lesson: because family relationships are so central to a child's survival and wellbeing children in the therapy room will often prioritise keeping parents pleased over expressing their feelings or viewpoint. Child-focused work can, therefore, be understood as an effort by therapists to ensure that the true voice of their clients can finally be heard.

Therapists' disengagement from families is also deeply rooted in the traditional, Westernised perceptions of children that have informed psychology and psychotherapy since their beginnings. If we consider two of the most historically influential theories in Western psychology, Piaget's theory of child cognitive development and Freud's theory of child's psychosexual development both share the idea that the child progresses through predetermined stages that are, to a great extent, independent from the environment. Moreover, both Piaget and Freud portray the child as very self-centred at the beginning of their life, learning socialisation and the importance of relationships as they grow. Although further studies have largely re-elaborated and developed such concepts to account for the child's context and relationships (e.g. Lurja and Vygotsky, with regard to cognitive theory, and Bowlby's attachment theory in the field of psychotherapy), psychotherapeutic practice remains influenced by this cultural imprinting: hardly surprising in a society which revolves around the pillar of individualism.

At this point, you might start to wonder whether bringing in concepts such as family dynamics, social context, and cultural identity might be, for the practitioner, a rather idealistic take on the business of psychotherapy. Is it worth embarking on such a mission instead of waiting for the child to be dropped by their parents for the counselling hour, focusing on what they bring to the session and forgetting about the rest? Of course, the answer will be different for each practitioner, depending on their values, interests, personal style of work, and professional background. However, it never hurts to bring some science into the conversation:

> Imagine a young couple at home on a lazy Sunday afternoon with their baby, just a few months old. Dad is playing with the child, tossing her up in the air just to catch her on the way back down. The child is laughing, while mum watches the scene and comments in a playful manner. From time to time, we might notice the baby briefly glance at mum. As the play goes on for a while, the baby might become nervous, agitated, or even cry. Dad then looks at his partner; they exchange a silent nod, and Dad gently hands the baby back to mum or places her in her cradle.

Because this is a traditional family scene, it can cloud our view of what's happening. Let's reimagine the scene with mum tossing the baby in the air and Dad watching the scene from a corner. Or, equally, they might be two dads or two mums. What remains unchanged in each scenario is that:

1. the child will often quickly look at the non-active parent while engaging in the play, and
2. as a result of this complex triadic interaction, the child's reaction will evolve as the play goes on, and they will laugh even

louder, encouraging the active parent to continue the play, or start acting distressed, thus stopping the play sequence.

What we just pictured is exactly what Margaret Fivaz-Depeursinge and her team observed while conducting their studies on the *primary triangle*. Their findings were revolutionary, revealing that children as young as three months old are capable of complex interactions with at least two conversational partners. Children will adjust their behaviour depending on the verbal and/or nonverbal feedback they receive from both parents, even when seemingly engaged with just one of them. A child's inner experience was found to be deeply entrenched in the family triangle.

These findings challenge our idea that children are born completely self-centred and only develop social competencies as they grow up. On the contrary, it seems that children are equipped with sophisticated social and interactive skills, and perhaps learn individualism along the way, when complex social emotions and feelings such as shame, pride, embarrassment, and guilt make their way into the child's view of the world.

Back to our initial question, then, an ecosystemic counsellor finds it helpful to consider the contexts within which their young clients exist. By doing so, counsellors become more aware of the deep, and sometimes silent, emotional scaffoldings that connect the child to their families. This provides space for new meanings to emerge in the conversation. But it also promotes authenticity, allowing the child's emotions to be connected to their relationship with significant others, rather than being read in isolation. The groundbreaking work of researchers such as Fivaz-Depeursinge, Maragreth Mead, and Gregory Bateson has shed light on family interactions, enabling therapists to make sense of the complex and at times chaotic world of family structures, interactions, and meaning making.

Families and Their Dynamics

Gregory Bateson proposed a radical idea that people are better understood by observing them within their significant network of relationships. This had a huge impact on the way practitioners around the globe made sense of key concepts such as the self and identity: what if, instead of being a predetermined infrastructure located within the individual, the self was an ongoing process influ enced by multiple contextual and relationship factors? It was with this question in mind that the Palo Alto research group started exploring the way interactions between people, and the feedback loops these interactions initiate, shape an individual's behaviours, feelings, and beliefs.

Watzlawick, Beavin, and Jackson offered the first systematic overview of this idea, proposing that human communication had a *pragmatic* purpose: showing how each person is trying to define a relationship, and trying to get the other person to go along with that. If we break this down into simple steps, we can see more clearly the patterns that emerge in communication between people:

1. In the context of an interaction, someone sends a message.
2. This message contains *explicit, verbal information, for example, the content*: "You know, this movie we talked about for weeks is finally out!"
3. *Nonverbal, implicit communications attempt to define the relationship, for example, excited body language*: for instance, if the person who gives the information about the movie is romantically interested in the message's recipient, they might accompany this communication with a plethora of nonverbal signs, ranging from a sensual voice tone, to suggestive eye contact, to intimate proximity, suggesting that they could go and watch it together, trying to turn the event into a date.
4. The person receiving the message replies with feedback that will convey not only their reply to the explicit, verbal message but also a response to the implicit level about the relationship. Such a response might:
   (a) confirm the sender's proposal, hinting that the person is excited to go and watch the movie together,
   (b) acknowledge the implicit message while also refusing the offer in it (e.g. "thanks, I have a partner"), and
   (c) completely dismiss or disregard the message, leaving the person confused and unable to decide how to pick the

communication from there (this could be, e.g. completely avoiding answering or answering by claiming they don't like movies).

According to Watzlawick et al., feedback influences the way relationships move forward but also how message senders feel about the relationship, themselves, and the other. With time, this dance of messages and feedback shapes interactions. Everyone involved develops general expectations about relationships, their own amiability, their capacity to influence events in the desired direction, and the way other perceive them. In a word, family and social feedback shape their "identity." For instance, someone who receives affirming feedback for their attempts at defining the relationship will develop high self-confidence, alongside, perhaps, a low tolerance for refusals and setbacks. On the opposite pole, someone who is constantly refused or dismissed might become inclined to enter new interactions with negative expectations and the idea that they will have to fight hard to be accepted.

If we translate this into our practice with children, in the therapy room, we meet clients who, despite their young age, have already developed expectations, core beliefs, and internal working models that dictate their initial moves in therapy. Some confidently trust us, some try to force us into confirming their ideas, some aggressively (or passive-aggressively) make us feel unwelcome, and some are guarded and wary. From the very first steps of discussing confidentiality and contracting, we participate in new interactions. These could confirm their pre-constituted assumptions about emotional expression or enigmatically place them in the wake of unexpected opportunities to cocreate something new.

Homeostasis and Morphogenesis

Moving further into Palo Alto's exploration of human communication, the concept of *homeostasis* is arguably one of their most groundbreaking concepts. According to this idea, the complex intertwining of messaging and feedback, involving all members of the family, has the specific function of protecting the family from unwanted change that could threaten their sense of identity as a group, or uncomfortably question their unspoken family rules. Feedback in a system such as a family is understood by Palo Alto not only as an individual response that people give to each other but also as an expression of the homeostatic tendency of the family to reaffirm itself against undesired transformation. Some behaviours are encouraged and others forbidden based on the family's need to resist change and promote continuity.

The idea that people respond to others' behaviour not only because of personal thoughts and feelings but also to maintain family-stabilising patterns might be difficult to grasp. To understand this further, below is an example from our clinical practice:

> Eleanor is a 21-year-old white, British female who recently experienced a sudden outburst of panic attacks. This began while she was taking the London underground on a Friday evening, and Eleanor described sweating, sudden shortness of breath, and her "heart about to pump out of [her] chest." She immediately called her boyfriend to pick her up from the station, and since then, she reported not allowing herself to leave home without her boyfriend or her mother. She took sick leave from work, and, when we met for the first session, she had been off for three weeks. Eleanor felt like her own body was betraying her, stealing her life from her. She has always been very independent, leaving home for boarding school at 14, gaining financial autonomy at 18. She resented having to go back to "live as if I am a child," depending on others for everything.

As therapists, our curiosity immediately takes us to explore the circumstances around the onset of her symptoms. Questioning revealed that Eleanor's relationship with her boyfriend had been strained in recent months, especially due to his reluctance to move in together. On an individual level, then, we might argue that panic was a response to this relationship rejection that impacted Eleanor's confidence and self-esteem. We might be interested in what core beliefs revolve around her self-esteem, her relational needs, and the emotional challenges of not feeling good enough for her partner.

In response to further curiosity, however, Eleanor explained that when she had the first attack, she was about to meet a new romantic interest on a first date, without her boyfriend's knowledge. Just as she was entering the tube station, conflicted feelings lingered, where the excitement of a new encounter was intertwined with feelings of guilt and fear. On a couple's level, we perceive another factor contributing to the panic was the presence of mixed feelings and ambivalence towards the relationship. The panic might have even emerged to protect the relationship with her boyfriend from becoming too dependent, and cheating is often linked to a person's emotional withdrawal from an intimate relationship.

Let's stay curious and consider what other changes were significant in Eleanor's life, close to the problem's onset. Eleanor explained that it was a time of family change. Ron, Eleanor's older brother, recently moved in with his partner and is now planning to get married. Since then, his contact with his parents has been reportedly "non-existent." Surprisingly, Ron (27 years old) had previously been considered a "mummy's boy." He had never had a significant relationship, and everyone in the family thought he would remain living at his parents' house "kind of forever." Eleanor described her mum's reaction to the news as "shocked and appalled" and hinted that she had been very depressed since. However, she seemed to have found new strength when she understood she had to help Eleanor get back on her feet. On this level, the panic attacks serve the "purpose" of reengaging Eleanor's mother, heavily suffering from her suddenly empty nest. In her new role, supporting her daughter's needs, she "forgets" about her depression, and Eleanor gives up on the prospect of marriage for herself. The family has reshuffled its roles but remains stable.

Eleanor noticed that her mother appeared to regain energy when supporting Eleanor through her panic. From a family systems perspective, Eleanor's symptoms may have had the effect of reorganising attention and care within the family. Her mother's focus shifted from the loss of her son's daily presence to supporting her daughter. Eleanor's difficulties thus coincided with a rebalancing of roles within the family, allowing connection and purpose to be maintained during a period of transition.

Now, if there is one thing we know about the human mind, it is that it is able to process and coordinate different layers of meanings, thoughts, and emotions at once. It is, therefore, possible that Eleanor's panic might simultaneously express her fear about dependency and support the family readjustment through a major transition, offering the most distressed member a new purpose. All this, of course, happens without any rational thoughts or planning from Eleanor, much like an emotional response to multiple triggers. The family system adds multiple layers to the client's inner world, being more like a web, where tension is distributed across many strands at once. When pressure increases in one area, the vibration travels throughout the structure. Eleanor's panic reflects strain within her own inner world, but it also resonates across the wider network, redistributing emotional weight and subtly reorganising relationships.

Ecosystemic counsellors read symptoms and problems not only as maladaptive, individual responses to a trigger but as adaptive responses to a family crisis. Two further family communication perspectives are helpful to hold in mind when working with children and young people. First, the Palo Alto researchers emphasised the constant tension between *homeostasis* (a family's pull to preserve the status quo) and *morphogenesis* (the push towards change, transformation, and development). Family life is shaped by the interplay of these forces, and family feedback can, therefore, be ambiguous, contradictory, or even paradoxical, especially during periods of transition. Second, they highlighted the importance of the nonverbal dimension of communication. Because verbal language is more easily managed and edited, it is often a more filtered channel. Nonverbal communication in posture, gesture, tone and pace of speech, proximity, gaze, as well as actions and choices, can express core emotional meanings more directly.

The Double Bind

As the Palo Alto group kept studying families, they noticed that feedback between family members was sometimes more complex than the supportive ("yes"), rejecting ("no"), or dismissive ("ignore it") exchanges that had initially been described. In some families, communication is so confusing that the recipient of feedback is left in a "checkmate" with no obvious way to respond. This pattern became known as a double bind, and it has four key features:

1. A high-stakes relationship: the bind takes place in a relationship that can't easily be left
2. Contradictory messages across levels (verbal vs. nonverbal communication)
3. No safe way to comment on the contradiction (can't meta-communicate)
4. Whatever you do is wrong (e.g. punishment/withdrawal/criticism)

Let's examine this further, using the example of a teenager who comes out as gay to his parents. This is a high-stakes relationship: the young person's safety, belonging, and emotional development depend, at least in part, on how his parents respond. There is also an inherent power imbalance. Parents have authority and often set the emotional terms of home discussions. As the parents respond to their son's disclosure, messages are communicated. Every message has two levels: the verbal level, conveying the content, and the nonverbal level, conveying the meta-message about the status of the relationship. Now, let's imagine that these two levels are in an open contradiction, so that a paradoxical loop is formed, making the message unintelligible. For instance, we could imagine these parents are conflicted between the need to accept and love their child no matter what, and years of cultural and religious conditioning that have led them into thinking that homosexuality is wrong. They might try to do their best to convey a message of acceptance, uttering words along the lines of "We love you the way you are," whilst their body becomes rigid, their mouth dries, and their eyes divert from their child's face. Imagine one of these parents trying to hug their child, doing what their mind tells them is the right thing, but the embrace is cold as their body betrays deep yet contradictory feelings. Even attempts to "do the right thing" can, therefore, land as emotionally incongruent, because the body is leaking feelings that the parent cannot (or dare not) put into words.

Over time, this can produce exactly the kind of confusion the Palo Alto writers were interested in. The young person may struggle to make sense of what is happening ("Am I safe or not?"), struggle to validate their own feelings ("Maybe I'm ungrateful"), and struggle to choose a response that protects the relationship. They may comply, minimise, or retreat emotionally. Inner-world distress shows up somatically in a tight chest, sweating, nausea, shaking, or behaviourally through shutdown, anger, avoidance, or self-harm.

Crucially, because the relationship matters so much, the teenager cannot simply ignore the mixed message. He cannot easily leave without major cost and cannot openly comment on the contradiction for fear of threatening the bond or provoking a backlash. That is why a double bind is best understood not as a simple misunderstanding but as a no-win relational position created when conflicting messages are delivered in a context where clarification and exit are not realistically available.

The idea of the double bind, then, is useful for children and young people's counsellors because it helps us notice when a child is being asked, implicitly or explicitly, to respond to conflicting messages in a family relationship. It directs our attention to communication on two levels at once: what is said in words and what is conveyed bodily. In practice, this lens explains why children look "irrational," shut down, compliant, or panicked. Their behaviour attempts to survive a no-win interaction. Using the double bind idea encourages counsellors to listen for mixed messages, name the relational dilemma in a safe, developmentally appropriate way and support the child to make sense of their experience, often by widening the focus from "what's wrong with you?" to "what is happening between you?"

Family as a Structure

Alongside the Palo Alto group, practitioners on the other side of the United States became interested in how repeated family interactions accumulate over time. Their focus was on how family history settles into stable patterns, transmitting roles, rules, and relationship templates across generations – even shaping how the family relates to the outside world. With these questions in mind, Salvador Minuchin, Julio Montalvo, and other key clinicians developed *structural family therapy*, grounded in a simple organising idea: to understand a child's presenting problem, you need to understand the family structure in which that problem makes sense. In the following section, we will explore several aspects of a family's structure: cohesion or bonding, flexibility, communication, boundaries, roles, and patterns.

Cohesion

Cohesion describes the way a family deals with the constant tension between the need for togetherness (feeling like an "us") and the promotion of individual differentiation, expressed in individual goals and development. We can think of this as the unique way in which each family tries to solve the dilemma between "I" and "We."

Some families privilege strong bonds and may go to considerable lengths to protect family boundaries, even at the cost of constraining individual ambition and identity. Such families are characterised by *high cohesion*, which becomes particularly pronounced when togetherness is prioritised over individual differentiation, which might be described as *enmeshment*. Other families, by contrast, emphasise individual autonomy, respecting personal schedules and adapting family activities around individual needs. In these structures, families may minimise shared rules and routines to prioritise personal choice and individual goals. These are described as *low-cohesion* families. Where cohesion is especially low and patterns emerge in which individual needs consistently override any sense of togetherness, families may be described as *disengaged*.

Pause and Reflect

- While you were reading about high cohesion and low cohesion, what feelings and thoughts came to mind?
- What was the model you felt was the "normal" one, and which one read as "awkward" or even "negative"?
- How does this resonate with your experience as a member of your own family (it can be the one you were born in, the one you spent most of your time with, the one you have chosen, or the one you created)?

Structural family therapists notice patterns at the different ends of this cohesion spectrum. Enmeshed families are often characterised by thick, almost impenetrable boundaries that separate them from the outside world. Strangers may be seen as irrelevant, untrustworthy, and even dangerous, according to family narratives. Often, these families begin to experience problems when the *outside* makes its entrance in their lives. This might occur because of school intervention, such as the influence or challenge of teachers, or at the point that young people's relationships with peers become important.

Ecosystemic counsellors see this reflected in a family's difficult relationship with helping professionals and their struggle to engage with educational or health processes that feel imposing or judgemental. As an embodied representation of the outside world, therapy may raise defensive responses in the family and can present a challenge to the child's engagement. The child might feel that talking to a therapist and building a rapport with them also means betraying the family. On the other hand, due to their strong mutual bonding, such families can become powerful allies of the therapist in promoting the child's wellbeing, if we are able to bring them on our side! Conversely, disengaged families might challenge a therapist, especially if they expect families to come together in the wake of a problem. A perceived lack of urgency in helping each other, or the prioritisation of adult wellbeing, might confuse the therapist and even translate into judgement. However, these families often grant more freedom to their members, including the younger ones, and this aspect can also be a precious resource in therapeutic work.

Flexibility

Flexibility is the family's capacity to embrace change without losing its identity. This concept is deeply connected with cohesion in determining the family's response to stressors. A family with *low flexibility* struggles to accept structural change, whereas a family with *high flexibility* can readjust and rearrange itself. Like cohesion, flexibility is a continuum where families at the extremes are more severely tested by change and transformation. A *rigid system* is one that completely rejects change to maintain the status quo. For instance, orthodox religious parents might stand against their child's marriage if the spouse does not share the family's faith. This reaction to change, of course, is typically understood by the family as a personal dilemma within the individual, who will have to choose between the wedding and parental disownment. In both cases, change tests the family organisation beyond its limit, resulting in either emotional cutoff or a dramatic emotional loss for one member.

At the other end of the continuum, a chaotic family responds to change by blurring roles, rules, and boundaries, responding with emotional dysregulation. For instance, a newborn baby raises the level of conflict in the marital couple, resulting in their teenage daughter taking on parental responsibility for the baby, without any negotiation or acknowledgement. Cohesion and flexibility are the family's scaffolding, combining to form unique structures such as a rigidly enmeshed family or a chaotically disengaged one, as we can see in Table 5.1.

Table 5.1 Different Family Structures

Flexibility ↕ / *Cohesion* ↔	**Enmeshed**	**Connected**	**Separated**	**Disengaged**
Rigid	Rigid-enmeshed: overly close, strict rules, resistant to change	Rigid-connected: close but rule-bound, limited adaptability	Rigid-separated: distant and inflexible, formal relationships	Rigid-disengaged: isolated, authoritarian, minimal support
Structured	Structured-enmeshed: close-knit, some adaptability but roles fixed	Structured-connected: healthy balance, predictable yet adaptable	Structured-separated: independent but organised, clear boundaries	Structured-disengaged: detached but orderly, minimal emotional exchange
Flexible	Flexible-enmeshed: Close but adaptable, risk of blurred boundaries	Flexible-connected: ideal functioning, balance of closeness and adaptability	Flexible-separated: independent yet cooperative, negotiable roles	Flexible-disengaged: Detached but roles shift easily, low emotional support
Chaotic	Chaotic-enmeshed: Overly close yet disorganised, unpredictable roles	Chaotic-connected: warm but unstable, inconsistent rules	Chaotic-separated: independent but erratic, unclear expectations	Chaotic-disengaged: isolated and disorganised, no clear structure

Communication

Communication is the "joint" that connects cohesion and flexibility, allowing families to form a repeatable structure. The complex exchange of verbal and nonverbal feedback that family members use to regulate distance, communicate presence, and allow or disallow conversations about feelings, goals, rules, and roles constitutes the foundation of the family's capacity to navigate change while maintaining identity. Good communication allows a highly cohesive family to stay "connected," without falling into the traps of enmeshed relational patterns. It can similarly support a highly flexible family to maintain functioning, without becoming chaotic. Family communication is made up of:

Speaking Skills: the ability of each member of the family to speak for themselves. This can be hindered when others speak for the individual, or the individual is unable to communicate for themselves.
Listening Skills: members' ability to actively listen and communicate empathy.
Self-disclosure: the ability to share feelings.
Continuity Tracking: the ability to remain on topic.
Respect and Regard: the affective tone of communication, reflected in how family members treat one another emotionally.

In work with children and young people, communication matters because it is through everyday interaction that families maintain connection and adaptability. Levels of cohesion and flexibility are not abstract family properties – they are continually negotiated through patterns of speaking, listening, emotional expression, and responsiveness. Communication is, therefore, a process by which families regulate emotional distance and make changes. It signals when togetherness is required, when separation is permitted, and how differences can be managed without threatening belonging.

For children and young people, whose access to language and decision-making is developmentally constrained, communication patterns are especially consequential. A family may advocate for values of openness or autonomy, yet communicate in ways that restrict expression, discourage disagreement, or prioritise stability over difference. Difficulties in communication can thus reflect inner-world tensions between cohesion and flexibility, such as when high cohesion limits emotional disclosure to preserve closeness, or when high flexibility results in fragmented conversations that leave children feeling uncontained.

Although most children and young people's counsellors work individually, family communication remains a vital lens. Patterns observed in the therapy room, such as hesitancy to speak, playing out conflict between hand puppets, or drawing depressing scenes of arguments, often mirror the communicative context in which the child is embedded. Similarly, conversations with parents reveal family rules around emotion, autonomy, and authority that form into a child's presenting issue. Attending to communication allows the counsellor to hold the individual experience of the child and the wider relational patterns in mind, without requiring direct family intervention. In this way, communication offers a clinically accessible bridge between cohesion, flexibility, and structure, enabling the counsellor to understand how relational dynamics are lived and felt by the child within their everyday world.

Boundaries, Roles, and Relational Patterns

Counsellors who attend only to communication risk locating difficulties at the level of individual skill or willingness, rather than recognising how such patterns are organised and maintained systemically. Assessing the family structure extends the therapist's curiosity beyond what is being communicated to how relationships are patterned, and where pressure, responsibility, and emotional labour are located within the family. This is particularly important in work with children, where symptoms or distress reflects structural tensions rather than individual pathology.

From a structural perspective, families organise themselves through boundaries, roles, and alliances that regulate closeness, distance, and power. One aspect of this organisation concerns the quality of *inter-systemic boundaries*, that is, how the family differentiates itself from the wider social context, such as extended family, schools, professionals, or cultural expectations. Boundaries that are too diffuse may leave the family overly exposed to external pressures, while overly rigid boundaries can restrict support and adaptability. Equally important are *intra-systemic boundaries*, which shape how different subsystems within the family maintain both autonomy and connection. For example, a couple subsystem may require privacy and emotional intimacy to function effectively, while also needing to remain accessible and responsive within their parental or co-parental roles. Children's difficulties can arise when these boundaries are unclear, collapsed, or overly rigid, leading to tensions that translate into their child's anxiety or low mood.

An analysis of family structure also attends to the distribution and clarity of *roles* within the family. When roles are poorly defined or inappropriately allocated, children may come to assume responsibilities that exceed their developmental capacity, such as becoming emotional caregivers to parents or acting as intermediaries in adult conflicts. Childhood role distortions place considerable strain on children and underpin a range of presenting difficulties. Typically, a child's wellbeing is impacted by small family subsystems. Patterns of *alliances and coalitions* form close or conflicted relationships between particular family members. These are often benign, emerging naturally through shared interests, temperament, or life stage. However, when such alliances become rigid and organised against a third party, they may develop into coalitions. Coalitions are of particular clinical concern when they cross generational boundaries, drawing children into adult conflicts and exposing them to themes or loyalties that are developmentally inappropriate. A child in a divorced family who forms a coalition against either parent generally has split loyalties that are carried in the body.

A family's subsystems often recruit children to regulate family tension. In some families, children may become *triangulated* into conflicts occurring elsewhere in the system, scapegoated as the "bad child" of wider relational distress, or positioned as "golden children" who must be perfect to maintain the family's image. While these configurations may stabilise the family, they often do so at a high cost to the child's wellbeing.

Cultural Considerations

Alongside family structure, it is also essential to consider the cultural, social, and historical contexts within which family organisation takes shape. This will be explored in greater depth in Chapter 7, but it is important to note that concepts such as cohesion, flexibility, boundaries, and roles are not value-neutral, nor do they manifest in the same way across cultural groups. Patterns that may appear enmeshed or rigid when viewed through a Western, individualistic lens may function as protective, adaptive, or ethically meaningful within collectivist cultures, migrant families, or communities facing ongoing marginalisation. Similarly, expectations around children's involvement in family life, caregiving, obedience, or emotional restraint may reflect cultural norms rather than dysfunction.

For counsellors working with children and young people, this means holding hypotheses about family structure tentatively and resisting the pull towards universal standards of "healthy" family functioning. Cultural meanings, migration histories, socioeconomic pressures, experiences of racism or exclusion, and intergenerational trauma can all shape how families organise closeness, authority, and responsibility. What appears as resistance to change may, in some contexts, represent an attempt to preserve identity or continuity in the face of external threat. Ecosystemic counsellors take a stance of cultural humility, remaining curious about a family's structure, rather than evaluating it against a cultural ideal. Structural exploration is ethically grounded when it asks how patterns support or constrain the child's wellbeing within their specific context, while remaining open to the possibility that change may need to occur at multiple levels, including beyond the family into the social world.

Structural Analysis

Approached with a stance of curiosity rather than judgement, structural analysis provides the counsellor with a framework for understanding how individual experiences are shaped by relational patterns. It allows distress to be located within the organisation of the family system, rather than solely within the individual, and supports therapeutic conversations that aim to reduce pressure on vulnerable members while increasing flexibility, clarity, and choice within the family. To help think about how a structural perspective can be helpful in understanding families, let's return to Eleanor, whom we discussed earlier in the chapter. Below is a description of Eleanor's wider family:

- Eleanor's mother: youngest of three daughters. Her father left when she was three, and her grandparents were the main caregivers for most of her childhood, due to her mother working long shifts to deal with the financial demands of being a single parent.
- Eleanor's mother's older sister: never married and still lives in the family home, where she takes care of Eleanor's grandmother, who developed dementia five years earlier.
- Eleanor's mother's young sister: she had a child with her former partner and is currently single.
- Eleanor's father: the only child of a couple that is still married, despite their relationship being described as "cold," "conflictual," and "strained." Eleanor's father grew up as his own mother's "best friend." This is still the case, as he frequently spends entire weekends at his parents' house.

If we consider cohesion, flexibility, and communication, we see that Eleanor's family presents with high cohesion and low flexibility. Family relationships appear to be enmeshed, with roles and boundaries often blurred. Several children are confidantes or caregivers of their own parents, and grandparents are surrogate parents. In this structural organisation, family patterns have been transmitted across generations. Finally, there are indications of resistance to change, with Eleanor's father maintaining the same role he had in his family of origin, even though he is now married and has children of his own.

We can also explore how the family responds to change. Eleanor's older brother Ron's decision to move in with his partner represents a significant test of the family's flexibility and cohesion. In a system characterised by high cohesion and low flexibility, such change is difficult to absorb. Rather than being distributed across relationships, the pressure generated by change becomes concentrated in one part of the family. To use a physical metaphor, when a joint cannot accommodate movement, strain is placed on an individual tendon, ligament, or muscle, leading to injury and symptoms such as pain and restricted movement. With Ron leaving, Eleanor's mother is left alone to deal with the loss, entering depression. Eleanor's symptoms intervene as a protective factor for the family's status quo, but the symptoms emerge from the pattern between mother-son-daughter. Eleanor's panic invites her mother to take on a caring role, and no other change is, therefore, required. The symptom redistributes the pressure, and the family maintains their structural functioning.

Structural Thinking with Children and Young People

At this point, it is important to pause and consider how structural thinking might be used in practice, particularly when the counsellor is working primarily with a child or young person rather than the whole family. After all, child-centred counsellors may feel cautious about family-oriented conversations that risk removing attention or autonomy from their client. The risk of jeopardising the one-to-one alliance with the child to gain more information about the family might also be perceived as exceeding the potential benefits.

Firstly, it is important not to lose sight of the wider context in which a child's wellbeing is embedded. Factors such as high levels of conflict within the household, critical life transitions, and significant family reorganisations can profoundly impact children and young people. When these contexts are overlooked, there is a risk of constructing a narrative in which the child is perceived as "flawed," "malfunctioning," or "broken." From an ecosystemic perspective, we understand the child's behaviour as an adaptation to relational and environmental pressures. Secondly, structural thinking does not require the therapist to intervene directly in family organisation, nor does it imply that the counsellor's task is to correct or reorganise family relationships. Instead, it offers a way of holding the child's experience in context, without collapsing into either individual blame or systemic overreach.

When working individually, the counsellor inevitably becomes part of the wider relational field. The therapy relationship may temporarily function as a new subsystem within the child's ecology, and this brings both opportunities and risks. Without care, the therapist may be pulled into implicit alliances, positioned as siding with the child against parents, or as an extension of parental authority, thereby reproducing the very patterns under exploration. Structural awareness helps the counsellor notice these dynamics as they emerge and respond with reflexivity. Importantly, structural hypotheses are not conclusions to be shared or imposed but working ideas held lightly in the background. They guide curiosity, helping the counsellor decide what to actively listen for and where caution is required. For example, recognising that a child is carrying family distress can prevent the therapist from inadvertently encouraging premature individuation or confrontation that might place the child at relational risk.

In this sense, structural thinking operates as an internal compass rather than a set of techniques. It allows the counsellor to remain anchored in the child's subjective experience while staying attuned to the relational pressures shaping that experience. Used in this way, systemic and structural perspectives support ethical, developmentally sensitive practice, even when therapy takes place one-to-one. Ecosystemic perspective explores aspects of family life similarly to exploring aspects of the inner world. Rather than relying on direct or interrogative questioning, therapeutic curiosity can be expressed through open, developmentally attuned prompts that invite reflection on family structure, boundaries, and relational patterns. Examples of such questions are:

- When there is an important decision to make, who usually starts the conversation in your family? Does anyone tend to have the final say?
- If you need help with homework, who do you usually turn to?
- When you moved house last year, who seemed most excited? Who found it more difficult?
- If you were to receive a poor grade at school, who might be most worried, upset, or disappointed? Who would be more understanding?
- Who would you go to first if you had a problem?
- Who would you share good news with?

These questions are intended as illustrations rather than prescriptions. Therapeutic curiosity unfolds over time and must be sensitively timed, with language and tone adjusted to the child or young person's age and communicative style. It is also important that such exploration remains meaningfully connected to the client's presenting concerns and goals for therapy. For example, a young person seeking support around academic performance may experience questions about homework routines or family responses to grades as immediately relevant, rather than intrusive. The child's problem might be the counsellor's best ally when it comes to exploring hidden aspects of family life!

A range of tools may also support this exploratory work with children, young people, and families. The genogram, for instance, has long been used to facilitate conversations about family dynamics, roles, boundaries, and intergenerational patterns. While its traditional formulation has been criticised for not capturing contemporary family structures or cultural diversity, more recent adaptations have increased its flexibility and inclusivity. Genograms can be constructed in ways that are responsive to a client's developmental level and abilities, using creative and nonverbal modalities such as drawing, toys, sandtrays, or three-dimensional materials like Lego. What remains consistent across these adaptations is the genogram's capacity to open reflective dialogue about family organisation and relational expectations.

From a counselling perspective, incorporating elements from the structural family therapy model might still carry the risk of subjugating empathy and unconditional acceptance. For this reason, it is important to maintain empathy and a stance of not-knowing, of nonexpert curiosity. We are not there to brand a system as dysfunctional, thus blaming families for their children's problems. The role of structural curiosity in the counselling process is to create a space to reflect, deconstruct, and question family patterns and to consider how these patterns may have developed in response to particular histories, stresses, and needs. Our entry point might remain with the child's inner world. Or we may enter counselling by focusing on the family, moving towards the child's feelings and emotions organically. In this respect, exploring family structures can promote our acceptance and empathy when working with behaviours that would be otherwise unexplained, difficult to understand, or even appalling.

Conclusion

Chapter 5 has argued for the importance of situating children and young people within the families that shape their experience, without losing sight of their individuality or agency. By drawing on systemic and structural thinking, we have explored how communication, cohesion, flexibility, boundaries, roles, and alliances organise family life and how children may come to carry distress when systems are under pressure. The final sections have emphasised that attending to family structure does not require family therapy as such. Rather, when approached with a stance of not-knowing curiosity, awareness of family structure can support counsellors to hold the child's experience alongside the wider relational context, deepen empathy, and open up new meanings and possibilities for change.

Chapter 5: Summary

Key Ideas

- A family is not only a place of attachment and nurturing but also a social context in which dynamics and communication cement into structures, rules, and roles.
- Family cohesion and flexibility express the family's capacity to balance togetherness with differentiation and navigate change while maintaining an inherent sense of "us."
- The child plays a dynamic family role and contributes to the system's structural functioning. The child's behaviour can protect family homeostasis or challenge it to strive for change.

Practice Implications

- When exploring family communication and interactions, counsellors can be curious about the quality of feedback exchanged and how it contributes to each member's identity, emotions, and beliefs.
- Counsellors can have a theory-informed approach to family structures, their boundaries, alliances, and coalitions, while maintaining a child-centred practice.

Reflective Prompts

- How much attention does your counselling work give to the role of family structure in the child's difficulty?
- How can you build more awareness and curiosity towards family dynamics and family structures?

Bibliography

Bowen, M. (1978). *Family Therapy in Clinical Practice*. Jason Aronson.

Bowlby, J. (1969). *Attachment and Loss* (No. 79). Random House.

Fivaz-Depeursinge, E. and Corboz-Warnery, A. (1999). *The Primary Triangle*. New York.

Freud, S. (2017). *Three Essays on the Theory of Sexuality: The 1905 Edition*. Verso Books.

Galloni, G. (2013). La localizzazione dinamica: lurija e il sistema funzionale come modello di una mente integrata. *Rivista Internazionale di Filosofia e Psicologia*. [Online] 4 (2): 161–169.

Minuchin, S. (1974). *Families and Family Therapy*. Harvard University Press.

Minuchin, S. and Fishman, H.C. (1981). *Family Therapy Techniques*. Harvard University Press.

Piaget, J. (1964). Cognitive development in children: piaget. *Journal of Research in Science Teaching* 2 (3): 176–186.

Vygotsky, L.S. (2012). *Thought and Language* (Vol. 29). MIT press.

Watzlawick, P., Bavelas, J.B., and Jackson, D.D. (2011). *Pragmatics of Human Communication: A Study of Interactional Patterns, Pathologies and Paradoxes*. WW Norton & Company.

Chapter 6
Family Stories and the Child's Sense of Self

The previous chapter explored family organisation, examining how communication, cohesion, flexibility, and structure shape the system. While this structural lens helps us understand where pressure accumulates and how families maintain stability, it does not fully capture how family members experience these patterns or how they make sense of their roles, relationships, and difficulties. In this chapter, we explore another aspect of systemic thinking: the role of meaning making in families. Using this lens, family organisation is held together by dominant stories and family scripts. We show that families operate as an interface between individual emotions, beliefs, and identity and the wider social, cultural, and moral landscapes in which they are embedded.

Narrative therapists focus on how stories and core emotional themes are shaped and sustained through family dialogue. They privilege stories and language, often exploring verbal discourse. Alternatively, there are dialogical approaches that are foregrounded in the relational and contextual nature of language, attending to how meaning emerges between speakers. Equally, there is the semantic polarities model that describes how nonverbal communication signals the emotional foundations of individual and family meaning making. For ecosystemic counsellors, these models offer valuable tools for understanding children and young people's meaning making. They support counsellors to move beyond individualised explanations of distress, while remaining grounded in the child's subjective world.

Stories Therapists Tell

As psychotherapy emerged as a tool for improving mental health, early practitioners framed themselves as neutral, external observers of their clients. This narrative positioned therapists as objective experts who worked to identify the dysfunctional aspects of the clients' functioning and to "fix" them. Over time, these views have been challenged, with humanistic ideas centring on the importance of the therapeutic relationship and the relational turn in psychoanalysis, emphasising mutual influence and intersubjectivity within the therapeutic encounter. Within systemic psychotherapy, the growing influence of feminist literature and social constructionism pushed practitioners to acknowledge that the simple act of observing is never neutral but positions the therapist within the sphere of their own observation. As such, ecosystemic counsellors do not observe families as a separate entity. Rather, we see that a new system comes into existence as soon as the family, or the child, begins interacting with the therapist.

Once the therapist is understood as internal to the therapeutic system, attention inevitably turns to their own subjectivity. The therapist's background, personal history, cultural positioning, emotional responses, and theoretical commitments do not remain outside the therapeutic process but actively shape which experiences and stories are invited, privileged, or silenced. Acknowledging this influence can be unsettling, as it requires therapists to relinquish the illusion of neutrality and recognise the limited nature of their point of view. One creative way we have explored this with students is to ask them to think of a therapeutic question that has no assumptions. Classes typically think for a moment and then make suggestions. One student asks, "How are you feeling today?" Initially, the student feels confident in having found a neutral question. But, we ask, Why do you privilege feelings? Why do you limit feelings to this day? Normally, the student explains that understanding the child's feelings today helps them assess current wellbeing and begin building rapport. Yet even this apparently simple enquiry carries assumptions about what counts as important experience, how emotion should be accessed, and what time frame is considered relevant. The exercise illustrates that every question reflects a position: a theory of mind, a view of change, and a set of values about what should be spoken. Rather than striving for impossible neutrality, the task becomes one of reflexivity – noticing how our questions arise, what they make visible, and what they leave in the background. In doing so, the therapist's subjectivity becomes less of an obstacle to be eliminated but a dimension of the therapeutic system to be held in awareness and used with care.

This shift in the therapist's position also raises important questions about professional expertise. If the therapist cannot occupy a position of objectivity, what becomes of their status as the "expert" in the room? Systemic and postmodern approaches respond by reframing expertise as contextual rather than absolute. The therapist's questions, assessments, formulations, and theoretical understandings are seen as informed and valuable perspectives but not as definitive truths. At best, they represent one possible account amongst many. For some practitioners, this can feel destabilising, as it challenges the idea that the therapist is in control of the therapeutic process or responsible for fixing the client. At the same time, it can be experienced as liberating. Relinquishing the role of the expert problem-solver allows therapists to move away from rescue and correction and instead focus on cocreating a relational space that is sufficiently safe, reflective, and responsive for clients to access and mobilise their own resources.

There are also important ethical implications here. If therapeutic contributions are shaped by the therapist's self, then ethical practice requires ongoing reflexivity. Developing the capacity to notice, monitor, and reflect on the professional, personal, and even private dimensions of the self becomes a central clinical skill, not to eliminate subjectivity but to work with it transparently and responsibly within the therapeutic relationship. Returning to our counselling trainees, we promote awareness of assumptions in every counselling interaction, but we don't stigmatise assumptive questions. The family therapist Gianfranco Cecchin said that every therapist carries "prejudices." Our objective is not to remove prejudices but to use them in a way that supports children's wellbeing.

Problem Stories

As children and young people's counsellors, we often receive referrals from a range of sources, including families, schools, social workers, healthcare professionals, and other agencies involved in a child's life. These referrals typically carry significant weight and may present themselves as objective accounts of a child's difficulties. Diagnoses, assessments, and outcome measures can further reinforce this sense of objectivity, offering what appear to be clear explanations and definitive formulations of a problem. Both therapists and clients can find reassurance in such accounts. For practitioners, diagnostic language can provide structure and a shared professional framework; for children, young people, and families, a diagnosis may offer relief in finally having "the facts" about what is happening. This reassurance, however, often comes at a cost, including the risk of stigma, over-identification with a problem, or the narrowing of how a child's experience is understood.

From an ecosystemic perspective, it is important to hold such information as context-bound understandings rather than fixed explanations. Referrals, assessments, outcome measures, and diagnoses can be understood as *stories*: accounts shaped by particular contexts, priorities, and positions of power. Rather than neutral descriptions of reality, these narratives foreground some aspects of a child's experience while obscuring or marginalising others. Furthermore, because these documents are typically produced within authoritative systems, they often carry a strong claim to truth. We may, therefore, be inclined to accept them at face value, much as a child in the 1950s watching a Western film might have uncritically assumed that cowboys were always the heroes, villainising indigenous peoples. Systemic thinking invites a more socially aware stance, encouraging counsellors to remain curious and critical of all accounts, including their own, and to recognise that the power to tell a story also confers the power to determine what is heard, what is muted, and what remains unspeakable.

From this perspective, part of the counsellor's task is not to replace one "true" story with another but to question dominant narratives and create space for alternative meanings to emerge. For example, when a school referral describes a child as "defiant," an ecosystemic lens prompts curiosity about the expectations, rules, and relational dynamics within that setting, and about whose interests those descriptions serve. Mara Selvini Palazzoli and colleagues captured this stance in their invitation to reflect on "the problem of the referring person," a line of thinking that has been further developed within post-Milan approaches to explore how dominant problem narratives contribute to the maintenance of difficulty.

For counsellors working with children and young people, this way of holding information has important practical implications. Rather than treating referrals or diagnoses as instructions for what to focus on or fix, they can be approached as starting points for curiosity. In the therapy room, this may mean listening not only for the problem that has been named but for how the child or young person relates to that description: whether they accept it, resist it, feel relieved by it, or experience it as shaming. It also involves attending to which stories are repeated across systems, which voices are amplified, and which perspectives (often the child's) are absent.

In practice, this multi-perspective stance allows the counsellor to remain aligned with the child while still taking wider contexts seriously. For example, rather than challenging a referral directly, the counsellor might explore how the child understands the expectations placed upon them, what happens when they comply or refuse, and how different adults respond to their behaviour. Such conversations can open space for alternative meanings to emerge, helping the child to locate their difficulties within relational and systemic contexts rather than internalising them as personal flaws. In this way, ecosystemic curiosity supports ethical, developmentally sensitive practice by reducing blame, widening understanding, and strengthening the child's sense of agency within the therapeutic process.

Family Stories

As we explored in Chapter 5, early systemic approaches tended to conceptualise the family as a coherent unit governed by its own internal rules and patterns. In the Palo Alto tradition, attention was paid to how communication regulated the tension between stability and change, while structural family therapy focused on how cohesion and flexibility organised boundaries, roles, and rules across generations. Both perspectives offered a holistic view of family life, privileging patterns and organisation over individual subjectivity.

As systemic theory developed, however, a central tension became increasingly apparent: how to retain a systemic, relational perspective without losing sight of individual meaning making, emotional experience, and identity. In other words, how could therapists continue to see the forest while also attending to the trees within it? At the same time, systemic thinking began to extend beyond the family itself, recognising that families do not exist in isolation but are embedded within wider sociocultural and political contexts.

Social constructionist and feminist perspectives were particularly influential in shaping this shift. These traditions foregrounded the role of power, language, and social location and emphasised both individual uniqueness and the ethical imperative to attend to marginalisation and inequality within and beyond the therapy room. They highlighted that storying girls as anxious led to increases in diagnoses of female anxiety disorders while underdiagnosis of autistic spectrum conditions in girls. From this standpoint, systemic enquiry is concerned not only with how family dynamics solidify into structures and dominant stories but also with how children position themselves within those narratives, and how broader cultural discourses shape family life. If neurodivergent girls are stereotyped as anxious, then their differences are misunderstood, their needs misread, and the support offered addresses the wrong problem. In this way, broader cultural narratives actively shape how those experiences are interpreted within families, schools, and clinical systems, influencing which stories are heard, which are dismissed, and which identities become seen.

To offer another example of these key concepts, let's return to Eleanor and her family from the previous chapter. In the trigenerational history of this family, we came across a few narratives and core themes that seemed to have influenced individual pathways and contributed to generating recurring patterns. The main story revolved around polarities of presence vs absence, distance vs closeness, and autonomy vs codependence. The roles of Eleanor's family members are, at least to an extent, defined by the stories they make together. We see four story-positions:

- **The Leavers**: family members who prioritise autonomy and personal goals and are retrospectively framed as selfish or abandoning (Eleanor's maternal grandfather; initially Eleanor; later, Ron).
- **The Loyalists**: figures whose worth is defined through endurance, sacrifice, and commitment to the family (the maternal grandmother; potentially Eleanor's mother).
- **The Preservers**: those who maintain closeness and continuity despite relational strain, valuing presence over resolution (the paternal grandparents).
- **The Dutiful Child**: children whose value is located in emotional availability, caregiving, and responsibility towards older generations (seen on both sides of the family).

These positions function as story-based roles rather than fixed traits, offering family members different moral standings within the narrative. Each position carries implicit expectations about what it means to be "good," "selfish," "responsible," or "loyal," and, therefore, shapes how individuals feel about family life. Both Ron and

Eleanor are called to position themselves within this moral landscape. Eleanor was initially the independent child who ventured early into the outside world and built her independence, whilst Ron seemed destined to follow a path similar to that of his Auntie, who remained in her family home her entire life. However, the unexpected change of Ron's positioning places him closer to his grandfather, who abruptly left to pursue his own life goals. As a response to this change, Eleanor finds herself in a dilemma: whether to protect her hard-won independence or to move into a more dutiful position in response to her mother's increasing need.

More space is dedicated in later chapters to exploring how wider social and cultural contexts shape children's beliefs, emotions, and identities. For the purposes of this discussion, however, we focus on how meaning-making approaches extend earlier systemic models by attending to personal experience and role interpretations. In Eleanor's family, shifts in one member's core narratives of autonomy, closeness, and responsibility reverberate across the system, creating dilemmas that are felt emotionally rather than consciously articulated. For an ecosystemic counsellor, this shift in focus is significant. Rather than understanding distress solely in terms of dysfunctional patterns or structural imbalance, meaning making invites curiosity about the stories that orient a child's sense of self, value, and belonging. Eleanor's panic, for instance, can be understood not only as a response to relational change but as an expression of a deeper narrative dilemma: how to remain a "good daughter" who responds to her mother's needs, without relinquishing a hard-won identity as an independent adult.

Individual therapy highlights family structure in the child's family narrative. Attending to family stories and the positions available within them allows counsellors to access emotional experiences that may be difficult to articulate directly. Feelings of guilt, fear, loyalty, or shame often make more sense when understood in relation to the roles a child feels compelled to inhabit or abandon. From this perspective, the familiar counselling question "How do you feel?" may sometimes illuminate a different one: "What story are you caught in, and what part are you being asked to play?"

Pause and Reflect

Think about Eleanor's story:

- What parts of your own self were engaged while you tried to make sense of that story, and how?
- What perspective did you embrace more naturally, and what voice was louder, or more silent, for you? Did you read the story through the eyes of a daughter or son striving for their independence whilst still trying to be loyal to their family? Were you a brother or sister, perhaps jealous of your sibling's freedom whilst you were trapped by the expectations of being "the good child"? Were you listening more to the voice of a parent trying to cope with an empty nest? Or that of a partner who feels dismissed by their other half, too involved with family business? Or what other voice helped you make sense of that story?
- Now, think: if you were to surrender your point of view in favour of any other of the aforementioned ones, how would it change how you feel about this story? What decisions or ideas would be different, as a therapist?

Negotiated Stories

As far as stories are concerned, we cannot ignore that the same story, told in the exact same way by the same person, has a different meaning depending on who's listening. It just takes us to look at the fandoms of popular TV shows, such as *Stranger Things* or *Squid Game*, to understand how differently a story can land: some fans love a plot twist, while others think it's stupid; some fans despise a character, whereas others love them. Meaning does not reside in the story itself but emerges in the interaction between the story and the listener.

This insight highlights a limitation of early systemic approaches, which offered powerful accounts of interactional patterns but paid less attention to subjectivity. While these models helped counsellors understand how communication shapes relationships, they often assumed that messages would be experienced in broadly similar ways. In response to these limitations, postmodern approaches, particularly those informed by social constructionism, have offered more nuanced models for understanding family and social communication. These approaches emphasise that meaning is not fixed or uniform but cocreated, with individuals actively shaping and interpreting messages at multiple levels.

The *coordinated management of meaning* (CMM) framework offers a structured way of understanding how this process unfolds. It proposes that the meaning of any communicative exchange is shaped by the coordination of several interrelated layers:

- The immediate episode or situation
- The relationship between those involved
- The speaker's sense of self
- The broader cultural context

Communication, from this perspective, is a dynamic, layered process in which individuals continuously negotiate and coordinate meaning. Although CMM is introduced here in relation to family interactions, its relevance extends across the child's inner world, family system, and wider social environment, as shown in Table 6.1.

We are usually able to coordinate multiple levels of meaning at the same time, which means we rarely notice how many layers are operating in everyday communication. Most of the time, higher-level frameworks, such as relational expectations, identity, and cultural norms, allow us to make sense of interactions with little conscious effort. In the example shown in the table, the speaker doesn't have to consciously puzzle over why his mother's voice sounded impatient, or why their sister rolled her eyes, or why they felt a pang of guilt and shame in their stomach. The structure of the situation or episode itself, his relationship with both family members, and the broader cultural narrative around being a "good child" come together to create an immediate and coherent interpretation.

Table 6.1 Coordinated Management of Meaning (CMM) Framework

Level	Description	Key question	Example
Speech act	The specific communicative action performed by the message (e.g. request, command, and promise)	*What is the speaker trying to do with this message?*	Mum barged into the lounge, announcing "dinner's ready," with a loud, firm tone and a stern lock.
Episode	The immediate context of the interaction or event	*What is happening right now?*	My sister and I were in the lounge, catching up on, as we had not spent time together in a while.
Relationship	The nature and history of the relationship between participants	*What does this interaction say about "us"?*	I have always been in a very close relationship with my mum, feeling her presence as caring and protective, whereas my sister was more of a rebel and resented mum's closeness as she felt it was an attempt to control her.
Sense of self	The individual's sense of identity and personal narrative	*Who am I in this situation?*	Hearing mum's voice made me immediately feel like I was doing something wrong, excluding her from an intimate conversation and kind of "conspiring" with my sister to leave her out. I also felt guilty for keeping everyone waiting at the dinner table. I guess it just clashed with how I see myself, as someone who's respectful and tries to do the right thing.
Culture	The broader social, cultural, and political norms influencing communication	*What cultural rules or values shape this?*	I come from a family where mums are expected to look after everyone and run the household. There's a clear sense that parents are in charge, and you're meant to go along with that. Dinner matters in my family because it's when everyone is supposed to be together.

But imagine the episode had unfolded differently. Suppose the two siblings had continued chatting, and no one came to get them. When one of them finally walks into the dining room, they see everyone already eating, seemingly unconcerned about their absence. Mum looks up and says, in a neutral tone, "Have a seat, please." This moment would likely feel far more confusing. The surface-level message doesn't align with the speaker's internal expectations about what dinner means in their family, or about how their mother usually behaves. The resulting confusion emerges not from the words themselves but from a mismatch between the episode and the layers of meaning the individual brings to it. In a different family, where dinner is an informal event, or where a parent's attention is regularly divided due to work or other commitments, the same episode might not be confusing at all. The siblings might simply sit down and eat without interpreting anything further.

This example illustrates how the CMM framework offers a nuanced and flexible account of communication. Rather than seeing meaning as inherent to a message, CMM invites us to explore how individuals construct meaning through layered interpretations of the episode, the relationship, the self, and the wider cultural context. When a young person brings a confusing or distressing episode into therapy, this model encourages us to stay curious:

- What does this moment say about their relationships?
- What does it evoke or challenge in their self-story or personal values?
- What cultural or family expectations are shaping how they make sense of the interaction?

In this way, CMM provides children and young people's counsellors with a powerful framework for exploring not just what was said but how it was understood and why.

Let's return to Eleanor one last time. We left her at a crossroads between protecting her autonomy and coming to mum's aid now that her beloved son has left the family household. Seen through the CMM lens, Eleanor's dilemma can be understood as a tension between different layers of meaning. Her sense of self, grounded in an identity as an independent young woman who built her life outside the family home, comes into conflict with how she understands her relationship with her mother, and with the sense of duty and responsibility that relationship carries, particularly in contrast to her "mummy's boy" brother. This tension does not exist in a vacuum. It is reinforced by broader societal narratives around gender, care, and the moral expectation that daughters remain emotionally available to ageing parents. The interaction between these cultural discourses and the family's own traditions and histories intensifies Eleanor's predicament, eliciting feelings of guilt, anxiety, and fear.

From this perspective, Eleanor's panic can be reframed as an emotional response to a self-reinforcing dilemma in which every available choice appears to threaten a core value. Remaining autonomous risks positioning her as selfish or abandoning. Stepping back into a caregiving role risks erasing her hard-won independence. Each option undermines the other, leaving her caught in a circular bind of meaning in which neither action offers resolution. This kind of recursive, no-exit dilemma is what is referred to as a *strange loop*: a situation in which attempts to resolve the problem repeatedly return the person to the same point of conflict. For children, this often evokes anxiety or a freeze response. Attending to the frozen inner experience can thaw it out, and so can exploring the child's inhibiting family story.

Stories in Therapeutic Practice

Viewing families as a frame of reference for individual meaning making enriches our understanding of children and creates space to engage with behaviours and feelings that might otherwise be labelled as "dysfunctional." From this perspective, distress is not located solely within the individual but emerges from the way meaning is coordinated across inner experience, family relationships, and the wider social context. For ecosystemic counsellors working individually, this offers a way of remaining relationally and systemically informed without requiring family members to be present in the room.

A useful illustration of this approach is the Daisy model, a counselling tool derived from CMM that functions as a simple, flexible conversational prompt. The model supports exploration of how a young person coordinates meaning across different domains of life, such as school, friendships, family, faith, or community, with the self at the centre. The child is invited to draw a daisy, placing themselves at the centre and using each petal to represent an area of life such as school, friendships, family, online spaces, faith, or community. They add words, symbols, or images to show how they experience themselves in each setting. The therapist then explores with the young person how meanings change across petals: Where do you feel most like yourself? Where do things feel harder? Where do the "rules" about how to be seem different? For example, a girl might write "quiet" on the school petal, "loud and funny" on the friendship petal, and "responsible" on the family petal. Rather than treating these as contradictions, the therapist becomes curious about how she coordinates these different ways of being. At school, being quiet may protect her from standing out; with friends, humour may secure belonging; at home, responsibility may maintain harmony. The focus is not on deciding which version is the "real" self but on understanding how each makes sense within its context.

This reflects CMM's view that people live within multiple, overlapping "stories" or contexts of meaning, and that difficulties can arise when these contexts clash or when one story becomes dominant and restrictive. The Daisy model makes these layers visible in a simple, child-friendly way. It allows the young person to notice patterns and tensions, all while the therapist maintains curiosity about how meanings are created. Narrative therapy reminds us that people do not simply have experiences; they make sense of those experiences through stories shaped by family relationships and culture. What becomes a "problem" is often linked to the dominance of a particular story that narrows how the child and others see them, while alternative meanings remain less visible. From this perspective, the task of ecosystemic therapy is to create space for different stories to be noticed and developed. Michael White talks about "thickening stories" of hope and empowerment, amplifying the self-understandings that best support a child's wellbeing. If the referral language pathologises the child, we intentionally unpack the language to create new words and meanings for the problem.

This narrative stance sits naturally alongside the Daisy model. As the young person describes themselves across different petals, they begin to recognise that no single context tells the whole story of who they are. The "quiet" child at school and the "loud" friend with peers are not contradictions but expressions of different storylines shaped by different relational settings. The Daisy, therefore, becomes a visual way of externalising the multiplicity of the young person's identity and experience, opening room for curiosity about how these stories are formed, maintained, and sometimes constrained.

It is at this point that the LUUUT model deepens the conversation, drawing attention not only to the stories that are visible across contexts but also to those that remain in the background or are difficult to voice. The LUUUT model similarly supports systemic curiosity by drawing attention to the multiple stories that coexist within any situation. These include stories that are *Lived* through action and interaction; *Told* as part of an official or socially acceptable narrative; *Untold* or *Untellable* because of fear, loyalty, stigma, or power; and *Unheard* due to marginalisation or exclusion. For ecosystemic counsellors, this framework offers a way of listening beyond what the child says, remaining attentive to silences, contradictions, and embodied expressions of meaning, without forcing disclosure or interpretation.

The Daisy and LUUUT models illustrate how CMM can be translated into everyday therapeutic practice. They enable counsellors to work systemically and ethically in individual settings, by foregrounding the child's meaning making, positioning them as experts in their own experience, and recognising that therapy itself becomes part of the ongoing coordination of meaning. We have in mind a 13-year-old boy named Cameron. His referral form said he was "aggressive and defiant at home," with a comment from his father saying he was "a complete nightmare to parent." School reports endorsed this view, noting Cameron's frequent arguments and his tendency to refuse adult instructions. Within the family story, Cameron had become known as "the difficult one," a child who "loses his temper over nothing."

At first hearing this, both the referral and the family's own language offered a single, pathologising account: Cameron is the problem. Through conversation, however, a broader picture began to emerge. Cameron rarely spoke of anger but much of the household shouting and the effort of "keeping things calm." He described stepping between his parents when arguments escalated and trying to distract his younger sister when she became frightened. Here we glimpse what the LUUUT model would describe as the lived story: a child moving, watching, and acting within a tense household, his behaviour shaped through moment-to-moment attempts to manage emotional intensity. Alongside this sat the told story, the official family account, in which Cameron was labelled as intentionally oppositional. This narrative made sense of real events but obscured their context. His outbursts were authored without connection to the wider strain in the family system. Individualistic counsellors can feel confused about narrative contradictions, but ecosystemic counsellors understand that contradictions form by simply moving position. Seeing from the parents' perspective, Cameron looks like the problem. It's only when we move positions that new and usually more hopeful perspectives emerge.

As therapy proceeded, space opened for Cameron's untold stories. He spoke hesitantly of feeling responsible for his sister and of fearing that "something bad" might happen if he did not stay alert. He felt that much of his temper was normal in his household but that, unfairly, his anger was more problematised. His concerns had not been voiced at home, where he felt it was his role to appear strong, not vulnerable, and caring. There were also unheard elements: his mother's acknowledgement that she relied on Cameron more than she realised, and his father's admission that he had mistaken hypervigilance for Cameron being defiant.

Through this widening of stories, Cameron's actions could be understood as expressions of protectiveness and heightened sensitivity to family tension. The work did not deny the difficulties his behaviour created but placed them within a family frame. As alternative descriptions took hold, we supported Cameron to work on how he can show his home worries and brotherly protection without becoming the "bad child." It was slow counselling work. But as he started to reexperience himself as protective and aware of family tensions, he showed less need for communicating through destructive behaviours. His parents, especially his father, showed him how proud they were of his improved behaviour. It is tempting to want families to see their role in the child's distress and to change from that perspective, but sometimes a change in the child is a change in the family, and this difference makes a big difference. Ideally, parents could be supported to use their relative power to connect with a child's inner struggles. But much of the family story and structure is unconscious, and it is reinforced by negative cultural stories about boys' behaviour. In Cameron's case, his parents eventually took greater responsibility for their home conflicts, and Cameron was gradually relieved of a protective sibling role he had assumed too early. In this way, the LUUUT model supported a movement from a narrow, pathological narrative towards a fuller account of the child's intentions and capacities. Ecosystemic counselling reinforces empowering narratives that help children shift positions in their families and social worlds.

Conclusion

This chapter has invited a shift in how family life is held in mind, from patterns and organisation alone, towards the meanings through which family relationships are interpreted, morally evaluated, and emotionally lived. By focusing on stories, positioning, and the coordination of meaning, we have explored how children and young people come to understand themselves in relation to others and how distress can emerge when available narratives constrain rather than support development. For children and young people's counsellors, this perspective offers a way of working that is both systemic and developmentally attuned. It allows therapists to remain close to a child's lived experience while staying alert to the wider relational, cultural, and moral contexts that shape it. Family stories, expectations, and values are already present in what the child brings to therapy, and they can be explored collaboratively through careful attention to meaning.

Having explored how meaning is made, negotiated, and coordinated within families, the next chapter widens the lens further, turning to the child's outer system. This includes the social, cultural, institutional, and political contexts that influence which stories become dominant, which identities are supported or marginalised, and how children and young people locate themselves within the broader world.

Chapter 6: Summary

Key Ideas

- Family therapy has evolved from a primary focus on dynamics and structures towards a deeper concern with how individuals make meaning of self, relationships, and their place within the family and wider social systems.
- Models such as the coordinated management of meaning, the LUUUT model and the Daisy model provide practical frameworks for exploring meaning making as an ongoing, relational process shaped across the life course of individuals and families.

Practice Implications

- Listening systemically invites counsellors to approach clients' stories with curiosity rather than certainty, exploring what is told, what is silenced, what the story protects, and how alternative meanings might become possible in therapy.

Reflective Prompts

- How much attention do you give to your clients' stories, and how do these resonate with your own?
- Do you tend to take stories at face value, or do you feel able to explore the gap between what is told and what is lived? If so, how?

Bibliography

Cronen, V.E., Johnson, K.J., and Lannamann, J.W. (1982). Paradoxes, double binds, and reflexive loops. *Family Process* 21 (1): 91–112.

Ekinci, N. and Tokkaş, B.G. (2024). A systematic review of narrative therapy. *Current Approaches in Psychiatry* 16 (1): 58–71.

Foucault, M. (1972). *The Archaeology of Knowledge* (trans. A.M. Sheridan Smith). Pantheon Books. (Original work published 1969).

Gergen, K.J. (1985). The social constructionist movement in modern psychology. *American Psychologist* 40 (3): 266–275.

Littlejohn, S.W. and Foss, K.A. (2011). *Theories of Human Communication*, 10e. Waveland Press.

Pearce, W.B. (2007). *Making Social Worlds: A Communication Perspective*. Blackwell Publishing.

Pearce, W.B. and Cronen, V.E. (1980). *Communication, Action, and Meaning: The Creation of Social Realities*. Praeger.

Ugazio, V. (2013). *Semantic Polarities and Psychopathologies in the Family: Permitted and Forbidden Stories*. Routledge.

White, M. and Epston, D. (1990). *Narrative means to Therapeutic Ends*. W. W. Norton & Company.

Chapter 7
Bringing the Wider World into Counselling

In the previous chapters, we explored how we can make sense of the difficulties that bring children and young people to therapy within the context of their inner worlds and family relationships. Chapter 7 widens this lens to consider the broader environments within which families and children live. An ecosystemic perspective acknowledges that children and families are embedded within sociopolitical systems. These form a backdrop against which relationships and identities are negotiated, shaping experiences of safety, belonging, and difference. While social forces are not always visible, they exert a steady influence that frames both a child's presenting problems and our therapeutic responses.

In the following sections, we will consider how a child's outer system can be worked with in therapy. We will explore culture's role in identity development, how young people's engagement with adult-led systems can be understood in context, and the ways in which digital environments have become a central part of many young people's social worlds. We will also consider the implications of these influences for counsellors' ethical reflexivity, considering ways to work openly with diversity and difference.

Locating the Child Within the Outer System

Careful attention to a child's inner and family worlds is not always sufficient to account for children's emotional challenges. In such moments, difficulties do not arise solely from what happens *within* the child or *between* family members but from the child's position at the intersection of multiple systems that hold different biased assumptions and social expectations. Drawing on Urie Bronfenbrenner's *ecological systems theory* (Figure 7.1 and Table 7.1), we can extend ecosystemic thinking beyond the family by making visible how wider social, cultural, institutional, and historical forces influence children's wellbeing. Ecological systems theory invites counsellors to consider how these multiple social layers present in the therapy room. In this section we pay particular attention to the child's *exosystem* and *macrosystem* and how these systems interact with the way the family and child make sense of their experiences. We begin with a macrosystemic example, before illustrating how exosystemic influences often enter children's lives through institutional decisions.

To understand the impact of the child's macrosystem more clearly, let's consider Sarah, a child from a family of practising Jehovah's Witnesses. An intergenerational transmission of values

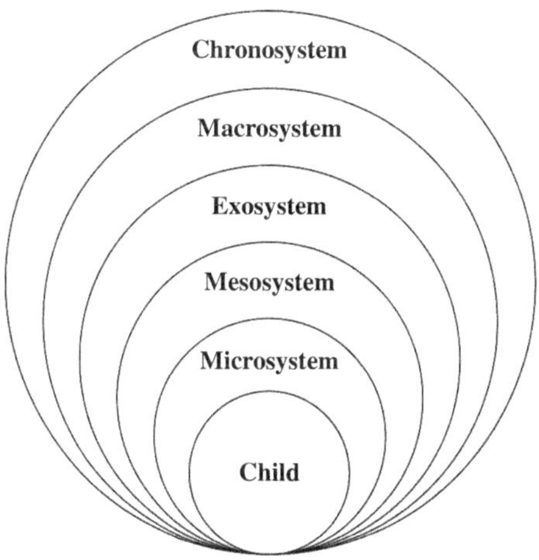

Figure 7.1 Bronfenbrenner's ecological systems theory.

Table 7.1 Bronfenbrenner's Ecological Systems Theory

Chronosystem: The dimension of time, capturing how developmental stage, life transitions, and historical change alter the meaning and impact of experiences across systems.
Macrosystem: The broader cultural, social, and ideological frameworks that organise values, norms, and assumptions across all other systems.
Exosystem: Contexts in which the child does not actively participate but whose decisions and pressures indirectly shape the child's relational and emotional world such as organisational and economic influences.
Mesosystem: The patterns of connection, alignment, or tension between the child's microsystems, which shape how experiences in one context carry over into another. For instance, how a teacher interacts with a parent about the child.
Microsystem: The immediate relationships that the child participates in directly, where experience and meaning are formed through everyday interaction. This includes family, friends, teachers, and therapy.
Child: The child's embodied, emotional, and meaning-making capacities, through which influences from other systems are taken in, organised, and responded to.

around purity, separation from "worldly" influences, and clear behavioural boundaries, contributes to family characteristics of high cohesion and low flexibility. Within this family microsystem, expectations around modest dress, avoidance of swearing, restrictions on friendships outside the faith, and clear rules regarding gender roles and sexuality are consistently reinforced and experienced as integral to family identity. Religion, therefore, forms a significant element of the macrosystem, shaping the values and assumptions through which other systems are organised and interpreted.

Now, let's imagine the moment when Sarah enters school and is progressively exposed to different ways of thinking. Classroom teaching, ideas from books in the library, and peer trends in the playground may differ deeply from what has traditionally been embraced by the family. Sarah encounters a social and educational environment shaped by different macrosystemic assumptions. In an RE lesson addressing world religions, Sarah expresses discomfort and repeats a belief learned at home, stating that other religions are "wrong." The teacher intervenes, reframing the comment as unacceptable within the school's commitment to inclusion, and other children respond with visible disapproval. Later, when Sarah recounts the incident at home, she questions the family's position on faith. Her parents respond by warning Sarah to be careful at school but also reaffirming that the family's beliefs must not be compromised.

Here, an important moment of transition for the family activates a moment of tension. The school operates within a cultural and legal framework that prioritises religious pluralism, while the family is organised around religious principles and communal norms. Sarah is positioned at the intersection of these macrosystems and is required to manage incompatible expectations about what can be said, believed, or expressed in different relational contexts.

From an ecosystemic perspective, Sarah's conflicting feelings are not located within her attitudes or behaviour alone. They are located in the relational work required to navigate belonging and safety across competing social systems. Her parents' heightened boundary-setting can be understood as an attempt to protect family coherence, while Sarah's oscillation between compliance and challenge reflects an effort to adapt to structurally conflicting demands. As children and young people's counsellors, we are committed to promoting the voice and safety of the child. When such conflicts arise, we might be tempted to dismiss the family's concerns as "oppressive" and even "retrograde", immediately siding with Sarah's right to her own independent thinking. However, we might also take a minute to step back and reflect on whether this new emerging thinking is truly "independent" or rather the expression of a different system's influence. If we see this problem through an ecosystemic lens, we might be curious about the creative attempts of the child and their family to deal with this clash. Our focus is to empower the child's creativity and resilience in making sense of it, and perhaps we even support the family in embracing this difficult change without losing their identity.

While Sarah's experience is primarily shaped by a clash of macrosystemic values, it is important to recognise how such tensions can also be carried into children's lives through exosystemic processes. Exosystemic influences refer to decisions, policies, and practices that are made without the child's involvement, yet significantly shape the conditions under which they live and relate. These influences are often less visible than overt value conflicts, but they can exert a powerful effect on a child's sense of belonging. To illustrate this, let's consider Leila, an 11-year-old girl referred to counselling following a noticeable change in mood and increased reluctance to attend school. She is black British, and her parents report that she has become increasingly resistant to getting ready in the mornings. In sessions, Leila speaks little at first, describing school as "stressful" but struggling to elaborate.

Several weeks earlier, the school introduced a revised uniform and appearance policy following a review by the senior leadership team. Amongst other guidelines, the policy specified that hair should be "neat, tidy, and of a natural style," with example photos provided. The policy was discussed at a staff meeting and communicated to parents via email. Shortly after the policy came into effect, Leila was challenged by a member of staff about her braided hair. Although the interaction was framed as a reminder of school rules rather than a disciplinary action, Leila experienced it as public shaming. She began asking her mother whether her hair was "wrong" and requested to change it so she would not "get told off again."

From an exosystemic perspective, Leila's distress can be understood as arising from institutional decisions that shaped how her body and identity were positioned within the school environment. A policy intended to promote uniformity and order entered Leila's lived experience as a message about acceptability, despite her having no influence over its creation or interpretation. In this context, Leila's withdrawal and anxiety can be seen as an adaptive response to navigating a system in which racialised cultural assumptions were embedded within seemingly neutral rules.

Whether working with macrosystemic or exosystemic influences in the therapy room, counsellors require self-reflexivity. Our own positioning is inevitably influenced by how a child's difficulties are interpreted. Attending to how our own exosystemic and macrosystemic locations intersect with those of the child and family helps sustain a stance of principled, non-judgemental curiosity. This creates a therapeutic space in which dilemmas and possibilities can be explored without requiring unhelpful assumptions or premature solutions.

Social Identity, Power, and Reflexivity

In his book on culture and reflexivity in systemic practice, Peter Rober highlights that, in Western societies, cultural diversity is an everyday reality. For ecosystemic counsellors, it is particularly important not only to acknowledge and respect cultural and social differences as they emerge in their relationship with the client but also to be reflexively aware and ethically responsive to the inevitable tensions and possible conflicts that multiculturalism may entail. In this respect, the Social GGRRAAACCEEESSS framework developed by John Burnham and Alison Roper-Hall offers a practical and reflective starting point for understanding how sociocultural factors influence counselling. Table 7.2 captures the different aspects of identity covered in the model (acknowledging that this can never be exhaustive) while giving examples of how these might emerge in therapeutic work. Burnham and Roper-Hall emphasise that some aspects of social identity are *visible and voiced*, while others remain *invisible or unspoken*, yet each can profoundly impact the therapeutic relationship.

For the ecosystemic counsellor, it is vital that we can reflect on our own Social Graces and how these influence our assumptions and interactions with clients. Having a clearer understanding of our own social and cultural positions helps us to be mindful of which aspects of identity are immediately visible. In our work with children and young people, some Social Graces are more at risk of being ignored or silenced, even when they may exert significant influence on the presenting problem.

An example of a subjugated Social Grace is "class." In our work with children excluded from school, social class is rarely named

Table 7.2 The Social GGRRAAACCEEESSS

Social grace	Description	Example in CYP counselling
Gender	Socially constructed roles and expectations linked to being male, female, or nonbinary	A young person may come to counselling questioning their gender identity and struggling with family expectations. The counsellor may have their own experience of sexuality and gender identity. The encounter between the client's and the counsellor's "gender" grace is likely to become a key factor in the therapeutic relationship.
Geography	Influence of location, environment, and cultural context	A child from a rural area may be feeling isolated compared to peers in urban settings. They may also experience embarrassment in raising this topic with the counsellor, and, therefore, let this grace be silenced for fear of judgement and stigma. It is a counsellor's responsibility to warm up the context so that there is space for this theme to emerge.
Race	Social meanings attached to racial identity and experiences of racism	A Black teenager may be experiencing microaggressions at school. How confident would they feel discussing this with a white counsellor?
Religion	Beliefs, practices, and values tied to faith traditions	A Muslim child navigating peer pressure during Ramadan. The tension between the desire to fit in with the rest of the class, avoiding possible stigma, and staying loyal to their beliefs and tradition might be a complex dilemma (you can, as a counsellor, consider dilemmas of this sort within the previously discussed CMM model as a strange loop between the level of relationships (with the peers and teacher) and the level of culture (his Muslim background), placing a tension at the level of their self-biography).

Age	Developmental stage and societal attitudes towards age groups	An adolescent may fear that their counsellor could dismiss their problem as "just a phase"
Ability	Physical, cognitive, or neurodiverse capacities and related social attitudes	A child with a disability may struggle to describe the full extent of their experience with a counsellor who does not share the same disability. The counsellor themselves may underestimate the level of hindrance caused by it or its psychological impact.
Appearance	How physical looks influence perception and treatment	A teenager experiencing body image issues due to social media comparisons may not be heard by a counsellor whose values do not place appearance in a position of priority.
Class	Socioeconomic status and related opportunities or barriers	A child from a low-income family may be feeling excluded from extracurricular activities. A counsellor from an affluent environment may be underestimating the issue.
Culture	Shared customs, traditions, and values shaping identity	A young person balancing collectivist family values with individualistic peer norms may meet a counsellor not fully aware of cultural differences, raising the risk that some cultural aspects and norms may go unvoiced and taken for granted.
Ethnicity	Cultural heritage and identity linked to ancestry	A child negotiating bicultural identity in a mixed-heritage family may experience dilemmas and confusion that a counsellor may feel unable to discuss due to the fear of offending their client.

(Continued)

Table 7.2 (Continued)

Social grace	Description	Example in CYP counselling
Education	Access to and experience of learning environments	A student may be feeling pressure to achieve academically due to family expectations. The counsellor's own values and perceptions about academic achievements and career goals may influence their approach to the situation and lead them to overwrite their client's experience with their own.
Sexuality	Sexual orientation and related societal attitudes	A teenager exploring same-sex attraction in a heteronormative school environment. How can the counsellor make sure that the context is warm and safe enough for this theme to be openly explored?
Spirituality	Personal sense of meaning and connection beyond religion	A Christian counsellor who is not reflexively and relationally in contact and monitoring this grace may look at other forms of spirituality lived by their client as "mere superstition" or even "blasphemy" and try to discourage them in their client.
Social Status (S)	Position within social hierarchies (e.g. popularity and influence)	A child feeling anxious about maintaining their online "status" amongst peers may meet a non-digitally educated counsellor who could easily dismiss this problem as irrelevant or childish.

but is nonetheless a significant factor. A counselling client named Lewis, a 14-year-old excluded boy, was referred for "lack of motivation" and "poor behaviour." He lives in a family where finances are tight, his mother works nights, and he shares a bedroom with two younger siblings. In the therapy room, the counsellor notices an assumption arising – that Lewis is disengaged or resistant – and pauses to reflect on how their own middle-class background shapes expectations about schoolwork and parental availability. When asked about school, Lewis shrugs and says he "can't be bothered." The therapist's question embodies middle-class values that can place pressure on some children to conform. It is important to recognise that there is no simple distinction between middle-class and working-class attitudes to schooling, and many young people from economically disadvantaged backgrounds engage with school in ways that reflect both structural constraints and personal priorities. Research on adolescent academic engagement shows that family socioeconomic status has a meaningful influence on how young people experience and relate to school, with adolescents from lower socioeconomic backgrounds more likely to report indifference towards school and education than their more advantaged peers.

Rather than assuming a lack of interest, a Social Graces lens invites curiosity about how Lewis' daily responsibilities, household pressures, and feelings of belonging inform his relationship with school. Instead of focusing solely on behaviour, the conversation opens towards questions of what school means to him and what support might help him feel seen and capable in that context. As Lewis speaks about helping at home and "not wanting Mum to worry," his actions can be seen less as apathy and more as constraint. The counsellor acknowledges the skills involved in managing family responsibilities while also exploring the cost to Lewis' own needs. This shifts the story from individual deficit to social context. By making class visible – without shame or blame – the counsellor helps Lewis recognise how circumstances affect his choices, while supporting him to identify areas where he would like more space or support.

Social Graces inform how children and young people engage in therapy. For example, children and young people may feel pressure to comply with, or align themselves with, a counsellor's perspective due to the age difference that implicitly positions the adult as an authority figure. A young person may find it difficult to explore intimate or vulnerable aspects of their identity with a counsellor whose gender, culture, or social positioning feels unfamiliar or unsafe. Similarly, a neurodivergent child may interpret nonliteral language, metaphors, or indirect communication differently from the counsellor, increasing the risk that their responses are misread as disengaged or judgemental.

These examples illustrate how a lack of reflexive attention to social positioning and difference can obscure important aspects of the therapeutic relationship, limiting the counsellor's capacity to attune accurately to the child or young person's experience. Using the Social Graces both reflexively and relationally, therefore, involves ongoing reflection on the counsellor's own assumptions and positionality, alongside a sensitive invitation for children and young people to make meaning of their experiences within family, school, peer, and community contexts. Naming social identity is the first ethical step, but ecosystemic counselling attempts to move beyond naming to directly exploring the impact of social differences.

The child's inner world is intimately tied up with their social identity. When a child feels an emotion, its expression and name are formed from social narratives. While the child's family structure is evident in their play and language, their cultural surroundings determine which structures are socially valued or demonised. Hence, when discrimination exists, the child's presenting problem embodies it. For some children, naming the difference is important. For others, naming the difference creates a rupture. In one example, a 13-year-old boy asked a white therapist for advice. The boy had experienced a racist incident on his way to therapy, having been called a racist name by two men in a park. The therapist, reflecting on power and privilege, said that offering advice felt inappropriate, as their social position might shape what seemed possible or safe in ways that differed from the boy's experience. The boy responded that this left him feeling more alone. By focusing first on the difference rather than on his immediate request for support, the counsellor had unintentionally added to his sense of isolation.

In another situation, a British Indian young person asked a white British therapist for advice about refusing a religious practice she experienced as unfair. The therapist named their social position and limits in understanding the cultural pressures involved, explaining uncertainty about giving direct advice. In this case, the young person experienced this acknowledgement as respectful. She later reflected that she had asked for advice out of habit and that she preferred space to explore her own position rather than adopt the therapist's.

Pause and Reflect

Thinking about the two case studies mentioned earlier, look at Table 7.2 and ask yourself:

- Which Social Graces are most immediately visible in your work with children and young people, and which may be less visible or more easily overlooked?
- How might this influence your understanding of the change and its identified issue?

Consider a child or young person you have worked with:

- How do multiple Social Graces intersect in their life, and how do these intersections shape their experiences within family, school, peer groups, or wider systems?

Despite its clinical usefulness, the Social Graces framework has attracted important critique. When applied unreflectively, it risks being used as a checklist or "tick-box" exercise, prioritising visible categories of difference over a more nuanced engagement with clients' lived experience. In such cases, attention to social positioning may drift towards performative forms of compliance rather than sustained relational curiosity. Additionally, organising the Social

Graces as discrete categories may inadvertently suggest that each dimension can be understood in isolation, obscuring the ways in which social locations are interdependent and mutually shaping.

An *intersectional* perspective extends the Social Graces framework by foregrounding how these social locations intersect and compound, shaping a child or young person's access to safety and support in context-specific ways. Rather than treating social identities as additive or static, intersectionality invites counsellors to attend to how power, privilege, and marginalisation operate dynamically across multiple systems. Engaging critically with the Social Graces through an intersectional lens, therefore, requires counsellors to remain alert to how wider institutional and cultural systems, such as education, social care, healthcare, media, and policy, interact with a young person's social positioning. This includes monitoring where structural advantage or disadvantage may be reproduced within these systems and how such dynamics may influence a child's wellbeing.

While counsellors must remain mindful of professional and organisational boundaries, there is an ethical responsibility to remain attentive to social injustice and to challenge narratives or practices that silence or disadvantage children and young people. Holding this responsibility with care allows the child's voice to remain central, particularly when issues of social identity and difference are at stake.

Rethinking the Self in a Liquid Age

When considering the impact of the exosystem and macrosystem on families' and children's lives, we need to be acutely aware of the era we are living in and the unique opportunities and challenges it presents. Zygmunt Bauman coined the term *liquid modernity* to describe contemporary social conditions in which traditional structures such as family, religion, class, and nation have become less stable and taken for granted. It would be misleading to assume that this represents a uniform or irreversible shift into a wholly new social era. Rather, the era in which we live can be characterised by ongoing tension between forces for change and forces for continuity. This tension bears some resemblance to the Palo Alto group's concept of *morphogenesis*, here applied at a societal rather than a familial level. Importantly, morphogenic pressures do not land evenly. Their impact varies across geographical regions, nations, communities, and, ultimately, families.

In some contexts, social forces contribute to significant changes, opening space for new identities and forms of belonging. In others, they evoke strong homeostatic responses aimed at preserving existing structures and values. This can be seen in rigid boundary-setting, dismissal of alternative viewpoints, or active resistance to perceived threats to the status quo. From an ecosystemic perspective, both patterns can be understood as attempts to manage uncertainty and maintain coherence in the face of rapid social change.

For instance, social constructionism and feminist literature have contributed to shaping the discourse around gender and sexuality, representing a strong pressure towards changing society's values and language. In some instances, this influence has led to marked cultural and institutional change, for instance, in UK universities or the NHS, where it is increasingly common to use individuals' preferred pronouns or language that is highly respectful of diversity. In other arenas, change has been resisted or even violently rejected, most clearly visible in the MAGA community in the United States, where social change has been responded to by enforcing a more restrictive discourse around gender and sexuality. Children and young people are, therefore, growing up in a cultural landscape of competing ideas, where change is happening in a sometimes unpredictable and erratic fashion, where identity is no longer fixed but constantly shifting.

As a result, children and young people's social identity might be expressed differently depending on the system with which they are interacting. This multiplicity of presentations can contribute to experiences of identity confusion, particularly during adolescence. Whilst confusion of roles and a blurred sense of self are widely recognised as developmentally normative at this stage, contemporary social conditions further intensify these processes. Rapid social change and competing value systems can leave young people feeling overwhelmed or hesitant to commit to future goals. For instance, just think about the implications of climate change's shadow of uncertainty on young people's future – or the impact of the COVID-19 pandemic on their experience of education and social connection. Such conditions can heighten feelings of fragility about what lies ahead, while also disrupting familiar pathways into adulthood. In this climate, identity formation unfolds in dialogue with wider societal anxieties. Young people are increasingly embedded in a global culture, and the need to navigate multiple conflicting narratives about what it means to live well.

Moreover, earlier and more sustained exposure to complex, evaluative forms of communication, particularly through social media, appears to be reshaping the developmental landscape in which children form a sense of self. As a result, processes of identity uncertainty and self-evaluation that counsellors have traditionally associated with adolescence are increasingly being observed at earlier stages of development. In clinical practice, this is reflected in the earlier emergence of difficulties historically linked to the "teenage crisis," such as body image concerns and restrictive eating patterns. These experiences are often accompanied by heightened levels of anxiety and hypervigilance, as children become more attuned to external evaluation and comparison. For some, this leads to coping strategies characterised by avoidance or attempts to tightly control aspects of the self or body, rather than the more exploratory identity experimentation typically associated with later adolescence.

Whilst counsellors and psychotherapists try to tackle these emerging problems by providing a secure base and consistent therapeutic presence, they also face the additional challenge of an increased mistrust of adults and adult-led systems, due to the sense of betrayal and failure experienced by young people as a consequence of political and social instability. One way of responding to these challenges is to support children and young people in developing their reflexive capacities: the ability to think about themselves in relation to others and to the systems they inhabit. It is important not to frame expressions of this mistrust as inherently dysfunctional or uncooperative; rather, we can help our clients understand their mistrust as a response to experiences of perceived failure at a societal level.

Crucially, this reflexive stance cannot be demanded of the child alone. The therapeutic relationship itself must also become a site of reflexivity, in which the counsellor remains attentive to how the young person experiences therapy as an adult-led system. Given the strong evidence that the quality of the therapeutic alliance is amongst the most robust predictors of therapeutic outcome, making space to reflect collaboratively on the young person's concerns within therapy becomes central to the work. In this way, reflexivity functions not only as a developmental capacity to be fostered in the child but as a shared relational process through which counsellor and young person negotiate a respectful and productive space.

Many counsellors will be familiar with clients whose distrust is expressed by sitting on the other side of the room or offering statements along the lines of "I don't even know why I am here" or "my father thought it was a good idea for me to come". Practitioners may understand these messages as reflecting patterns of attachment insecurity or relational trauma. While this is often the case, an ecosystemic perspective supports counsellors to question how such responses may reflect other aspects of the child's ecosystem, where frictions between the client's inner world and the exosystem and macrosystem are at play.

Being curious about what this reluctance to engage may be, communicating is a way to not only defuse the tension but also plant the seeds of a therapeutic alliance. For instance, early therapeutic conversations can be used to make visible the multiple systems that shape a young person's presence in therapy. Rather than interpreting reluctance or ambivalence as resistance, counsellors can invite reflexive exploration of whose concerns are being represented, which expectations are being negotiated, and how the young person understands their position within these adult-led systems. Questions such as those below are not intended to elicit compliance or insight but to support the child or young person in articulating their location within a network of relational and cultural influences.

- *Why do you think X wants you to be here?*
- *If you were to persuade X that you don't need counselling, what would be the most convincing behaviour?*
- *If this space were to, at some point, become safe and useful for you, what would need to change?*
- *You just told me all the reasons why you were sent here today. Is there anything you agree on? To what extent?*
- *You told me about what people around you would like you to change. Is there anything that you would like to be different?*
- *I can see X would like you to change this behaviour. What do you think about it?*

Provided a positive therapeutic alliance can be established, counsellors then require strategies to support children and young people as they navigate the uncertainties of liquid modernity and the fragile sense of identity that may accompany it. A common therapeutic aim in this context is to support the development of a sense of inner stability that is less dependent on external validation, though healthy social relationships are usually balanced on self-worth and feedback. Helping a young person cultivate an identity that is not wholly organised around others' expectations or evaluations can offer an important source of psychological continuity.

This emphasis on inner stability is not without risks. If handled unreflectively, it may be experienced by the young person as a lack of empathy or acceptance, as though the counsellor were encouraging a retreat into the inner world as a way of managing the unpredictability of the outside world. Such a move risks minimising the real impact of external systems on the child's experience and may inadvertently reproduce the very sense of disconnection the work seeks to address.

An ecosystemic stance, therefore, calls for a balance between supporting internal coherence and remaining actively curious about the child's outer world. A therapeutic position that combines unconditional acceptance with non-judgemental curiosity allows us to join the young person in exploring how identity is being shaped across contexts, rather than attempting to neutralise or bypass those influences. This requires attending to the social, digital, and relational spaces that matter to the child or young person. Let's be curious about why a particular TikTok personality holds significance for a young person's sense of self, or why a single "like" on Instagram can meaningfully alter their self-perception. Similarly, let's ask about the significance of online gaming: Who does the young person play with? What needs does the virtual world meet? Or why can they allow themselves to play at brave warriors in a party of people they have never met, whilst struggling to enjoy playtime with their classmates? Being in touch with dimensions of existence that may be unfamiliar to many of us can ultimately help our clients explore their identity across contexts.

If identity is a story, we might be able to tell it differently.

Children and Young People's Digital Worlds

As part of the intricate ecosystemic layers that influence children's lives, we cannot ignore how young people today are the most digitally connected generation in history. Social media, online gaming, and instant messaging are integral parts of their social world. This phenomenon, defined as *hyperconnection*, has multiplied the opportunities for children and young people to interact with each other, so much so that the social elements of the self often take over or regulate more private and inner aspects. For example, think about moments when you were enjoying a concert, a holiday, or a meal, and felt the urge to post a picture on social media so that all your contacts could participate with you. How this kind of sharing impacts our experiences of such moments is still a fertile area for research. From a clinical perspective, this creates a complex relational landscape in which high levels of digital interaction and visibility do not necessarily support experiences of felt connection. Counsellors are, therefore, required to attend carefully to how hyperconnection shapes young people's relationship experiences, rather than assuming that frequent contact equates to relational depth.

In approaching this dimension of our clients' lives, it is important to remain attentive to how cultural dynamics within the digital outer system shape identity formation and self-experience. These influences may be observed through several interrelated processes:

- **Heightened Social Comparison and the Growing Performance of the Self**: Digital environments often amplify comparison and encourage rapid, visible self-positioning. Practices such as virtue signalling, the pressure to be on the right side of any conversation, and the expectation to respond quickly to online prompts can reduce space for reflective thinking and ambiguity.
- **Premature Exposure to Adult Content, Discourses, and Ideologies**: Digital spaces may draw children and young people into conversations, images, and value systems for which they are not fully equipped. While extreme manifestations such as online grooming or radicalisation are well recognised, even when the influence does not reach such a critical threshold, we can come across children with very complex experiences of exposure to adult material.
- **Challenges in Forming and Sustaining in-Person Relationships**: For some young people, digitally mediated interactions may feel more predictable or less emotionally risky than face-to-face encounters. This can make in-person relationships feel more demanding or uncertain, a pattern that has become particularly visible following periods of social disruption associated with the COVID-19 pandemic.
- **The Emergence of Digital-Specific Relational Risks and Identity Concerns**: Phenomena such as cyberbullying, AI use, and the management of digital identity now play a significant role in many young people's lives. These experiences may be unfamiliar to counsellors who are not digital natives, yet they can exert a profound influence on self-esteem, belonging, and relational safety.

Taken together, these dynamics highlight how the digital world has become an integral part of the child's ecological environment, rather than a peripheral influence to be managed or minimised. From an ecosystemic perspective, online spaces function as powerful exosystemic and macrosystemic contexts in which identities are rehearsed and evaluated, often in ways that intersect with family, school, and peer systems. For counsellors, the task is, therefore, not to counterbalance the digital world by privileging the "inner" over the "outer," but to remain curious about how these spaces are being used, what needs they meet, and how they contribute to the young person's evolving sense of self. Attending carefully to these digital dimensions allows identity to be explored as a relational and narrative process unfolding across contemporary systems.

Conclusion

An ecosystemic perspective invites counsellors to look beyond the child and family and to remain attentive to how cultural, institutional, and political forces shape children's experiences of self. Attending to the outer system helps prevent the individualisation of difficulties that are, in many cases, rooted in wider social conditions. This work requires reflexivity as much as technique. Counsellors are not neutral observers of the outer system but active participants within it, carrying their own social positions and values into the therapeutic space. Holding this awareness allows counselling to become a place where competing meanings can be explored with curiosity rather than judgement, and where children and young people can be supported to make sense of their lives within the complex systems they inhabit.

Chapter 7: Summary

Key Ideas

- The outer system plays an important role in shaping a child's beliefs, emotions, and ultimately behaviours. Social justice is a major context for mental health concerns in children and young people.

- Societal influence can manifest directly, as the child engages with the different groups and agencies that constitute the exosystem, or indirectly, through the relationship between the individual and the cultural landscape represented by the macrosystem.
- The cultural and social changes that can be summarised by the concept of "liquid modernity" place new challenges for young people, and this is often reflected in counselling.
- The importance of a reflexive and socially aware counselling practice is crucial.

Practice Implications

- The counsellor can be an agent of social change in tackling marginalisation and injustice by being aware of how different Social Graces influence the clients' relationships inside and outside the therapy room.

Reflective Prompts

- How often do you reflect on who you are in your clients' perception? What social discourses, infrastructures of power, and groups of influence do you represent in their eyes? How does this influence your relationship with them? How can you use your own power to empower your clients?

Bibliography

Bauman, Z. (2000). *Liquid Modernity*. Polity Press.

Burnham, J. (1992). Social graces: a practical tool for working with difference and diversity. In: *New Ways of Working with Families* (eds. J. Mason and S. Alcock), 19–32. Sage.

Cole, E.R. (2009). Intersectionality and research in psychology. *American Psychologist* 64 (3): 170–180. https://doi.org/10.1037/a0014564.

Crenshaw, K. (1989). Demarginalizing the intersection of race and sex: a Black feminist critique of antidiscrimination doctrine, feminist theory and antiracist politics. *University of Chicago Legal Forum* 1989 (1): 139–167.

Crenshaw, K. (1991). Mapping the margins: intersectionality, identity politics, and violence against women of color. *Stanford Law Review* 43 (6): 1241–1299. https://doi.org/10.2307/1229039.

Roper-Hall, A. and Burnham, J. (2012). Family therapists' engagement with social differences and the Social GGRRAAACCEEESSS framework. *Journal of Family Therapy* 34 (2): 117–133. https://doi.org/10.1111/j.1467-6427.2011.00554.x.

Chapter 8
Time and Transition Through the Eyes of the Child

It's almost dark. Nine-year-old Freddie sits staring from his window, watching the streetlights begin to flicker as dusk falls and daylight fades. His little sister calls him from the hallway, but he is deep in thought, so he barely notices. Tomorrow is a big day for his family, tomorrow is moving day! The day he moves from the house he has grown up in, the house with the marks on the kitchen door frame, where mum took great pride in measuring him and his growth, with little lines and ages next to them. The house where he tripped on the doorstep and broke his arm, the house where Nanna and Pappy would come to visit, and the doormat that Nanna would wipe her feet on whilst shouting "woo hoo, only me" to mark hers and Pappy's arrival. Pappy would huff and puff in behind Nanna, always a little embarrassed that they walked in without knocking. This is also the house where, six months ago, his parents sat down with him one day and told him that they loved him very much, but they could no longer be together. The house that dad moved out of six months ago, so now Freddie sees his dad at Nanna and Pappy's every weekend.

So far, ecosystemic counselling has focused on the child's inner world, their family, and their social environment. We have missed something integral to counselling, which is the impact of time on a child's developing sense of self and wellbeing. In the opening vignette, we can see that Freddie's perception of time is an ongoing adjustment to his dad no longer living with him. He loops between excitement and fear, the prospect of something new, but what if he doesn't like it, what if his friends can't be bothered to walk the extra distance to call for him, and what about this "having to tighten our belts when we move" stuff that mum keeps talking about, what is that and what does it mean? Freddie has a knot in his stomach as he imagines his mum's face with the frown of worry that he has seen before. What Freddie does not know is that, alongside the physical changes in his environment, his history, and what has come before, as well as his anticipation of the future, will impact his present and shape who he is and who he will continue to become. This is what authors such as Bowlby, Ainsworth, and Guidano argue when discussing how our attachment relationships shape our internal working models. Our internalised perceptions of how the world will respond to our needs say a lot about who we are. And, as we evolve through time, these models, these nuclear scenes about us and our significant others involved in a dance of mutual exchanges and feedback, gain nuances and complexity: in some cases, they will further thicken, becoming unchangeable, often rigid stories that we keep reliving in any new relationships; in some others, they will progressively transform and reshape into new opportunities, new chapters, and new stories to be rewritten.

The Time System

Within the ecosystem model, time is an invisible system that shapes each layer of life. Just like the water surrounds the fish, time holds Freddie's development. And like the translucence of the water, time is all around us. Failure to address the water over time will cause decay; however, acknowledging and addressing its presence creates a rich environment for growth. We can think of these processes in the context of temporal shifts. When we explore the temporal dimension within an ecosystemic framework, we refer to everything that unfolds or changes over time. The term temporal simply means relating to time. Children's experiences, relationships, and sense of self are not static; they evolve moment by moment, day by day, across developmental and generational timelines. Attending to the temporal aspects of a child's world invites counsellors to notice how time is felt and expressed. This allows the child to be understood by considering rhythms of routine, emotional change, and the ways past, present, and anticipated futures intersect within the therapeutic process.

In counselling, time frequently sits in the background as we anticipate how much time we have in the session, whether it's now too late to open up something new, whether six sessions are enough, and whether Dad has time to leave work and drive across town to get Freddie to therapy for four o'clock. Time is all around us, and its ebb and flow interact with everything we do. Time is the medium in which children grow, relationships unfold, and the family evolves.

Pause and Reflect

- What significant shifts or changes did you have in your childhood?
- How might these changes influence your work as a therapist?

In the example above, the nine-year-old Freddie experiences time as strongly influenced by emotional and relational factors. Following parental separation, time is often organised around routines such as school schedules and custody arrangements; each daily ritual provides him with predictability and continuity. However, the child's internal experience of time remains dynamic: periods of separation from a parent may be perceived as prolonged, while moments of contact may be experienced as brief. Anticipation, uncertainty, and emotional meaning modulate the child's perception of temporal flow, indicating that time is not experienced as static or linear, but as flexible and context-dependent within the child's cognitive and emotional framework.

On a broader scale, time will also progressively reshape these perceptions: dad's absence will mean something for nine-year-old Freddie, and something different for 16-year-old Freddie, when new interests and new areas of the outer system become available and perhaps attract Freddie's interest. Time operates also biologically; as Freddie grows, his voice will deepen, and puberty will change his body at a speed so rapid that he experiences "growing pains" as his body adjusts to the new growth spurt. He grows psychologically through memory and anticipation, socially through school terms, calendars, and interactions with his peers, as well as through transitions and cultural rituals to be observed. He also travels through history as generational narratives shape the family he is embedded in, and as generational narratives shape what being a child means in the era he is raised in.

In therapy, the counsellor may attend to the client's thoughts, feelings, and behaviours while overlooking the temporal currents that surround the work. Developmental change and distress are inherently temporal. The child who suddenly withdraws may be responding to a change in teacher, or the family in crisis may be responding to the daughter who broke the family's rules and moved out aged 18, leaving the family to reconfigure into a new identity. To think ecosystemically is to recognise that the child's inner world and external context are like a kaleidoscope of moving shapes, with the child moving through evolving internal and external landscapes.

Development as a Systemic Process

Historically, traditional models of child development have portrayed growth as a linear process or a trajectory with distinct stages; each milestone met and then left behind as the child moves forward into adulthood. Whilst child development frameworks, such as Piaget's cognitive development or Erikson's psychosocial stages, provide valuable signposts, they are somewhat limited by the linear perspective that struggles to account for the child's lived experience. Let's, for instance, have a look at the following clinical vignette:

Ravi is eight years old and was removed from his family into the care system at age six. Due to abuse and neglect by his mother, Ravi was the primary carer for his sister in the early years of his life. At age five, he had the developmental capacity to make a bottle of formula milk for his sister, including using a kettle and cooling the milk to a safe temperature. From a linear perspective, we could view Ravi as developmentally advanced for his age. Ravi, however, sleeps under his bed with a teddy called Dave and a book light for company. He is sure that Dave will keep him safe, as Dave will be his lookout if the angry men come to the house. Ravi is also a frightened little boy craving for love and protection.

Ravi invites us to think of time and development in a fluid fashion, as a multifactorial process where different dimensions converge at their own pace. As argued by authors such as Bronfenbrenner and Stern, child development is not a vertical climb but a mutual dance between the child and their environment as they oscillate amongst relationships, biology, and culture. Humans are relational beings, and so children grow through relationships. Ecosystemic counsellors refer to the "contact boundary," which is the constantly shifting, dynamic interface where the individual meets the world (other people, objects, ideas, etc.) and where experience is organised into meaningful "gestalts." Each new capacity from bonding and attachment to co-regulation and moral reasoning is experienced in the interplay between the contact boundary of self and otherness.

Freddie's anticipation about moving house illustrates this interplay. His bodily sensations (tight stomach, quickened pulse) are bound up with relational and social meanings: leaving friends, a new school, and continuing to come to terms with his parents' separation. The process of development is thus less about forward progress and more about adaptation to evolving time-bound and relational conditions. Ravi, on the other hand, may experience a transition from one school lesson to the next as a frightening move into the unknown. Ravi's history has taught him that the world is an unsafe place; people cannot be trusted and will harm you, so his body is wired for threat. Where developmental trauma has been experienced, the individual's capacity to adapt to change will be different from that of a child who has been afforded, in the main, a secure base.

Developmental Pathways over Time

Children's development is like a Harry Potter-style series of moving staircases with many intersections that are influenced by internal and external factors. Freddie's developmental capacity will directly impact how he experiences the world. His ability to reflect on "what if my friends don't come and call for me anymore," and "what if daddy is sad now, mummy and he do not live together," demonstrates an emerging cognitive capacity to think in abstract terms. His body may feel the sadness as these thoughts enter his head, and he may begin to link cognitive and bodily sensations. His linguistic development may shift from a capacity to describe feeling sad to one of feeling concerned and a little bit excited, depending on his cognitive, language, and bodily connections. When considering the sliding staircases in both Ravi and Freddie's stories, we can begin to see how profoundly early environments can shape a child's temporal development. Freddie's worries about moving house and the expected challenge of change are shaped by his experiences in a loving and attuned environment. The first five years were significantly different for Ravi, living in an environment of chronic neglect, emotional abuse, and periods of sustained threat to survival for himself and his sister. Like Freddie, his early experiences will shape the architecture of his developing brain and his perception of safety in relationships. Trauma is not an event that Ravi simply remembers; it is a context in which he developed and was embodied in the first five years of life.

Ravi's caregiving routines, such as preparing formula milk, using a kettle, and soothing his baby sister, were not early skills to celebrate. They were survival strategies imposed by living in an environment that failed to meet his or his sister's needs. He learnt to take responsibility because the adults around him were unable or unwilling to keep him and his sister safe. At the same time, he slept under his bed with Dave the teddy, believing danger might reappear at any moment. These seemingly contradictory behaviours make perfect sense when we understand that development under neglect is fractured yet adaptive. Ravi's system developed skills where the environment demanded them, while simultaneously, essential emotional needs went unmet.

Whilst it is often easy for a trained counsellor to immediately sense how Ravi's outstanding practical skills are also signs of pain and worry, it's not as simple to look into other skills that are often celebrated in children – those align more with cultural values that we might inadvertently be buying into, if we do not assume a reflexive stance. For instance, let's stop and ask ourselves how many children are praised for learning to play piano at five or being able to read competently at six? How many teenagers are the light in their parents' eyes due to their outstanding athletic performances, or how many young girls are admired for being thin and pretty? Do we really take enough time to reflect on how each of these outstanding skills and qualities may also hide an excess of compliance or conditional love?

Let's get back to Ravi. Now, aged eight, he is living in a stable and safe foster placement with his sister. It will take time to reconfigure his system, for his brain and body to learn safety. Time, consistency, and repeated positive interactions will teach him that things are different now. To him, time does not unfold smoothly. It jumps, stretches, and collapses depending on the level of perceived threat. Minutes can feel elongated, especially when waiting, a sensory reminder of earlier years, where waiting meant hunger, fear, or unpredictable adult reactions. Nights were not restful but long stretches of scanning and listening. Even now, in safety, a sudden sound can rupture his calm: a door slamming makes his shoulders tense before he has consciously processed the noise. His foster carer, Janet, says, "He watches everything ... his eyes move faster than anyone I've ever known." Although Ravi is safe, he is still in a state of high arousal.

Pause and Reflect

- Based on their experiences, what might Ravi and Freddie's views of themselves, others, and the world be?
- How might this impact how they form and manage relationships?

For Ravi, trauma can simultaneously fragment and freeze time. The body and central nervous system are caught in history, whilst cognition and the not-yet-developed frontal cortex of the brain battle to update themselves to the now and present moment. His future may feel vague and unsafe, as his past teaches him that safety can be stolen in the blink of an eye, and that adults may turn from the unfamiliar territory of predictability and safety to the familiarity of neglect and abuse. When his foster carer, Janet, says, "I'll be back in five minutes," his body prepares for abandonment, his stomach tightens with the anticipation of starvation, and his psyche goes into overwhelm. To deal with the overwhelm, he involuntarily numbs into dissociation, now losing the "here and now" as well as the "there and then." Minutes later, he notices himself standing in precisely the same spot, yet his carer is now wearing her coat and carrying a rubbish bag to the door. He is back in the "here and now," but time has again moved on without his control.

Ravi's lived time is also shaped by the role he held as a young child, when he was thrust into needing the wisdom of an adult and the skills of a parent for his baby sister. Children are keen observers and copiers, sponging up everything their environment offers. Their mind is a complex design where an immense capacity for empathy and relational connectivity is deeply intertwined with egocentric instances. They are immediately capable of attuning to the complex emotional climate of their household, thanks to an in-depth perception of the grown-ups' emotions and mindset. At the same time, they often assume that others' views are the same as their own and tend to generalise circumstantial information. An adult can filter complex information due to their layered understanding of social interactions: for example, when greeted by a friend with a cross face, they may think, "Maybe they are having a bad day, I wonder what's happened." In contrast, the child may shift rapidly into thinking "they are cross, what have I done wrong?" Survival in the early days requires a world that is "all about me." It is this literal thinking that also impacts our capacity to filter what we experience. The child who struggles in class quickly assumes "I am stupid." The child with a punitive parent learns, "I must try harder." The child who is rejected concludes "I am unlovable"; all of these generalisations are made to allow us to take in the rapid temporal pace of new information. This early underdeveloped filtering system is also why core beliefs about us, the world, and others are formed mainly during the early years of our lives, as like a tiny bird in a nest, we swallow whole what is provided to us.

Mum had her "better" days when Ravi was very little. As a keen observer, he watched mum scoop formula into a bottle, add hot water, and cool it before propping it under his sister's chin. He also noticed it repeatedly fell to the floor, and his sister cried. Crying made mum angry, so he also quickly learnt to hold the bottle for his sister. As mum slipped emotionally further away from them and her anger and disgust towards them grew, Ravi realised that when she cried, he needed to make her bottle, because no one else did. When danger escalated, he hid his baby sister beneath the bed with him. His internal world measured time not only through his own sensations but through the need to attune and attempt to comfort hers. Every moment of fear stretched twice as long because he was monitoring her as well as himself. Every silence felt loaded with threat because he was listening for cues that she might be in harm's way. In this way, Ravi's lived time became relationally doubled: he lived both his own timeline and hers. Ravi would reassure his sister, telling her it was ok, whilst on the inside he screamed with terror and fear.

Paradoxically, although a child himself and in need of protection, Ravi was thrust into the role of protector, and it became an integral part of his identity from an early age. Fast-forward 20 years and consider how this script may play out in his future. Ravi may become a devoted father, ensuring that his own children never go without. A protector of his family, friends, and everyone around him. Working tirelessly to ensure that everyone's needs are met. Endearing and loyal qualities without a doubt. What if he has also not learnt to recognise his own needs or believe he is worthy of love and care from others, and the only person he can truly rely on is himself? The interplay between the system that surrounds him and the ebb and flow of the past, intertwined with the present, will determine not just the now but also his future.

Pause for Reflection

- What role or roles did you play or were you invited into in your family growing up?
- Did this influence or have an impact on your decision to train as a counsellor?

Now Ravi is in a safe and stable environment, and his foster carer, Janet, is tending to his needs. He does not experience the shift in role as a relief or that somehow now he is liberated back into childhood. The role of carer for his sister gave him purpose, albeit at a tremendous emotional cost to him and his sister. This role also gave him a level of control over an environment that, in many ways, he had little or no control over. He learnt that appeasing his mother would reduce the likelihood of aggression, not disturbing her whilst she slept reduced the possibility of her waking up in rage, hiding himself and his sister under the bed, protecting them from his mother. Ravi experiences loss and grief for the role. His sister no longer needs him in the way that she did. When she falls, she often seeks comfort in Janet; he feels monumentally lost. His nighttime anguish and fear have now changed but not disappeared. He now sleeps in a separate room from his sister. What if his sister is not safe right now? What if Janet is hurting his sister, what if she forgets to pick his sister up from school, what if she doesn't know the difference between a cry of sadness and a cry of pain ... what if ... what if ... what if! As well as structure and routine, this change in environment brings grief and fear.

For Freddie, time has always been scaffolded in routine and, in the main, a level of predictability. Attunement of his parents, discussed in previous chapters, offered him a secure attachment, teaching him that the world is a safe place, people can be trusted, and he is lovable. Freddie has also experienced adversity in his life: when his parents separated and, some six months later, when he moved to a new house. He can still recall the marks on the doorframe in his old house as his parents marked his growth. He now has two new door frames with marks, one at his mum's home and the other at his dad's and Leah's (his dad's new partner's) house, where he goes every other weekend and once on a Tuesday for tea. Freddie knows he is loved, but he still wonders what if there was something he could have done to stop his parents from splitting up. Sadly, when Freddie is seven, his Nanna dies. Nanna and Pappy's home was his consistent safe space when his parents split, and the smell of Nanna always brought comfort to Freddie at a visceral level. School and home are worried about Freddie, since Nanna died; he is not his "normal happy self."

When we consider Freddie's story, we see that although he was embedded in a secure developmental pathway, time can still bring about destabilisation when transitions, loss, grief, and adversity cluster together through time. Although held in secure relationships, these experiences still require emotional reorganisation. The separation of his parents and the loss of his Nanna still require emotional reorganisation as his and the family's worlds reconfigure to accommodate change. Pappy is now learning how to manage the house and bills. Freddie's dad is now grieving for the loss of his "we will sort it" mum, but who will be his "we will sort it" person now? His dad's girlfriend, Leah, is moving into the role of comforter for dad, and his mum, who knew Nanna for 20 years, is grieving at a distance, not knowing what her place is in this side of "the family" anymore. Freddie's withdrawal and sadness are not the signs of a pathology but a system working hard to accommodate and integrate cumulative experiences of loss.

Ravi's position on the temporal spectrum differs. Although he is now physically safe, his body, thoughts, and nervous system taught him to expect that danger will return at any moment. This is not a cruel act on the body's and the mind's behalf but an attempt to stay on guard, stay alert, and maximise the chances of survival. For Ravi, the trauma from his early years remains active in the present, shaping his expectations of adults. It is through this contrast that the role of therapy becomes clear. The role of therapy is not to erase the past but to offer a relational space, and, in this space, time can be slowed to sit with feelings avoided or expedited to work through a trauma memory in a tolerable way. Time can be adjusted and attuned to the child's emerging needs. From an ecosystemic perspective, the therapy is embedded within the broader context of family, school, and wider support networks.

The ecosystemic perspective also embeds what came before in the scripts, narratives, and experiences of our ancestors and how that has shaped our present. The therapist's role is to help the child integrate past, present, and anticipated futures. It is in this context that we turn our attention to how we work with time therapeutically and how an ecosystem lens shapes practice for children such as Freddie, Ravi, and many more.

Time is a great healer but only if the conditions are in place for healing to occur. Only within the wider ecosystemic conditions that make healing possible will Ravi and other children experiencing developmental trauma heal. Ravi's brain and body will only learn that the world is safe when the microsystem around him, his foster carers, daily routines, and school environment provide consistent evidence that adults are reliable (see Figure 8.1). The mesosystem, including the connections between home, school, therapeutic support, and social care, must communicate a coherent, stabilising

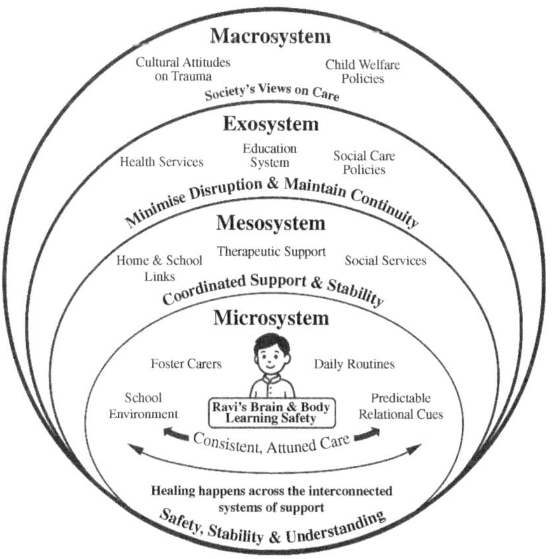

Figure 8.1 Ravi's ecosystem.

message that Ravi is valued, protected, and understood. At the exosystem level, the services around him, health, education, and social care, need to minimise disruption and maintain continuity, reducing the temporal ruptures that previously shaped his development. Even the macrosystem plays a role, as cultural narratives about trauma, safeguarding, and children in care influence how adults respond to him and how he comes to understand his own story. Time can, therefore, function as a healer only when all these ecosystemic layers work together to create the conditions for safety, attunement, and reliable caregiving. For children whose early years were shaped by fear and unmet needs, healing emerges not only from the passage of time but also from the steady, repeated experience of safety across the interconnected systems that now hold them.

For a child who has experienced parental separation and the loss of a grandmother, such as Freddie, the capacity to process these events and to reengage in future-oriented planning emerges through relational validation within the family system. Shared family narratives and culturally embedded norms play a crucial role in supporting the child's developmental continuity. From this perspective, healing is a relational process, co-constructed within the family and its broader sociocultural context.

Working Therapeutically with Time

Working therapeutically with time requires the therapist to hold multiple temporal layers simultaneously. A child enters therapy carrying a history, an embodied experience of the present, and an imagined or anticipated future. These temporal dimensions are not sequential but co-present, continuously shaping the child's lived experience in the here and now. Within an ecosystemic framework, therapy does not seek to extract the child from these relational, developmental, and sociocultural contexts. Rather, the therapist actively engages with them, bringing these temporal layers into visibility, naming them, and working with them within the therapeutic relationship.

In working with Freddie, the therapist will support him in making sense of the changes he has experienced over time. His internal world has been organised around expectations of community, embedded within a developmental system shaped by prior experience: one in which adults are anticipated to help him understand what will happen and why. Within this process, it is essential that the therapist remains responsive rather than rigid, moving with the emergence of new meanings and information. To presume an absence of trauma or significant adversity would risk silencing unspoken experiences and constraining the co-construction of a narrative that can hold complexity.

As counsellors, we also maintain awareness about other nuances of suffering and challenges that impact children and young people. During the trajectory of our careers, we become progressively exposed to the more extreme forms of child abuse, neglect, and trauma, and we risk becoming inattentive to the pain and struggles that can hide within the small behaviours or disclosures from children. Similarly to what happens to our clients, time transforms counsellors as well – and experience can become a dangerous friend when it blinds us towards unspoken challenges. A privileged child, who has never experienced instability, can carry a burden of fear that will need therapeutic care and support to heal. Our empathy towards children who have gone through trauma and extreme abuse and neglect must not thicken our skin towards more subtle forms of challenges that other children and young people experience. Hence, ecosystemic counsellors pay close attention to the overt and the microscopic indicators of trauma.

How Do We Know What Has Come Before?

The ecosystemic therapist learns to go beyond the therapy room and move temporarily into the future and past. This includes an interest in intergenerational scripts, including intergenerational trauma. On a surface level, Freddie's family seems, in the main, to be steady and emotionally attuned. We cannot assume that this status quo has existed through the generations. Freddie's grandparents were raised by parents who lived through the Second World War. Loss, separation, and rationing were all familiar to Pappy and Nanna, and his mum's parents, nanny and grandad. They learnt the stiff-upper-lip "smile and carry on" attitude. They also learnt that food was not to be wasted, and Freddie's mum often refers to uneaten food as waste because Nanny told her that, as Nanny's mum could not allow a scrap of food to go to waste. Many family rules were absorbed into what could and couldn't be talked about or endured privately.

The therapist may pay attention to the language Freddie uses to locate himself in time. He may refer to "before I moved," "when I was little," "when mum and dad were together," all indicators of temporal markers for significant periods of his life. Part of the therapeutic work is to help Freddie hold all these narratives and explore his world in and beyond them, helping his meaning making around being loved by both parents. Grief and loss can hurt, but the memories can live on, change can be painful, and feelings can shift. The therapist may consider the future by exploring Freddie's anxiety around change. For example, they may use statements that show insight into his inner experience of time: "When you think about moving, I hear that part of you is feeling excited, but another part of you is also worried." During therapy, the therapist works with the child to develop temporal integration, which involves the capacity to hold past experiences, present feelings, and future imagining without becoming overwhelmed.

The therapeutic work with time is fundamentally different for Ravi. Ravi does not simply remember his past; his past is active in his nervous system; the past is embodied in the now. Trauma is not time-tagged and does not emerge sequentially. Like a lava lamp, the therapist needs to be flexible in working with what bubbles up in the process, moving through time as trauma breaks non-sequentially into the conscious. Time is a core component within the therapeutic work with Ravi, as at the core of trauma therapy is processing the trauma so that it moves into a memory from the past, and his body and psyche learn that the past is over and the present is safe.

The therapist becomes a temporal anchor, predictable by arriving at the same time each week, maintaining consistent, predictable boundaries, and attuning to and responding to Ravi's emotional states, helping him remain within the window of tolerance as he processes what has come before, only by anchoring it in the now. Over time, the therapy itself becomes part of Ravi's ecosystemic recalibration. The therapy offers a relational rhythm of consistency and predictability that contrasts with the chaos and fear of his early experiences. Ravi's system, over time, tests the therapist and the therapy as he ebbs and flows with the possibility that people are safe and can be trusted.

Pacing, Presence, and the Therapeutic Use of Time

In ecosystemic therapy, pacing is central to the therapeutic intervention. Children whose development has been marinated in threat may experience the adult's urgency as danger. In contrast, being too slow may be experienced as "pending doom". Like riding a horse, the therapist needs to hold the reins: too fast, and the horse will bolt; too slow, and the horse will become frustrated and agitated. The therapist needs to attune to what is within the window of tolerance and hold the pace with the child or young person, enabling them to work within this window. Too fast, the therapist needs to stabilise and reground; too slow, the therapist needs to support resistance or avoidance.

Freddie's sense of time is more linear, not fragmented by the psychological defence of dissociation or by the body staying on guard, unaware that the danger has passed. Freddie's experiences of loss and distress were relational and reflective as opposed to survival-based. He may learn over time and through experience that feelings will pass, that uncertainty can move back to stability, and that adults will remain emotionally available. The therapist can support him to learn that sadness, grief, and loss do not need to be fixed quickly but worked through, held, and supported by the system around him.

It is crucial that the therapist is aware of their own relationship with pace and time. Ravi's story may pull the therapist towards rescue and, in turn, acceleration, a desire to take the pain away in an instant, with the therapist's awareness that Ravi has endured so much for so long already. The therapist needs to take stock and ground, reminding themselves that the developmental trauma has occurred in a relationship. Therapeutic healing also happens in part through the relationship with the therapist. We must be acutely aware, as practitioners, that working relationally with children who have experienced developmental trauma invites them into the place with the highest potential for danger: a close relationship. As a result, the work will take time. The child will expect you to hurt them, harm them, and let them down; only time, predictability, and consistency in dispelling this fear will change this process. The ecosystemic approach requires the therapist to reflect on how their own temporal assumptions, relating to progress, endings, and "good outcomes," interact with the individual child's lived experience.

Pause and Reflect

- What factors outside of the therapy room may influence the speed at which you work with the child?
- How might you manage this if it does not fit with your own pace?

Working Across Systems: Time Beyond the Therapy Room

At the core of ecosystemic therapy is the recognition that the child is embedded in an ecosystem, and so change does not occur in isolation. The therapist must not only align with the systems around the child but also work actively alongside them. The therapist must align with the temporal rhythms of school, home, and the wider professional network, holding the "team around the child" as partners in the work. Disparity or mixed messages across systems can create challenges or undermine the work. That said, it is also essential for the therapist to keep in mind that each profession may have its own agenda while still acting in the child's best interests. The teacher who cares deeply about the child's distress and recognises the dysregulation in their behaviour, whilst also managing the needs of 30 other children and delivering a curriculum focused on academic achievement. The parent is frustrated as they feel that school is not doing enough or the school feels that the parent is "blaming everything on the school." The community wants to embrace the child but is frustrated with the "naughty" behaviour they display. All have their own rhythms, time pressures, and expectations imposed on them by one another and by the larger societal expectations and agendas. All of them are embedded in an ecosystem of influences from the past, present, and anticipated future. Therapeutic conversations may, therefore, extend beyond the child to include foster carers, teachers, and social workers, helping them understand how the child experiences time.

With an ecosystemic consideration of time as an essential component of the therapeutic work, also comes an encouragement for counsellors to always embrace the space outside the therapy room when evaluating results. Too often, during our work as supervisors, we hear therapists assert that the child has shown improvement because "they open up with me more" or "they started being more forthcoming," or "it seems that they built a stronger relationship with me." Whilst the above are all potentially good indicators of therapeutic process, if isolated, they can also be misleading. What if, for instance, the child opens up with you more because the world around them has shrunken further and they have no one else left? What if the growing trust in you pairs with a progressive mistrust in other key relationships such as family, teachers, peers? Being sensitive to how time transforms relationships inside and outside our small office is an important skill for an ecosystemic counsellor.

The ecosystemic approach recognises that this integrative process is not shaped primarily by what happens in the therapy room alone but by the interplay between this and the broader systems and context in the ecosystem, in the past, present, and projected future. As new temporal rhythms emerge, the therapy works to support the child to manoeuvre within their own unfolding life story.

Conclusion

This chapter has explored how time is lived and experienced by children within the ecosystemic model. Time isn't simply something that passes; it is carried in bodies, relationships, routines, and expectations. Children do not experience time in isolation. Their sense of continuity, safety, and possibility is shaped by the relational environments that hold them across moments of change, loss, growth, and repair. Freddie and Ravi illustrate very different relationships with time. One has mainly known predictable and relational scaffolding, even when faced with disruption and grief. The other has known time shaped by survival, vigilance, and fractured rhythms. Neither experience exists in a vacuum. Each is embedded within a family context that both reflects and transmits patterns of coping and expectation across generations. What a child learns about time, whether it can be trusted, whether endings are survivable, and whether needs will be met are learnt first and foremost in a relationship.

From an ecosystemic perspective, therapy does not attempt to correct a child's relationship with time. Instead, it attends to how time is organised and experienced within the child's wider world. Change becomes possible when children are repeatedly met with consistency, attunement, and emotional availability, not only in the therapy room but across the systems that surround them. Over time, these repeated experiences begin to soften rigid expectations, allowing new rhythms to emerge and new meanings to take root. This naturally draws our attention beyond the child and into the family system itself. Families hold time in powerful ways, through routines, roles, stories, silences, and intergenerational scripts. They carry histories of loss and resilience, of rupture and repair, often long before the child is born. To understand how a child experiences the present and anticipates the future, we must also understand how time has been lived, spoken about, and managed within the family. It is here that the ecosystem widens. Having explored the child's relationship with time, we now turn, in the following chapter, to the family system, the relational context in which time is organised and transformed, turning to how families shape and are shaped by the temporal experiences of the children within them.

Chapter 8: Summary

Key ideas

- Children's development is temporal: their past experiences, present context, and anticipated futures constantly intersect. Time is *felt*, not only measured. Emotional states, transitions, routines, and relational safety shape how children experience their flow.
- Children grow through relationships and across multiple environmental layers (micro–macro systems) in a nonlinear way.
- Early caregiving environments shape neural pathways, bodily responses, internal working models, and expectations of others.
- Ecosystemic practice recognises that therapeutic change is relational and systemic, not contained in the therapy room.

Practice Implications

- Notice how the child talks about "before," "after," "when ...," or anticipated futures.
- Explore temporal ruptures (e.g. loss, separation, moves, and trauma) and temporal scaffolding (e.g. routines, consistent caregiving).
- Make sure you consider how time flows across different life areas of the child, such as school, home, peer relationships, and therapy.
- Understand how these shape children's meanings around time, safety, endings, and needs.
- Not all distress stems from dramatic events; subtle adversities or internal pressures also shape development.

Reflective Prompts

- How might your accumulated experience dull sensitivity to "small" forms of suffering?
- How does your own pace typically feel – fast, slow, contained?
- What emotional responses do Freddie-like children evoke in you?
- What about Ravi-like children – do you feel pulled to rescue, speed up, or soothe quickly?
- How does your personal relationship with change, endings, and uncertainty influence your therapeutic stance?

Bibliography

Bronfenbrenner, U. (1979). *The Ecology of Human Development: Experiments by Nature and Design.* Harvard University Press.

Guidano, V.F. (1987). *Complexity of the Self: A Developmental Approach to Psychopathology and Therapy.* Guilford Press.

Hughes, D.A. (2017). *Building the Bonds of Attachment: Awakening Love in Deeply Troubled Children,* 3e. Rowman & Littlefield.

Perls, F.S., Hefferline, R.F., and Goodman, P. (1994). *Gestalt Therapy: Excitement and Growth in the Human Personality.* The Gestalt Journal Press.

Perry, B.D. and Szalavitz, M. (2017). *The Boy Who was Raised as a Dog* (Rev. ed.). Basic Books.

Stern, D.N. (1985). *The Interpersonal World of the Infant.* Basic Books.

van der Kolk, B.A. (2014). *The Body Keeps the Score: Brain, Mind, and Body in the Healing of Trauma.* Viking.

Chapter 9
The Child's Development Within the Family Life Cycle

As counsellors, understanding change is vital. This is either because we are tasked with promoting and encouraging therapeutic change or because we need to understand how change is affecting the wellbeing of our young clients. Arguably, it is impossible to understand change without understanding time, which is the precise unit against which change is measured. We want to know if depression reduces in six weeks, if families argue less after coming to therapy, and if time with a counsellor is more beneficial than time on a waiting list. Clinically, the flow of time has often been categorised into different developmental stages. This chapter explores how counsellors can engage with those stages. How does a family reorganise when a child moves from dependence towards greater autonomy? What happens to parental roles when a young person begins to make confidential decisions about counselling? How might sibling relationships shift when one child's needs require increased attention? How are children's emotional difficulties intensified at different developmental stages?

It is with these questions in mind that structural family therapists conceived of family life cycle theory, a framework used in counselling, psychology, and social work to understand how individuals and families develop over time. If we approach counselling through the lens of the family life cycle, we will, therefore, focus on the different stages of family development, the tasks and challenges at each stage, and the horizontal and vertical stressors that influence family members, especially children and young people.

In family life cycles, "horizontal stressors" are those events that occur simply because of the flow of time and that can have an impact on families and/or individuals. For instance, grandparents becoming progressively older and transitioning from being caregivers and helpers towards needing care and help – this is a common horizontal stressor. These stressors, although often predictable, can still apply enormous physical and emotional pressure on families and their members, due to the necessity to reorganise around the changes that each of these stressors is likely to bring.

In counselling children and young people, horizontal stressors often appear in the form of normative transitions that nonetheless require considerable adjustment. A child starting secondary school, for example, may be navigating shifting peer groups and increased academic demands at the same time as parents renegotiate supervision and trust. Similarly, the birth of a sibling or a child preparing to leave primary school can alter routines and emotional availability within the household. None of these events is inherently problematic – they arise as part of the family's natural movement through time. Yet for a child already sensitive to change, such transitions may be experienced as perturbing loss, and they can manifest in challenging behaviour and mood swings. From a life cycle perspective, the focus is, therefore, not only on the child's symptoms but on how the family system is adjusting – or struggling to adjust – to the ordinary yet demanding shifts that accompany development.

On the other axis, vertical stressors are events that occur abruptly and often have a shock-like quality for the system. These include sudden illness, bereavement, separation, redundancy, migration, or traumatic incidents. Vertical stressors can disrupt a family's sense of continuity and predictability, and may distort how time is experienced, with members feeling either stuck in the moment of crisis or propelled into unwanted change. For example, parents mourning the sudden death of a 13-year-old son not only are forced into an unanticipated family reorganisation but must do so while carrying profound grief and attempting to make sense of the loss. In such circumstances, children's responses may reflect the wider emotional climate: increased anxiety, regression, anger, or heightened caretaking. The life cycle lens widens the focus, encouraging counsellors to understand these reactions as embedded within collective attempts to absorb shock and restore some sense of stability.

Vertical stressors are arguably more impactful on family life due to their sudden, often traumatic nature. Yet, the lasting influence of horizontal stressors in testing the family's cohesion and flexibility should not be overlooked. It is no coincidence that quite a few of our referrals, as counsellors, come in times of transition. Some of these present themselves as vertical stressors (migration, death of a family member, change in school motivated by a parent's job, etc.), but quite often they are simple and totally expected horizontal transitions (moving from primary to secondary school, approaching school examinations, leaving the family home to begin adulthood).

Monica McGoldrick and Betty Carter modernised and extended Duvall's earlier work around the life cycle, producing a stage-based model of family life that, although subjected to criticism due to its heteronormative nature and rigid structure, is widely used in family therapy and counselling. It is popular amongst social workers and children's mental health practitioners. This is due to the model's effectiveness in capturing and helping to make sense of children's issues that emerge during family transitions, some of which are slow and smooth, whereas others are sudden and abrupt.

The Six Stages of the Family Life Cycle

The stage-based conceptualisation of family life cycle offered by McGoldrick and Carter is characterised by six distinct phases of life, each one presenting with its unique challenges and opportunities (see Table 9.1). The life cycle pictures members of the family as in a continuous flow between differentiation (e.g. as they leave home as young adults) and togetherness (as new families are formed through

Table 9.1 Life Cycle Stages

Stage	Key transitions/tasks	Emotional process of transition
1. Leaving home: single young adults	Develop autonomy and emotional independence from the family of origin and establish work and relationships.	Accepting emotional and financial responsibility for oneself
2. The joining of families through marriage or commitment	Form a new couple system, realign relationships with extended family and friends.	Commitment to a new system
3. Families with young children	Adjust the couple system to make space for children, take on parenting roles, and manage demands.	Accepting new members into the system
4. Families with adolescents	Increase flexibility of family boundaries, allow for children's independence, and refocus on the couple and career.	Shifting of parent–child relationships to permit independence
5. Launching children and moving on	Release young adults into the world, renegotiate couple relationships, accept in-laws and grandchildren.	Accepting multiple exits and entries into the family system
6. Families in later life	Adjust to retirement, ageing, loss, and generational shifts in power and responsibility.	Accepting the shifting generational roles

mutual commitment). Ecosystemic counsellors use this model to assess whether their client's family has successfully navigated key developmental tasks associated with each life cycle stage (e.g. boundary-setting, communication) or if they are stuck at a previous stage.

By looking at the stages listed above, the reader can perceive how the model stems from a view of the family informed by cultural values of heteronormativity and stability, where the family is conceived as a unit secured by marital commitment and perpetuated by bloodlines. As such, the model in its original formulation seems unable to capture the complexity of different life choices and alternatives to the traditional idea of family. If used to evaluate and assess family life from a clinical perspective, it is at risk of conveying a judgemental perspective on families unable (or unwilling) to match this model. However, it remains an essential guide for the ecosystemic counsellor's curiosity when confronted with family organisations that differ from their internalised models of what "family" means. As such, we can ask ourselves questions such as how stage 3 is experienced by adoptive families or single parents, or how stage 1 plays out when there is no marriage and the commitment is between people of the same sex and/or gender. These questions can help shift the therapist's position from a stance of heteronormative judgement (where the model is used as a textbook to dictate what is right or wrong) towards a stance of curiosity, with the model serving as a tour guide to take us around in search of new and unexpected landscapes.

It is also important to mention that, in response to the aforementioned criticism, McGoldrick and Carter further developed their conceptualisation of the family life cycle into a systemic and culturally sensitive version, more in tune with the evolving social sensitivity.

The central idea, that families may be understood as emotional systems developing through recognisable stages and transitions, each accompanied by particular tasks and emotional demands, remains intact. What has shifted is the manner in which this development is conceived. Families are no longer regarded as moving along a single, stable path but as shaped by changing circumstances, varied forms of living, and the contexts in which they are situated, including culture, gender, migration, and social class. For therapists, the value of the model lies in its capacity to offer a guide to the unfolding of family life over time, while also requiring attention to the wider social conditions within which that life is lived. The notion of a predictable trajectory must, therefore, be held alongside an awareness of social inequality, the marginalisation of minority groups, and the constraining effects that dominant assumptions about gender and sexuality may exert upon families' possibilities for living.

Pause and Reflect

- Try to recount a time of your life, as a child or teenager, in which the tension in the family was high, or either you or any other family member was branded as "difficult," "troublemaker," or otherwise challenging.
- If you were to think about that specific moment in your family life through the lens of the life cycle model, what stage do you think your family was transitioning through?
- What aspects associated with that stage, as displayed in Table 9.1, played a role in increasing the family tension?
- How does it sit with you to think about that time in these terms?

Systemic Perspectives on Family Life Transitions

Each individual's development occurs within the context of the family system.

Changes in one member affect the functioning of all others. With this in mind, a counsellor working within an ecosystemic framework might be curious about how these two trajectories of individual and family development interact with each other. For instance, in the "families with adolescents" stage, normal family tensions may intensify and reach a "dangerous" threshold. Counsellors with an understanding of the life cycle can help parents adjust boundaries, encourage autonomy, and communicate effectively. They can also normalise family stress during transitions, promoting a non-pathologising view of family life and helping both parents and children understand that challenges are part of healthy family development.

Let us consider a family in which one sibling is approaching the transition from primary to secondary school, a period marked by the interplay of biological, social, and psychological change. This shift may bring anxiety as the young person navigates unfamiliar social and physical environments, yet it may also open opportunities for new peer relationships and the exploration of emerging interests. When we add the knowledge that the family migrated to the current country only a few years earlier, the different levels of experience begin to interweave in shaping emotional and behavioural responses.

Difficulties in forming new friendships, for instance, may be intensified by changes in sibling relationships. The older child's move to a new school may leave a younger sister behind, altering their sense of closeness and increasing the risk that the younger child feels more peripheral or excluded. At the same time, the parents are faced with their own developmental tasks. Having already navigated the demands of migration, they now encounter the unfamiliar terrain of a new school system and its expectations. Such a moment may evoke both loss and hope: loss of familiarity and continuity, and hope for opportunity and belonging. How parents make sense of these mixed feelings, and how they help their children understand and regulate similarly complex emotions, becomes central. It is also relevant to consider how earlier family decisions, including who carried responsibility and influence in the move to a new country, continue to shape patterns of meaning and care within the family at this stage.

The Rhythms of Time, Power, and Constraint in Family Life

An ecosystemic understanding of time also invites us to consider whose time is being prioritised, whose pace is being respected, and whose experience of time is rendered invisible. For children and young people, particularly those living in contexts of adversity, time is seldom neutral. Decisions are often made about children, rather than with them. Transitions are frequently imposed rather than negotiated, and the onus to "adapt" frequently sits disproportionately on the child. From this perspective, the family life cycle is not only a descriptive framework but also a lens through which power and vulnerability must be considered. Children experiencing adversity may live within compressed or distorted temporal worlds. For some, development is accelerated by necessity, as in the cases of developmental trauma, parentification, caregiving roles, or exposure to adult responsibilities long before emotional readiness. For others, development appears "delayed" or arrested, not because of a deficit but because the system around them has not provided the safety required for growth. In these contexts, the question for the counsellor is not whether the child is "on time" but what has shaped their relationship with time itself.

An ecosystemic approach encourages us to be curious about potential mismatches in temporal rhythm within families. Parents may be oriented towards future outcomes, such as academic success, independence, or becoming the greatest achiever, while children may be anchored in the immediacy of present emotional experience. Adolescents, in particular, often straddle competing temporal demands, both physically and psychologically, as they are expected to prepare for adulthood while still emotionally embedded in family systems. When these demands fall out of sync, distress may emerge as a signal of systemic strain. Importantly, time for the family is also shaped by broader social and structural forces. Poverty, migration, racism, disability, and involvement with statutory systems can significantly disrupt the family life cycle. Families may find themselves repeating transitions, skipping stages, or remaining "stuck" in survival mode. From an ecosystemic standpoint, this is not a failure of the family to progress but an adaptive response to external circumstances and constraints. It is imperative that, as counsellors, we resist deficit-based narratives and instead support families to make meaning of their experiences within a wider socio-cultural context.

Blameful perspectives creep in at every ecosystemic level. When the child fears parental judgement, we look to the parents for change. When parental criticism forms in response to discrimination in the social environment, especially as their child's differences are targeted by unfair systems, we look to society for change. These responses are understandable, but the ecosystemic model encourages counsellors to avoid blameful perspectives. We invite counsellors to see the interconnectedness of the inner world, family, outer world, and time. This vast interacting, intersecting relational web has no ultimate cause. We aim interventions at whichever system is accessible, child-centred, or useful. By integrating these considerations, time becomes more than a backdrop to therapeutic work; it becomes an active dimension of the ever-evolving formulation. Attending to how time is experienced, negotiated, and constrained within families enables counsellors to work with greater compassion, reflexivity, and ethical awareness, particularly when supporting children and young people whose developmental pathways have unfolded under conditions outside of their choosing.

Multigenerational Transmission

As discussed in Chapter 7, ecosystemic counsellors observe an intergenerational transmission of communication patterns, core narratives and themes, and internal working models. It is important to highlight that this transmission does not follow a deterministic, linear cause-and-effect pathway. Quite the opposite, this transmission occurs loopingly within harmonious family conversations, conflicted breakfast arguments, social policy, school sick days, and grandparental Christmas gifts. As such, we can observe certain "traits" (behaviours, values, beliefs) that seem dominant in the first generation, "disappear" in the second one, only to present again, maybe with slightly different characteristics, in the third generation. Let's continue the example of the presented on page 173. In their case, the problem seems to have been triggered by multiple factors, amongst which a prominent one was the change of cultural environment, with the consequent language barrier and necessary readjustments that families, and especially children, face when moving to a different country. If we review the family genogram and move up one generation, we see how the grandparents on both sides of the family organised life around stability, tradition, and a rigid distribution of roles. The family structure was quite hierarchical, and great importance was given to men having a stable, full-time job, with women being home-based caregivers for their children.

In this respect, the second generation operated a corrective family script, privileging change and the exploration of new territories, feminist rules, and roles. During the therapeutic conversation, it was plain to see how both parents perceived the constraints of having to live by a strict set of rules. James (the father) did not want to spend his entire life at a desk like his father did, doing a job he hated for the sake of breadwinning. Instead, he wanted his job to be fun, even if that meant earning less, and wanted to have space for hobbies and other passions. Laura (the mother) felt the same sense of constraint at the idea of being a housewife, confined forever in the village she was born in, waiting for her husband to come back from work. She wanted to pursue a career, make a difference, and see the world.

When they formed their own couple, they implicitly renegotiated those rules, roles, and values. They chose to accept the risks of moving overseas and organised family life around a breadwinning woman and a man working part-time in jobs that were unstable yet often enjoyable. It is interesting to consider the family's request for help: they came to therapy in response to the younger child's presenting difficulties, namely anxiety and depression. When the symptoms were explored more closely, it came to be understood as expressing a sense of nostalgia for familiar roots, a longing to return to a place where one's language is spoken and one's identity is recognised, and a desire for belonging and the stability once provided by earlier family rules.

This example illustrates how families may move between replicative and corrective family scripts across generations. A replicative script refers to patterns and expectations that are carried forward, often implicitly, because they are familiar or associated with safety and belonging. A corrective script, by contrast, emerges when a generation organises itself in deliberate contrast to the previous one, seeking to avoid what was experienced as limiting, painful, or unjust. James and Laura's life choices – migration, flexible gender roles, and prioritising fulfilment over stability – can be understood as corrective responses to the rigidity they associated with their families of origin. Yet their child's difficulties hint at the possible re-emergence of needs linked to the earlier script: stability, continuity, and rootedness. From an ecosystemic perspective, neither script is right or wrong; each represents an attempt to solve the dilemmas of family life. Therapeutic work involves making these patterns visible, so families can choose which elements to retain, which to revise, and how to integrate security with change across generations. When counselling individual children and young people, this involves supporting them with linking their values and beliefs with their inner experience of family.

Useful Tools for Exploring Time and Change

Given the importance of time in children's counselling, several authors have developed ways of exploring time in their work with clients. A technique that is often useful to make sense of time when working individually with children and young people is the use of a timeline to identify crucial life events that might be involved with the onset of the problem. Timelines can be co-created by the therapist and the client in a conjoint, creative space involving drawing, sculpting, and the use of toys. They can be creatively adapted to match the client's unique way of making sense of time and events. For instance, with one young person who regularly travelled to and from London by tube, we adapted the timeline into the form of a new underground line. Each significant life event became a station, and the direction of the line reflected where the young person felt that moment was leading them. One station was labelled: "April 2022 – change here for my parents signing their divorce and me doing really badly at school."

If you wish to engage with time and change more systemically, you might decide to organise the information you collected about these dimensions in a chronological table, such as in Table 9.2. This might take a bit of time and energy; however, it offers the possibility to look at time and change from two different perspectives.

Table 9.2 offers the therapist the opportunity of two different readings. If we read the table vertically, we can appreciate the individual trajectory of each family member and bear witness to important narratives. For instance, all mum's main events have to do with her career, whereas dad's table is quite empty. Equally, we can decide to read the table horizontally and have some curiosity about co-occurrences in the family timeline. We can be curious to understand how dad managed to be a father whilst perhaps feeling the calling to care for his own mother, whose health deteriorated drastically just a few months after Jenna's birth. In this case, we have horizontal and vertical stressors combined, generating pressure on the family's cohesion and flexibility.

We can also become curious to understand how each morphogenic movement on the mum's side (graduating and finding her first job, being promoted, moving to the UK, and further climbing the ranks of her organisation) falls together with her own mother's depressive episodes. We can use our timeline for hypothesising, and we might wonder whether 2024, a year in which the family seems to make roots in the UK (even dad finally finds a job!), landed particularly harshly on the maternal grandmother, who seems to struggle with her daughter's progressive autonomy and distance. Does Louise's anxiety and desire to go back home have anything to do with these stressors?

Table 9.2 Family Timeline

Year	Mum/Laura	Dad/James	Jenna	Louise	Maternal grandma	Paternal grandma
2024	Promoted to head of the local firm's branch	Finds a part-time job at a supermarket		Anxiety and depression, miss home	Hospitalised for depression	Health further deteriorated
2020	Moved to the UK	Moved to the UK	Moved to the UK	Moved to the UK	Hospitalised for depression	
2017				Born		
2013			Born			Health deteriorated, needs care
2011	Engaged	Engaged				
2010	Got promoted at work				Hospitalised for depression, increased medication	
1992	Graduated in Law, first job for a firm				Diagnosed with depression	

This is an example of time's role in testing the family's resilience, cohesion, and flexibility and how we can use time to make sense of a child's problem in a broader landscape. As counsellors, we can use our questions to explore time, irrespective of whether we are working with families or individually with children and young people. For instance, we can ask horizontal timeline questions like "When did the problem start?" "When is it more likely to happen?" and "When is it less likely to happen?" These questions can assist the counsellor in understanding the timing of the problem and the problem's developing storyline. We can also project into the future, with future-oriented questions like "if nothing changes, how do you imagine your family in one year from now?," or, conversely, "let's imagine tomorrow you wake up and the problem is gone, how would this change everyone's life"? We can zoom in to analyse triggering circumstances or zoom out to see from a distance how everyone in the close family network responds to the problem. As ecosystemic counsellors, time offers us a four-dimensional approach to our therapy sessions and an opportunity to accompany our clients as they make sense of their own positioning in family history and the broader cultural landscape.

Children, Time, and the Work of Becoming

When we speak of family development, it is easy to fall into the language of stages, transitions, and tasks, as though time moved evenly and predictably for all. Yet children do not experience time as theory describes it. They live it, and they feel it in the waiting outside offices while adults speak, in the long afternoons when a parent is absent, and in the suddenness of change that arrives without warning. For the child, time is not measured in developmental charts but in moments of closeness and distance. From this perspective, children's symptoms may be understood as communications about time as much as about emotion. A child who becomes anxious at the move to secondary school may fear not only new peers but also the speed with which childhood seems to be receding. The adolescent who withdraws during family conflict may be attempting to halt the emotional acceleration of events they cannot organise within themselves. The child who regresses following the birth of a sibling may be protesting against a tempo of change that has outpaced their sense of belonging.

In this way, children's symptoms can be seen as efforts to regulate the family's time-bound rhythm. Some children slow the system down, drawing attention, care, and pause. They regress to earlier points and begin to speak like toddlers or cling to stuffed toys. Others appear to speed it up, enacting crises that force decisions long deferred. Neither position is chosen deliberately by the child. Each arises within the child's developing attempt to remain connected in a world of shifting relationships. The ecosystemic counsellor, therefore, listens not only for what the symptom means but for what it says about when something is happening in the life of the family. This attention to timing brings into view an essential task of counselling: the processing of psychological time. Therapy offers a rare space in which experience may be slowed, revisited, and re-sequenced. Stories that felt overwhelming can be approached in fragments through role-play or storyboarding; transitions that felt abrupt can be placed within a longer narrative arc by speaking it, slowly, out loud. In doing so, ecosystemic therapy becomes part of the family's life cycle. A session may mark the first moment a loss is named, the point at which a parent recognises a child's need for autonomy, or the pause that allows a family to move forward with greater coherence.

For children, whose lives are often governed by decisions made by others, this temporal function of therapy carries particular significance. It may be the first setting in which their pace is respected and where their imagined futures are encouraged. The child who speaks of "going back home" may be expressing a longing for a time when identity felt secure. Regression typically gets seen as a defence in counselling. But regression can be the body's way of living for an extra moment before a family transition – a nostalgic break from the present anxieties. The task of counselling is not to deny this longing, nor to hasten adaptation but to help the child hold past and present together without losing the possibility of what comes next.

Family life cycle theory reminds us that no moment exists in isolation. Each difficulty stands at the intersection of histories, expectations, and emerging possibilities. Yet this understanding must be paired with a recognition of children's inherent developmental movement. Even within constraints, children grow. Even within disrupted systems, they imagine. The ecosystemic stance recognises the child as an active participant in the ongoing negotiation of meaning. Thus, counselling supports families in finding a rhythm that allows growth without lessening childhood wellbeing. When time is experienced as bearable, symptoms need not carry the full burden of signalling distress. Mental health issues will soften, especially when the family has found a way to move through its life stages together.

Chapter 9: Summary

Key Ideas

- Time is an important dimension for both the counsellor and the client to explore.
- The exploration of time does not need to be limited to an individual perspective but can embrace how the client's family and close network respond to the challenges and opportunities presented by their life cycle.
- Family life cycles evolve through stages and transitions that, depending on the family structure and organisation, can present unique challenges and opportunities and impact family members differently.

Practice Implications

- When exploring the relationship between life cycle and the evolution of our client's problem, we can broaden the extent of our curiosity beyond the individual's life cycle, with a theory-informed approach to what happens at a family and close network level.

- As counsellors, it is important to be receptive and open to understanding transitions in the individual and family life cycle, identifying horizontal and vertical stressors.

Reflective Prompts

- How open are you to exploring the full extent of the family timeline? Do you focus on one dimension mostly (present, past, future), or are you curious to explore them all?
- Do you consider your client solely when exploring time? Are you ever curious to understand how everyone else in the family is managing life cycle transitions?

Bibliography

Carter, E.A. and McGoldrick, M. (1980). *The Family Lifecycle: A Framework for Family Therapy*. Gardner Press.

Carter, E.A., McGoldrick, M., and Garcia-Preto, N.A. (2011). *The Expanded Family Lifecycle: Individual, Family, and Social Perspectives*, 4e. Pearson/Allyn & Bacon.

Duvall, E.M. (1971). *Family Development*, 4e. J. B. Lippincott.

Chapter 10
Holding the Inner and Family Worlds Together

Counselling is a practice and not just a set of theories. Our intention in these two chapters is to train you to use the ecosystemic model with anonymous transcripts from real clients, guiding you through how to make child-centred decisions. It is tempting to view a therapy model like a set of flatpack furniture instructions, especially because this gives you certainty. But unlike a dining table with its different components, a child in distress won't always respond to the same set of tools in the same way. We can be confident that the ecosystemic layers are present, but we never know how the child will respond. For this reason, we encourage you to see the model as a guiding set of principles that you must fit creatively to each child's responses.

Let's say we take on a referral together with a view to deciding how we make use of ecosystemic practice. The client's name is Anna, she is 13, and when she arrives at our centre she sits upright in the waiting room, hands folded as though waiting for instruction. Her mother is a little brisker in tone and late for work. She made the referral after noticing what she called a "change in attitude." Anna, she said, had become "unusually quiet" and "less herself." The school had noticed, too. Once animated in class, she now seemed detached and easily shut down when people talked to her. The presenting issue was vague, as it often is with young people.

Pause and Reflect

- How does ecosystemic counselling make sense of the child's situation?
- Which ecosystem are you most drawn to: the inner world, the family, the outer world, or time?

We were drawn to reflecting on the child's outer system. Reflecting on peer relationships, in the context of becoming a teenager, our ecosystemic curiosity wanted to know more about the influence of identity on the changes seen in Anna. But what were you drawn to? Perhaps you were reflecting on the child's inner world? Beneath the ordinary developmental disturbance of adolescence, there was something slightly amiss, a shrinking of confidence that seemed to come from a deeper emotional place. Or maybe adolescence and puberty were the key influences that came to your mind? Noticing the time system's impact on the young person's confidence brings the focus to bodily changes, identity formation, and a lack of safety with becoming independent.

It is a professional hazard that we become all too curious here and forget the child in the room. So, our advice is, wherever your curiosity goes, learn to hear where the child takes you. You will have plenty of time to explore the other curiosities that surface later.

Contracting and Relationship Building

When we first meet Anna, she gives a polite but distant smile. She looks at the floor, then at the table, and finally at us with eyes that seem filled with tension. "Mum says I should come," she says sluggishly. We respond with active listening, using a restatement, "Mum says you should come?" She shrugs, "Yeah. But ... It's fine." Here we can make a decision to sit with the tension and tolerate it, or to move into discussing the procedure of therapy. Neither is the right way, and both have their merits, but we are juggling the need to build a relationship with the need to set the boundaries of counselling, known as *contracting*.

What Would You Do?

Intuitively, we decide to sit for a while in the shared quietness, just two people waiting to know what might be safe to say. Anna struggles to manage the quietness and says, "Am I supposed to say something?" Contracting, the ecosystemic way, means being led by the client while ensuring we cover the key boundaries in counselling, which are confidentiality, safeguarding, session structure, and goals. And so, we respond by giving our definition while inviting the young person, saying something like, "for us counselling is a place where you can talk and explore your feelings or relationships ... you don't have to speak, but what do you think counselling is all about?"

The client might withdraw, engage, or do something unexpected. Our role is to begin to create the boundaries early on, to give us the safe foundation needed for exploring the ecosystemic problems that bring clients to see us. We find a natural way to say:

- **Confidentiality**: What you share here stays private, unless I'm worried about your safety or someone else's, in which case we'll talk together about what needs to happen.
- **Safeguarding**: My job is to help keep you safe, which means if I ever think you're at risk, I will act to protect you, but I'll always explain what I'm doing and why.
- **Counselling Structure**: We'll meet at the same time and place each week for an agreed number of sessions, giving us a counselling routine where you can explore what's going on.
- **Counselling Aims**: This is your time to understand yourself, your relationships, and your world more clearly and to find ways of coping or changing things that make sense for you.

Contracting may happen at the beginning of the session or be interwoven throughout, according to what the child brings. We know that creating a shared sense of safety, even if a little procedural at first, contains the child in the long term. Contracting gives us the opportunity to begin to explore the client's issues and goals. Now, the base of the ecosystemic model is the child's inner world, but that doesn't mean we have to start there. It's less a beginning and more a single layer of a multilayered problem. Let's consider how to work on this level while we are beginning to get to know Anna.

The Child's Inner World

As we have described throughout this book, the child's inner world is the sphere of sensations, images, and meanings that arise before language can fully label them. To enter this world, counsellors must listen to the words and the body's cues in parallel. In Anna's posture, she shows restraint by crossing her arms and a slight tremor in her leg, and we sense her withholding. We invite her, with an open question, to describe how things feel "on the inside, right here in the room." This attempts to use immediacy, which is naming the emotional signals from the client's body language. She hesitates, "I don't know," she says. "I feel normal, I guess." We stay present with her and restate the idea of "normal." Her normal, it seems, is an effort not to feel too much. As the session unfolds, she begins to share fragments of her life. "Sometimes it feels like I'm watching my life on the TV but not actually living it," she says. "Like everyone's talking but I'm not really there."

An ecosystemic counsellor sees no pressure in having to connect the child's words with other levels, such as time or family. We enter the child's frame, knowing they will frame their experience in one or more of these levels. Our theory is that people who can access experiences across the levels of the inner world, the family system, the social world, and the time system are more adjusted to their reality and congruent in themselves. With Anna, this means we continue to be present in what she brings to us. We offer a reflection: "It sounds lonely, like you're close enough to see people but not quite able to join them." To which she nods, her eyes opening wider. "Yeah. It feels like they don't see me either." In this moment, our counselling task is not ecosystemic interpretation but therapeutic presence, to sit beside her as she finds language for her invisible inner world.

This is because the client's inner world is rarely organised around logic. It forms through emotion, sensation, and early memories. Her cognitive system, so her thinking, is linked with her emotional system, and each part of herself conspires against being emotionally present. For Anna, much of this comes out in her language, which is mostly visual language. She often describes scenes like sitting in a classroom, lights flickering, the sound of pens scratching, and being at home with the television murmuring in the background while her mother cooks. These details are her way of grounding her abstract experience in something tangible, but she feels disconnected. When asked where she feels her feelings, such as sadness, she struggles to locate or experience them, telling stories and analogies, and this contributes to her dissociation.

In attending to these small moments of Anna covering over the emotion with stories, ecosystemic therapy invites her to notice how her body and emotions are intertwined. Active listening, using immediacy, restating and intensifying her words, and paraphrasing to show empathy – these inner-world techniques expand her self-awareness, providing Anna with acceptance for feelings that inevitably begin to surface. Our decision to stick with the inner world was guided by her insinuation of it in her behaviour, though she was unintentionally hiding from it.

Pause and Reflect

- How is ecosystemic counselling helping Anna at this point?
- What are the positives and drawbacks of focusing on the inner world?

The Therapeutic Relationship

Anna's inner world could only be reached through a safe relationship. For young people, the counsellor often becomes a temporary mirror, reflecting emotions that may have been obscured by family life. Early sessions are often marked by testing. She might say something self-critical like, "I'm just weird like that", and glance sideways to gauge our reaction. When met with acceptance, she will begin to risk more emotional honesty. Perhaps she is really feeling that other people dislike her? Perhaps there is a sadness behind the humour?

We strongly believe in the core conditions developed by Carl Rogers. Empathy, unconditional positive regard, and authenticity are the foundation of the therapeutic relationship. The Lambert et al. studies from the early 90s found that, for positive therapy outcomes, the relationship was more important than the model. And our model takes this research very seriously. By empathising with Anna's inner world, we trust that she will become more congruent with it and aware of her genuine feelings. Statements like "My mum doesn't really get emotions" hint towards a developing sense of safety in sharing feelings, and this accompanies slight improvements in self-awareness. But clients rarely travel in one emotional direction. When we attempt to centre the inner world in our counselling, our inattention to the wider system can lead to friction. For example, we might ask Anna what she meant about her mum not "getting" emotions. She replies, "She just says, 'Don't overthink it.'" There is a hint of irritation, quickly covered over by "It's not a big deal." This minimising tone reveals family loyalty and self-protection. To criticise her mother outright would feel disloyal. It feels safer to silence her own experience.

While the therapeutic relationship allows Anna to experiment with emotions and new relationship patterns, those patterns come out in how she engages with our questions. Freud identified this as transference, when the client transfers onto the counsellor assumptions and emotions from old, often parental, relationships. In situations like this, the ecosystemic model encourages counsellors to move into the family system directly, whether by naming the shutting down that's happening in the room or by being curious about how the loyalty to mum connects with her emotional withdrawal.

The Family System

Anna's story could not be understood in isolation. The ecosystemic view invites us to imagine the family as a living organism, each member affecting and being affected by the others. Moving into the family system doesn't require a noticeable change for the client. We decided to explore the family system because (a) the client's emotional shut down connects to her role in family life and (b) the response the client was having to our questions started to mirror withdrawal-based family dynamics. For an example of making this subtle shift, we ask Anna to speak about her mother. We notice that the language of care and control intertwine. "She worries about me," she said. "Like if I'm late from school, she calls five times." We ask how that feels. "Sometimes it's nice. Sometimes it's too much. Then, she gets angry if I don't answer."

This push–pull dynamic echoed classic patterns in families that are negotiating adolescence, a struggle between autonomy and attachment. Her mother's anxiety appeared to mirror an earlier generation's coping style, which is about keeping things emotionally tidy and presentable. Now we work with Anna on exploring those familial influences. Our questions become more circular, more focused on relationships. We ask, "How do you respond to your mum's anger?" "What kind of values is your mum trying to show you?," or "What does being late to school mean to your mum?" Here, we remain empathic and non-judgemental, but we have moved from an internal frame of reference to a systemic family frame of reference. Systemically, we can also frame the question about transgenerational patterns. Something like "How has your mum's experience of being parented impacted how she parents you?" Circular questions, like the Waltzer ride at a fairground, can be dizzying, and so we may need to repeat, break it down, or have the client draw it out on some paper. We say again:

> "How has your mum's experience of being parented impacted how she parents you?"

Anna describes her grandmother as "very proper," someone who "doesn't talk about feelings." The transgenerational resonance is clear. Emotional restraint has been modelled as a form of strength, and one effect is that emotions are interpreted as weakness. Working systemically means holding these patterns in awareness without stigmatising them. Our non-judgemental stance moves from the inner world to family behaviours. For example, when Anna recounts an argument, her mother accusing her of being "ungrateful" for wanting space at home, we explore both positions *neutrally*. "What do you think your mum might be feeling when you say you want to be alone?" Anna might think for a while and say something like, "Maybe she feels like I don't need her." We ask, "And how does that make you feel?" ... "Guilty," she says delicately. The guilt, we wonder, might be her way of carrying the family's fear of disconnection.

John Byng-Hall, who developed the idea of family scripts, said that family scripts often operate beneath awareness. Moving from the internal frame of reference to the family means exploring the unspoken rules that contribute to the child's feelings. In this case, the unspoken family script is something like, "Don't upset others with your feelings." When we introduce this idea tentatively, Anna's eyes widen yet again. "That's exactly how it is," she says. "Mum always says, 'Don't make things harder than they are.'" By giving language to the family script, therapy creates space for choice. Anna can begin to try out small acts of differentiation, such as taking time for herself or expressing mild disagreement, and noticing the consequences with the counsellor's support. The inner world alone might not help Anna make the changes needed for her and her mother to renegotiate their relationship, especially as she slowly becomes a young adult.

Pause and Reflect

- How is the family frame influencing the counselling conversation?
- Do you gravitate more towards reflection on the inner system or the family?

Emotional Inheritance and the Family Script

We're reminded of a therapy session with an Irish family. The 13-year-old daughter, much like Anna, was emotionally shut down. We had the privilege of having three generations in the room. The daughter said her mum never shows emotions. Her mother said this is because she wants to be strong. And anyway, her mother, who was in the room, also never shows emotions. The grandmother spoke reservedly, describing the huge risk of emigrating from Ireland, without money or social support, and she vowed never to be broken by the experience. She was a tough and courageous woman who risked everything to start a new and safe life for her family. Her granddaughter, caught in the emotional inheritance of her toughness, could see the tears on her grandmother's face. The mother leaned in while the three of them hugged. Unfortunately, this rule that had served grandmother well, a few generations back, had stuck the family to a detrimental script. We had opened space to reauthor this inherited script about being tough and unemotional. Whether exploring family beliefs with individual clients or families, the inner world begins to connect more vividly to genuine feelings, instead of ritualistically hiding them. The ecosystemic model sees the inner and family worlds as two parts of the child's experience, and counselling one part affects the other.

As the family patterns come into focus, counselling's emotional texture changes. We needn't have the family in the room to explore this. Returning to Anna, she brings a series of dreams into the session. Most therapists would not think to use dreams in an ecosystemic way. But like all counselling material, dreams can be emotionally processed for their inner, family, and social connotations. Like play, drawings, or metaphors, dreams carry the child's emotional world while also holding traces of relationships, roles, and developmental shifts. In one intense dream, Anna was on a train moving too fast, unable to find her seat. Her mother was somewhere on the train but out of sight. We begin with the inner world. What is it like to be on a train that cannot be slowed? Where does she feel that in her body? What emotions come with not finding a seat? Anna speaks of a tightness in her chest and a sense of being "swept along." The dream gives shape to an internal experience of acceleration, of life moving forward before she has found a stable place within it. The missing seat becomes an image of uncertainty about who she is becoming.

Ecosystemically, we explore the inner-world elements of the dream to find that each image resonates with the family's developmental phase, which is adolescence as a train departing childhood. The mother's out-of-sight-ness captures Anna's ambivalence about letting go – she needs her mother but not always visibly. The dream images are like memories or emotional photographs; they visualise feelings and family connections. By asking about a train departing or about an out-of-sight mother, the dream is a rich resource for exploring the child's ecosystem. Our counselling integrates the personal and the relational, helping the young person discover that her inner world and her family's development are travelling on the same emotional journey.

Pause and Reflect

- In what ways could you ecosystemically continue to work with Anna's dream?
- How would you use the dream to think about the outer system?

Dreams and metaphors provide a bridge between cognitive insight and emotional reality, but the crucial thing to grasp is that we change to a circular way of thinking about dreams. Or, if easier, we change to a relationship way of thinking. In the dream, Anna loses confidence partly because she holds tension and anxiety (inner world), but the context for the inner world is a lifetime of family rituals around avoiding emotions (family). When she describes the dream, we might ask, "What do you think your body feels on that train?" She might say, "Tight ... Like I can't breathe properly." We practise grounding, focusing on breath and sensory details (inner world). But slowly, she imagines herself finding her seat, noticing the peaceful scenery outside. "It's calmer now," she says. These experiential shifts mirror her growing independence in the family. Switching between the two frames gives us extra options for supporting Anna. And, crucially, she experiences us therapeutically as present and containing.

Holding Complexity

Counselling with young people often means becoming the translator of unspoken emotional languages. Anna's family, like many, had learned to equate love with reservedness and protection with emotional absence. Our role was not to correct this but to expand Anna's emotional vocabulary and circular (or relationship) awareness. When she expressed emotions like "I felt scared" rather than "It was fine," she disrupted a generational pattern of minimisation. That change happens right there in the room. As Gregory Bateson said, her inner-world change was a difference that made a difference in her family world.

The ecosystemic model requires the counsellor to think in several directions, not necessarily at once but over the course of a session or a counselling journey. When clients speak of loneliness, we listen both for their individual experience and for the family relationship patterns in which their experience was formed. Was this an embodied loneliness or a symptom of emotional disconnection in the family? Often it is both. These are different descriptions of the same problem. At times, systemic insight must be balanced with therapeutic presence. One afternoon, the real Anna, on whom this case study is based, arrived upset after a disagreement with her mother. “She said I’m selfish,” Anna said, close to tears. Our urge to explain the developmental push for independence was strong, but instead we chose to stay with her felt sense. “That sounds painful ... Where do you feel it?” She pressed her chest. “Here. Like a massive punch.” We sat together for a while, tolerating the painful stigma of the label “selfish.” Only later did we explore what the word selfish meant in her family.

This illustrates that counselling theories must leave space for the client’s emotions. The ecosystemic model is not a checklist, it’s more like a lens, helping the counsellor to orient their attention. In Anna’s case, attention moves fluidly between body, emotion, relationship, and family system. Each layer reveals another facet of meaning. Integrative trainees often find themselves confused at first, being pulled between a world of emotions and a world of family patterns. But our advice is to be present with the child in whatever they say, being able to hear the difference between feeling and family. Our perspective is that when we are trained in a single model or layer, while expert and specialist, we lose the ability to hear and hold complexity.

The Self Between Worlds

In this chapter, under the surface, we are discussing three theories of change. One is that Anna begins to integrate truthful feelings into her self-image. And by doing so, Anna organically grows into a healthier and more grounded person. This is a humanistic or person-centred theory of change, which says that people become incongruent with their experiences when they are taught to emotionally hide. Intensifying experience, naming it, and tolerating it, as Gendlin describes, give the child a chance to process and work it through.

At the same time, we are arguing for a relationship between the child’s feelings and their thoughts and behaviours. This cognitive-behavioural model, which is supported by deep psychological research, describes the mechanism for how children like Anna come to shut down emotionally. They think "emotions are scary or unsayable,"; they behave by not sharing emotions; and they feel shutdown. Cognitive cycles of this kind maintain the client's problem, and hence a change in thinking, feeling, or behaving creates positive ripple effects. Aaron T. Beck and other cognitive scientists found exactly what Carl Rogers did, that empathic counselling attends to thoughts and feelings, assisting clients in overcoming emotional issues.

With Anna, while the cognitive and person-centred roots of the model are evident, empathy, congruence, and unconditional positive regard were also catalysts for systemic change. Empathy allowed her inner world to surface, congruence modelled emotional honesty, and unconditional positive regard countered the intergenerational fear of "broken" by emotions. These conditions, held consistently, allowed the ecosystemic process to unfold. This hints towards the third idea about change, which is that childhood problems stem from relationship patterns and beliefs in the family system. Being curious towards family roles, scripts, and experiences unravels destructive influences on the child's inner world. We might draw a family genogram, use drama to enact family life, paint an emotion, or use the sandtray to explore dreams, but each piece of practice comes into direct contact with theory. That is, each therapeutic technique implicitly explores the interconnection between the child's emotions, self-image, and family context – sandtrays and face painting, used ecosystemically, work on all levels of the child's ecosystem.

Pause and Reflect

- Can you describe the three theories of change just mentioned?
- What are the benefits and limits of each theory of change for a counsellor?

Reflections on the Model in Motion

Anna's therapy illustrates the ecosystemic model's circularity. The work began with the child's inner sensations, extended into the family's emotional scripts, and looped back as personal insight. No single theory dominated. The humanistic stance created safety; the cognitive lens clarified patterns of thought; the systemic awareness illuminated relational dynamics; and the phenomenological approach sat with lived experience. In practice, this integration is less about theoretical blending and more about therapeutic flexibility. When Anna described physical tightness, we worked somatically. When she spoke of guilt towards her mother, we worked systemically. When she questioned her worth, we engaged cognitively. Each intervention arose organically from the dialogue, guided by what the moment required. Working solely within one of these layers, for example, working only with emotional presence, could have been *as* beneficial to Anna but would have missed her fuller ecosystem.

By the final session, the real Anna reflected on her change. "I still get nervous," she said, "but it's different now. I don't think something's wrong with me for feeling it." We asked her what helped most. She thought for a while and said, "I think talking and not being told what to feel ... Just someone actually listening ... It was almost gentle in a way"

Her words captured the essence of ecosystemic counselling, which is a model that listens not only to individuals but to the networks of meaning around them. The child is never a separate unit; she is the living intersection of personal, familial, social, and temporal systems. To counsel a child is to counsel the world that made her. And her experience of therapy was interesting. For her the therapy was about "listening," where another child's experience might be about "teaching" or "behaviour change." Embedded within each description, subtly, will be the mutually influential ecosystemic layers, and our description, while different from the child's, complements theirs. The ecosystemic model is, after all, a theory of living systems. Change is never static; it ripples outward, touching family dialogues, peer relationships, and future choices. At the end of therapy, we reflected on Anna leaving the counselling room for the final time. At the door, she paused and said something to the effect of "I actually think Mum's trying, too." And though she might not see it, that simple observation illustrated the silent revolution of ecosystemic counselling, which is that one child's change can break the chain of generations of unspoken sadness.

Chapter 10: Summary

Key Ideas

- A child's inner world forms within a relational field. It is an internalised form of early caregiving systems, not a private, isolated realm.
- Inner experience is embodied, patterned, and systemic: nervous system regulation, internal parts, and relational scripts together create a self-organising internal ecosystem.
- The inner world functions as a social survival system, rehearsing relationships and preserving coherence and connection, even when this means constraining spontaneity or growth.

Practice Implications

- The child's way of expressing themselves in therapy, whatever form this takes, communicates relational history and tests how adults will respond now.
- Symptoms often reflect adaptive strategies that once preserved connection or safety in a specific relational environment.
- Working "inside" (with feelings, beliefs, scripts, parts) is still systemic work. Shifts in the child's inner world can initiate change in family, school, and care relationships.

Reflective Prompts

- Where do you tend to individualise what is actually formed relationally?
- How might you listen differently to a child if their "symptoms" are understood systemically?

Bibliography

Bateson, G. (1972). *Steps to an Ecology of Mind: Collected Essays in Anthropology, Psychiatry, Evolution, and Epistemology.* San Francisco: Chandler Publishing.

Beck, A.T. (1976). *Cognitive Therapy and the Emotional Disorders.* New York: International Universities Press.

Bowen, M. (1978). *Family Therapy in Clinical Practice.* New York: Jason Aronson.

Bowlby, J. (1988). *A Secure Base: Parent–child Attachment and Healthy Human Development.* London: Routledge.

Byng-Hall, J. (1985). The family script: a useful bridge between theory and practice. *Journal of Family Therapy* 7 (3): 301–305.

Byng-Hall, J. (1995). *Rewriting Family Scripts: Improvisation and Systems Change.* New York: Guilford Press.

Carter, B. and McGoldrick, M. (1999). *The Expanded Family Life Cycle: Individual, Family, and Social Perspectives*, 3e. Boston: Allyn & Bacon.

Dallos, R. and Draper, R. (2010). *An Introduction to Family Therapy: Systemic Theory and Practice*, 3e. Maidenhead: Open University Press.

Egan, G. (2014). *The Skilled Helper: A Problem-management and Opportunity-development Approach to Helping*, 10e. Belmont, CA: Brooks/Cole.

Erikson, E.H. (1963). *Childhood and Society*, 2e. New York: Norton.

Freud, S. (1923). *The Ego and the Id.* London: Hogarth Press.

Gendlin, E.T. (1978). *Focusing.* New York: Everest House.

Lambert, M.J. (1992). Psychotherapy outcome research: implications for integrative and eclectic therapists. In: *Handbook of Psychotherapy Integration* (eds. J.C. Norcross and M.R. Goldfried), 94–129. New York: Basic Books.

Lambert, M.J. (1999). Are common factors the central issue in psychotherapy research? A review of research and a critique of methodology. In: *The Heart and Soul of Change: What Works in Therapy* (eds. M.A. Hubble, B.L. Duncan, and S.D. Miller), 33–55. Washington, DC: American Psychological Association.

Lambert, M.J. and Barley, D.E. (2001). Research summary on the therapeutic relationship and psychotherapy outcome. *Psychotherapy: Theory, Research, Practice, Training* 38 (4): 357–361.

Minuchin, S. (1974). *Families and Family Therapy*. Cambridge, MA: Harvard University Press.

Norcross, J.C. and Lambert, M.J. (2011). Psychotherapy relationships that work II. *Psychotherapy* 48 (1): 4–8.

Patterson, J. and Fisher, C. (2002). *Clinical Applications of Bowen Family Systems Theory*. New York: Haworth.

Rogers, C.R. (1951). *Client-centered Therapy: Its Current Practice, Implications, and Theory*. Boston: Houghton Mifflin.

Satir, V. (1983). *Conjoint Family Therapy*, 3e. Palo Alto, CA: Science and Behavior Books.

Stern, D.N. (1985). *The Interpersonal World of the Infant: A View from Psychoanalysis and Developmental Psychology*. New York: Basic Books.

Wampold, B.E. and Imel, Z.E. (2015). *The Great Psychotherapy Debate: The Evidence for What Makes Psychotherapy Work*, 2e. New York: Routledge.

Winnicott, D.W. (1965). *The Maturational Processes and the Facilitating Environment*. London: Hogarth Press.

Yalom, I.D. (2002). *The Gift of Therapy: An Open Letter to a New Generation of Therapists and Their Patients*. London: Piatkus.

Chapter 11
Moving Between Social Worlds and Time

When we meet a child in therapy, it is tempting to imagine that what happens between the two of us is the whole story. As discussed in the previous chapter, systems theory challenges us to think differently. It says that every feeling that arises in the room has already travelled through a web of relationships, way before it reaches the child's speech or body language. The ecosystemic model asks us to notice how inner experience, family life, community, culture, and time itself shape the child's presenting problem. It is a profoundly thoughtful way of working that refuses to reduce a human life to any single system. Instead, it invites counsellors to hold multiple contexts in view and to move fluidly between them.

The work of Carl Rogers, Aaron T. Beck, Monica McGoldrick, Salvador Minuchin, Jay Haley, and others has sketched an accurate picture of the child's inner world and family system. These authors illuminate the child's emotional life and relationship patterns. In this chapter, we shift our focus to the outer and time systems, which Bronfenbrenner and Erikson describe as the wider social world and time-bound processes that hold every relationship together. These are the domains in which children learn who they are in the eyes of others and how they fit into the long story of their families and communities.

The outer system includes school, friendships, neighbourhood, community groups, and the cultural frameworks that define what counts as normal or acceptable. A child's anxiety may strengthen the parents' relationship, but the values and social norms of any family household are inherited from the surrounding culture. Parents from different communities do not create the same types of relationships with their children. In fact, writers such as Pearce and Cronen argue that culture sculpts family beliefs. In their view, anxiety is not produced in isolation from the powerful stories that society tells. For instance, the sole concept of "anxiety" will differ deeply in its meaning and expression if our frame of reference is a Westernised society, characterised by a focus on the individual's self-actualisation. Anxiety in this frame is treated as an individual weakness or deficit to be corrected. If our frame of reference is made from collectivist cultures, such as those in East Asia, then our social expectations revolve around prioritising group harmony over individual emotions. Anxiety in this frame is tied up with preserving group values. Anxious attachment is higher in some collectivist cultures like Japan and South Korea because children are socialised to stay highly attuned to others' approval, while secure attachment is roughly the same across societies.

Some nations, such as the United Kingdom, produce more anxiety-related eating disorders in predominantly young females because of body image ideals. In this context, subcultures such as upper-middle-class schools produce more performance anxiety and self-harm because of high-pressure schooling. When a child says, "I feel sick every time I go into school," it could be easy to brand the sickness as "dysfunctional" and believe that the counsellor's role is to fix it. The ecosystemic model encourages therapists to be curious about the multiple layers of meaning involved in such sickness. At what point of the developmental stage does this problem arise? At what stage does the problem appear in the family's life cycle? What transitions and horizontal and vertical stressors are involved? What does this sickness say about the child's beliefs, emotions, and values? In which ways do cultural norms and expectations inform emotional expression? What emotions are welcome in the social context and can, therefore, be mentalised and acknowledged, and what emotions are forbidden and discouraged? Does this sickness emerge as a response to all ecosystemic layers of complexity, rather than just being an individual sign of weakness?

Pause and Reflect

- What are the main cultural values that help or hinder childhood mental health?
- How does your culture of origin influence your counselling style?

The outer system is the domain where power, belonging, and difference are negotiated, and the time system (the "why now") adds another dimension. Compare the influence of English political or religious values in the Middle Ages with today, where democracy is the norm and religion has a shrinking political influence. Conversely, in areas like sub-Saharan Africa, religiosity has grown dramatically. Gay rights, civil rights, and women's rights, each affected by religious and political values, show themselves in the family home and in the child's emotions. Hence, the proportion of children with trauma, depression, anxiety, and anger problems changes according to the time-bound cultural context in which they live. When is religion resourceful and when is it restraining? How does social pressure motivate a 10-year-old or provoke anxiety in a 16-year-old?

Time reminds us that no culture is fixed. Together, the two systems ask the counsellor to think dynamically, to see the child as part of an ever-changing network of relationships that extends way beyond the family, out to the far reaches of society and forward through time. Gregory Bateson thought that mind itself was an ecology. That our experience owes itself to the interwoven fabric of our society. Thinking this way, he said, requires a certain kind of openness and curiosity about how meanings are produced in different contexts. Further developments in systemic thinking also highlight the importance of life cycle transitions that happen at individual, family, and cultural levels. According to this perspective, culture itself is a living entity going through different stages, from birth to cultural maturity, towards decline and, at some point, transformation into new social forms.

Counselling theories model the cultural association between a child's issue, developmental stage, and life cycle. From an ecosystemic perspective, we encourage counsellors to integrate these three levels by "zooming out" to understand the point at which the child's issue intersects with family and cultural demands. When a child says, "I hate school," the ecosystemic counsellor doesn't rush to interpret them. Instead, we wonder: What is the story of "school" in this child's world? How does it sound at home, amongst friends, and in the body? What expectations or inequalities are carried in that single word? The answer isn't located in the child alone and is found in the intersection between ecosystems.

Ecosystemic counselling begins in one system and flexibly shifts to another. A 12-year-old describes a tightness in her chest before school (inner system). Asked about what happens next, she mentions the shouting at breakfast (family system). As she talks about the dread of entering the classroom, she recalls comments about her accent and the way she tries to sound "more British" (outer system). The ecosystemic counsellor combines the different levels of change into one model. Our idea is that the body is at the centre of family life and that the family forms out of a shifting culture. Nearly every change in one area affects the others. Thus, a counsellor does not aim to master this complexity, let alone change it or correct it, but to stay in dialogue with it. By holding the outer and the temporal dimensions of a child's world, we come closer to the lived truth of human development, that identity is co-created with others, and that experience depends on social life.

The Outer System in Practice

Michael White, one of the pioneers of narrative theory, says that to understand the child in the outer system is to see them as a participant in multiple, overlapping social worlds. Each world has its own rules or "narratives" about who belongs and who does not, what counts as success, what earns shame, and how emotion is displayed. These worlds, through conversation and social feedback, form the social architecture of a child's daily life. When we work ecosystemically, we are interested not only in how the child navigates these structures but also in how the structures themselves sustain or restrict their wellbeing.

Seeing the Social Field

One of the first tasks in outer-system counselling is to map the social world. The counsellor helps the young person describe their unique world in concrete terms: Who or what matters? Where do they spend time? What happens in those spaces? We listen for patterns of connection and disconnection, which are the hidden forces that shape belonging. One way of doing this is to ask the child to draw their world, such as a classroom, a lunch table, or a playground. Each line within the drawing becomes infused with social meaning. Who sits close? Who is missing? Who holds the power to include or exclude? Through these small acts of mapping, we begin to see the structure of the outer system as the child encounters it.

Take, for example, a child who is asked to draw their experience of school. Figure 11.1 below is an example. What kind of social world is communicated in this drawing? How would you respond to it as the counsellor?

The child was referred for "disruptive behaviour." Teachers reported that she shouted out, left her seat, and refused to follow instructions. In the first session, she described herself as "the bad one." Using small figures, we invited her to build her classroom.

Figure 11.1 A digital replication of a child's drawing.

She placed her own figure at the edge of the group, near the door, explaining that she sat there because she was "too loud" and "the teacher doesn't like noise." When asked what it felt like to be sat away from others, she said, "Like everyone's looking at me and laughing all the time." The problem shifted from an internal trait to an ecological one. The difficulty was not defiance but one of exclusion. We asked her to go deeper into the activity and to draw her experience (Figure 11.1). The drawing holds traces of the child's inner world, but her social environment is depicted richly, too. There's a panicky sense of overwhelm with the wide, worrisome eyes, overstretched, upturned mouth, scattered teardrops, and a tension between a faceless group of teacher-like figures and a mocking crowd of children. To explore the outer world, we make use of:

Circular Questions

"If your sadness could talk to your classmates, what would it say?"

"Who is best at understanding when you are sad without having to talk?"

Story Building
Invite the child to give the face a name, a story, and a social world. Ask who this character meets during the day at school, on the playground, and in their neighbourhood.

Role Reversal and Perspective Taking
Encourage the child to speak from the point of view of someone in their outer system, such as a teacher or classmate, looking at her crying face.

The approach here is that social problems are often mislabelled as individual problems. By making the social world visible, counsellors help children and adults see behaviour as communication, a signal about the state of the environment, rather than a defect in the child.

Michael White and David Epston argue that labels like "behaviour problem" cause a stigma and a rather corrosive one at that, because behaviourist language finds fault with the child's actions. Having discovered that behaviour change is possible by, in Skinner's words, "reconditioning" the child in the classroom, White and Epston argue that this construction reinforces social divisions. Locating a child's problem within themselves and branding it as a behavioural issue unfairly perpetuates pre-existing power dynamics and the elements of social injustice and marginalisation that lie underneath. For example, it is convenient for upper-class and middle-class people to stereotype working-class people's behaviour as "wrong" or "dysregulated," because this masks the inequality that the "wrong" behaviour communicates – ensuring that the best chances of academic success remain in the same hands.

Arguably, an explanation for a behaviour often conveys at least as much information about the speaker as it does about the behaviour itself. While it is true that attention to the child's disruptive or anxious behaviour can support a change, the "fact" of change can be modelled in a variety of ways. In ecosystemic counselling, we take the narrative view that we ought to question when our model is a form of social control. Asking circular questions, building stories with the child, or inviting them to take different perspectives are attempts to make changes in behaviour by reflecting on the social context in which that behaviour makes sense. As Peter Lang said, "Every problem is a frustrated dream." What is the frustrated dream behind the child's exclusion behaviour?

Embracing key elements of the narrative approach within an ecosystemic framework helps the counsellor get rid of the stigma associated with some of the inner-world models. As discussed in Chapter 6, we are curious about the power held by those who are allowed to tell the story and be heard. Social institutions such as school are amongst the most powerful narrators of a child's identity; most often, their voice is louder and more authoritative than the child's voice itself. Some children are affirmed by the school process, while others are pathologised by it. Asking the child, "If your sadness could talk to your classmates, what would it say?" allows the child to perceive and process the possible disadvantage they experience in the classroom. We are less interested in helping children idealise false responses from classmates and are more focused on helping the child articulate their authentic social experience.

Pause and Reflect

- What other aspects of identity influence the child's peer group?
- How would you respond, ecosystemically, to a child who feels they don't fit in?

Think Process, Not (Only) Content

The tools of ecosystemic counselling are the same as those in general counselling with children and young people. We encourage you to use drawing, figures, puppets, sandtrays, talking therapies, drama, sculpting, empty chair work, and a whole host of engaging and therapeutic resources. Our model differs simply by situating those traditional tools within an integrated theory. While the sandtray might traditionally be projective, communicating the unconscious attachment system, for example, it equally communicates family and culture, such as social norms around education and intimacy. Traditional models simply miss the opportunity to widen the lens in therapy.

Take Haniya, aged 12, who said in her third session, something like, "They [classmates] think I'm quiet, but I'm just tired." Our technical response, as in what activity we do with this statement, is a matter of low priority. We could repeat this back in a child-centred way, "Your classmates think that you're being quiet, but really you're just tired?" She might begin to describe more details, and we follow her thought process, paying close attention to the social aspects like her beliefs and values, her relationships, and the meaning of emotive words and phrases. But we could have taken a different approach. For example, we could have role-played the classroom scenery and narrated the thoughts in her mind and those projected onto her classmates. Either way, the content and technique involved are likely to end up in the same process. We move in the same direction towards the social aspects like her beliefs and values, her relationships, and the meaning of emotive words and phrases.

"Content" refers to what is talked about and the method of talking or playing, whereas "process" refers to how the content is talked about or played with. Hence, the child could talk about school, home, or the last meal they ate (content) but each time they do so in a low tone of voice with a lack of self-belief (process). They could draw their family, populate a sandtray with figures representing teachers and peers, or play with dough autonomously and confidently, or, on the contrary, they could engage in these activities hesitantly and constantly looking for the counsellor's guidance and reassurance.

Ecosystemic counselling encourages you to pay attention not only to the outcome of any conversation or activity (the content) but also to the patterns, dynamics, emotions, and relational exchanges occurring in the moment (the process). This rests on the assumption that the process gives you the living experience of the client's social patterns, not just the story about them. As a result, it doesn't always matter if we select a drawing or a sandtray. Probably

Figure 11.2 A drawing of two contexts.

the most effective way is to ask the child, to allow their organic way of languaging or depicting their world to come forth. Let's revisit the "quiet" child's situation above, imagining that Haniya likes to draw. Using drawing, she creates two scenes: one of herself in class, surrounded by speech bubbles filled with noise; the other of herself at home, listening to the sound of prayer (Figure 11.2).

The drawing reveals that Haniya is navigating the norms of a British secondary school while adhering to family values rooted in Pakistani culture. In the counselling space, she begins to explore what quietness means to her. It isn't passivity but a form of self-protection. Her drawings illustrate that her feelings about quietness are context-dependent, a skill in one environment, a burden in another. The counsellor helps her build language for this complexity, so that quietness becomes a choice. Sometimes we work within the context and can help schools or other systems reflect on the meaning of the child's behaviour, but typically we have no influence on the context, only the child's sense making and responses.

Peer work involves strengthening the child's sense of agency in social systems they cannot fully control. We help them identify allies, recognise moments of micro-connection, and rehearse small acts of authenticity. It may be as simple as naming one teacher or friend who "gets them," or scripting a sentence they can use when boundaries are crossed. Each act supports self-esteem within the social world. But challenging the "Quietness is Weird" label is a political action as well as a therapeutic one for Haniya.

Pause and Reflect

- How are politics involved in Haniya's relationship with quietness?
- In what ways can counselling help to alleviate some of the negative consequences of social disadvantage?

Power, Culture, and the Wider Environment

As we have seen, the outer system is never culturally neutral. John Burnham and Alison Roper-Hall's social GGRRAACCEESS remind us that gender, race, age, class, ethnicity, and sexual orientation continually shape access to safety and belonging. These dimensions of identity are not abstract categories but are lived realities that influence how children behave and how others interpret their behaviour. Ecosystemic counselling demands cultural reflexivity, which is an awareness of our own position as counsellors and of the power we hold in naming or not naming difference. The systems theorist, Heinz Von Forester, named this "second-order" positioning – we see ourselves as part of the system.

For instance, when working with a child from a global minority background, the counsellor may sense hesitation in speaking about discrimination. By naming that hesitation, we legitimise the topic, "I notice we haven't talked much about how people at school treat you. Is that something that feels safe to talk about here?" Such invitations shift power by allowing the child to author the conversation about identity on their own terms. When the child's social reality is mirrored without judgement, therapeutic safety deepens. Had we focused on the inner world alone, we would have risked contributing to the power imbalance inherent in our social identities. All presenting problems arise in relation to forms of power and discrimination. A position like this can sound extreme. But can you think of an inner-world issue that would not shift if power and discrimination shifted?

It's important we don't idealise, because we cannot reduce the overpowering social systems in a child's world. But we can help them notice and cope with the effects, which are otherwise unseen. Language makes it so. And the languaging of the social world makes it possible for a child to be empowered by new self-understandings. The child's culture, whether that be linked with class, age, religion, geography, gender, ethnicity, to name a few, also provides resilience. Communities carry rituals, values, and collective narratives that can ground children in belonging even when other systems are unstable. Part of outer-system counselling is to connect the child to cultural sources of strength. We ask, "Who in your community helps you feel most yourself?" or "What traditions or places feel like home to you?" These questions remind the child that identity is not only individual but communal, supported by a network of meanings that stretches beyond the therapy room.

These approaches share one goal, which is to transform invisible systems into visible, malleable ones. Once the child can see the system, they can begin to move within it. This movement, a shift in posture, a new conversation, a change in understanding, is where therapeutic change occurs. And to be consistent, this change happens organically with counselling core principles like empathy and authenticity, but typically those therapeutic positions don't hear or see into the collective social context. The outer system is, therefore, not something we visit occasionally – it's always present, shaping the child's inner and family worlds. By engaging directly with it, counsellors respect the full context of the child's experience and create conditions in which change can extend into the child's everyday life.

The Time System in Practice

When counsellors think about therapeutic change, what they imagine is a difference over time. Erik Erikson observed that the human personality develops through eight stages across the lifespan. Each stage demands that the person reach psychological and social milestones, which we discussed in Chapters 7, 8, and 9. Erikson's individual account of development was made systemic by American sociologist, Evelyn Millis Duvall. She proposed that families similarly change over time in predictable ways. Moving from childrearing to the launching stage, for example, where children are (metaphorically) launched into adulthood, akin to a bird flying the nest for the first time.

When Erikson and Duvall observed how people change, they noticed that failed attempts to move into the next bio, psycho, or social stage create inner-world tension. This implied emotional turmoil arises from developmental delays. If, for example, a couple has a child without transitioning emotionally and behaviourally to being parents, someone, or everyone, in the family system pays the emotional price. It could be that the child gets neglected while the couple maintains its unrealistic levels of intimacy. But more often, in a male-designed society, it's a mother having to negotiate the child's needs for a parent and her partner's need for a mate. And hence the development delay, the tug of war between roles, ends up with a child or a father facing rejection.

As far as the sociologists were concerned, the two models of change missed the bigger picture. Even those who realised the power of Erikson and Duvall's theories couldn't avoid the question of why these developmental delays occur. Bronfenbrenner, to take the most famous example, argued that the explanation for developmental delays lies in historical time. Human evolution and culture force human beings into traditions that, in many cases, resist change. For example, the family history of a father might be that he was rejected as a child. Coupling, therefore, might be an extremely rewarding moment in his life, being able to experience an acceptance beyond what his childhood could offer. But in becoming a father, when his partner's change in role evokes a double sense of rejection, he demands more sexual contact and sinks into depression when intimacy is replaced with parenting.

It is an interesting reflection on the nature of children's psychological issues that most counselling models sidestep the idea of time. Ecosystemic counselling points out that time is the only candidate for a theory of change. Most theories imply time but never quite model it. For example, Carl Rogers believed that counselling clients move from being out of touch (incongruent) with their feelings to being in touch (congruent). Or Sigmund Freud believed that clients move from unconscious drives (ID impulses) to conscious awareness (psychodynamic insight). Time is the foundation of these belief systems but nevertheless remains unnamed. In our model, we say that time itself is an important "world" for exploring. And, to complicate matters further, we must add another dimension of time. This is the course of counselling, the seconds, minutes, and hours within a session, coupled with the arc of time from beginning to end of therapy. We may call this "therapeutic time," the beginnings, middles, and endings of interventions, sessions, and ultimately therapy itself. Ecosystemic counselling involves listening to how the four dimensions of time intersect in the present moment. Let's break those down into clear and usable ideas.

Developmental Time

When we meet a child, we are meeting someone in the middle of becoming themselves. Their capacities for thinking, feeling, and relating are changing from month to month. What looks like regression is sometimes a sign of growth, something like a reorganisation of the self that temporarily unsettles their normal equilibrium. As Erikson suggested, each stage of growth carries its own psychological task: trust, autonomy, competence, and identity. These tasks are ongoing dialogues between the self and the world.

For example, a 14-year-old who begins to reject parental guidance may not be "defiant" but simply working on the important task of autonomy. The counsellor's role is to hold this process with compassion, helping the child understand that conflict can be developmental. Similarly, younger children who re-enact themes of safety and danger in play are often revisiting the earliest task of trust. When we track development through time, we begin to see behaviour as an intelligent response to the demands of growth. A recent case example illustrates this view. A mother was estranged from her eight-year-old daughter and came to family therapy to rekindle their relationship. The child, seeing the mother for the first time in many months, began sucking her thumb and speaking babyish. Uncomfortable with the child's regression, the mother became strict about sitting up and speaking age-appropriately. We supported the mother to see the behaviour less as defiance but as a return to an earlier need for safety and to respond with reassurance and attunement rather than correction. After a very short while, the child naturally grew up in the room and acted her age.

Practical techniques help bring this temporal perspective into focus. Timelining is one such tool because it allows the child to map their life visually, locating memories, transitions, and emotional peaks along a line or spiral. The counsellor invites the child to add symbols or drawings for significant events, a move, a friendship, a loss, or a new sibling. As they do, patterns emerge. They may notice clusters of change or recurring feelings that resurface at certain ages. The example in Figure 11.3 can help to reflect on the effective simplicity of timelining.

In the session with Zofia, aged 15 and suffering from panic attacks, we laid out a long sheet of paper and asked, "What are the moments you remember, when you think about the time in which the panic entered your life?" Zofia placed a marker at age 12, "Dad left," another at 14, "new school," and a third at 15, saying, "moved house." As she reviews the sequence (Figure 11.3), she notices that "It's always when something big changes." That recognition transforms her narrative because instead of seeing panic as random, she begins to understand it as a signal of transition. The inner

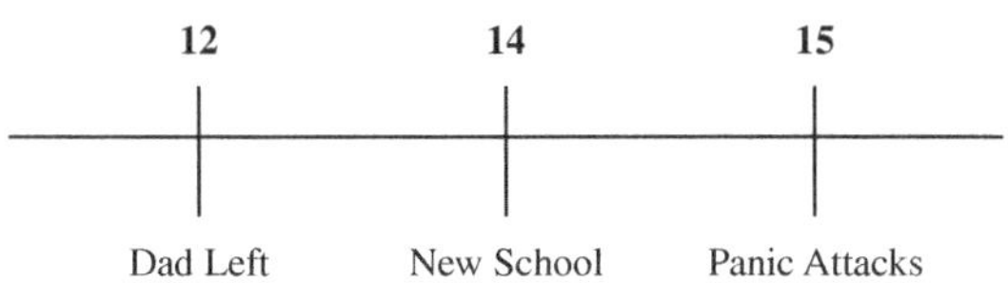

Figure 11.3 Timeline with Zofia.

experience of anxiety, the behaviour of panic – each personal difficulty – is a response to change. Together we explore what helped her cope in earlier transitions and how those strategies could be reactivated now – or how new ways of coping can help in future transitions. Timelining thus turns time from an adversary into an ally, a rich source of insight and continuity. With the regressed child above, we didn't need to use a physical timeline to achieve the same effect – we knew to view the regression as part of the family timeline, and hence we weren't worried about it; we simply helped the family build trust.

Family Time

As the work of Duval and McGoldrick has shown, families also grow and change through predictable stages, such as coupling, childrearing, adolescence, launching, and ageing. At each transition, boundaries and roles are renegotiated invisibly. Problems often arise when the family struggles to keep pace with developmental time. Parents relate to a teenager as if she were a small child, for example. The counsellor listens for these family time-based mismatches, exploring moments when the family's internal clock is out of sync with the child's growth.

Consider Rory, a 12-year-old client. His mother's remarriage and his father's withdrawal placed the family in transition. Rory's stepfather is adjusting to a parenting role he never anticipated. At the same time, his mother is balancing loyalty to her son with the demands of a new partnership. In this context, Rory's irritability and withdrawal are not simply emotional symptoms but signs of untimely disruption. That is, the family has changed faster than its members can emotionally reorganise. An ecosystemic response is to slow the family's time down. The counsellor might use a family timeline, inviting the child to place key events on a line: "When did this story begin?" This exercise often reveals differences in perception; one person's "fresh start" may be another's "ending." When these perspectives are made visible, empathy becomes possible. The child can begin to see that they are all adjusting to the same change but at different speeds.

The counsellor may introduce an activity called *the constellation map*, designed to explore how relationships realign after a major transition. The child or young person is invited to draw a set of circles and to place the people in their lives according to how close or distant they feel at present. Using different colours or shading for "before" and "after," we can make invisible shifts visible, such as a parent who has moved inward, a stepsibling hovering on the edge, or a once-central figure now feeling remote. The purpose is not to assign blame or repair bonds on the spot but to make relationship changes explicit. Seeing these constellations side by side invites empathy, allowing the child to understand the family time's process of adjustment. In this way, mapping becomes a bridge for helping the child slow down, recognise the patterns that change creates, and find language for the pull of connection they are still navigating (see Figure 11.4).

This example of the constellation map (Figure 11.4) allows Rory and his mother to notice that his father has become more distant during the transition. We can explore how the child wants the future family constellation to look, but equally we can make sense of the impact of time and change on the child's current presenting issues. Visualising time allows young people to perceive change from a concrete perspective, and the counsellor can

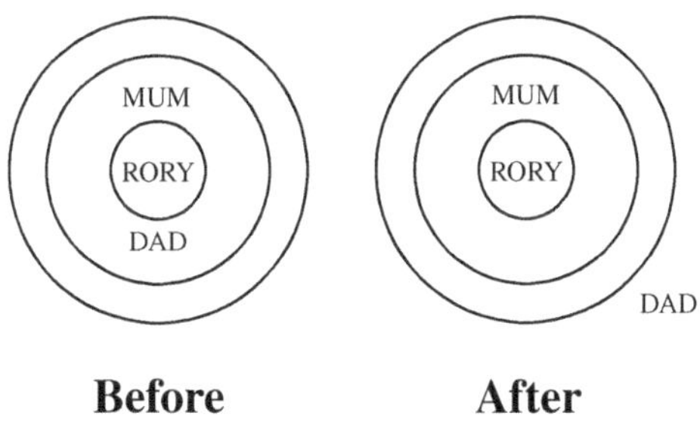

Figure 11.4 The constellation map.

creatively add to the map thoughts, feelings, social contexts, and other expressions of the child's ecosystem.

Historical Time

Historical time lies beyond the immediate household. It represents the transgenerational patterns and cultural histories that shape family life. Some families carry legacies of migration, loss, or trauma that influence how they manage emotion and connection. As John Byng-Hall reminds us, some families inherit powerful family scripts about gender, duty, or resilience that dictate who is allowed to need help, who is expected to help, and who must carry their own burden without asking for support. Each one of these scripts is influenced by the decade and century in which it exists.

When ecosystemic counsellors explore the child's feelings and stories, we want to make the connection between the past and present. The therapist asks, "Who in your family taught you how to handle anger?" or "When someone in your family feels sad, what usually happens?" Such questions open doors to the past, allowing the child to locate themselves in a lineage of coping styles and beliefs. Ryan's family, for example, had a history of conflict avoidance. His grandmother, who emigrated during political unrest, had once told his mother, "We don't talk about pain, we survive it." In therapy, Ryan realised that his habit of smiling through distress was part of that legacy. Recognising this didn't destroy the pattern, but it gave him a choice. He could appreciate his grandmother's strength while also developing a new emotional language.

These conversations link naturally to creative mapping tools like genograms or family scripts. By diagramming relationships across generations, the child and counsellor identify recurring themes of caretaking, absence, secrecy, and endurance. Seeing these patterns externalised allows the child to hold compassion for their family while loosening the grip of inherited expectations. As a reminder of Gregory Bateson's view on this, recognising the *pattern that connects* can allow the counsellor to bring *news of difference* in the therapy room – thus offering the possibility of seeing the old story from a new angle. This is what makes change possible, as new perspectives allow for new stories to be voiced, with brand new emotions suddenly emerging and new thoughts and behaviour becoming possible.

Pause and Reflect

- What social inheritance is useful for a child's wellbeing, and what is hurtful to it?
- What family scripts have influenced your choice of becoming a counsellor?

Therapeutic Time: Beginnings, Middles, and Endings

When the outer and time systems are held together, the work becomes more than symptom relief. The child begins to experience what Michael White calls narrative coherence, the sense that their feelings, relationships, and history belong to the same story. Within the counselling relationship, we recognise that time has its own life. Each session, and the overall journey, moves through phases of contact, exploration, and separation. Children and young people often live intensely in the present, and so endings can feel abrupt or confusing unless they are prepared for and ritualised. The counsellor's awareness of therapeutic time helps transform closure from loss into growth.

Rituals are especially useful here. They provide structure and meaning to transitions, mirroring the rhythms of family and cultural life. A simple ritual might involve revisiting the first drawing or map made in early sessions, noting what has changed. Some counsellors create a "growth timeline" of the therapy itself, marking key insights or turning points. Others use routine outcome measures (ROMs) to map changes. These acts consolidate learning and reinforce the idea that endings are part of an ongoing

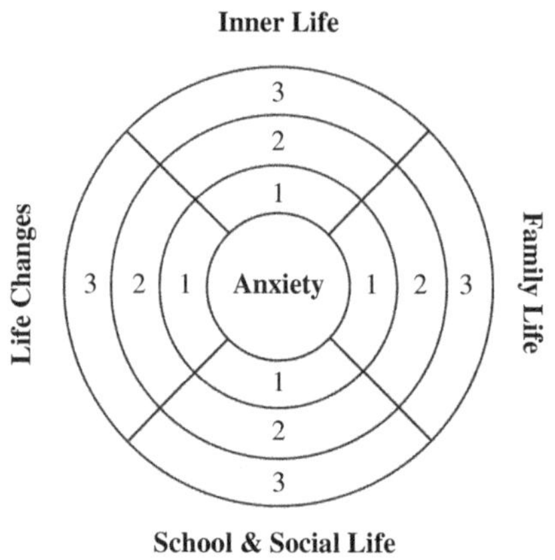

Figure 11.5 The child ecosystem measure.

story. A simple example of an ecosystemic ROM is to write the child's presenting problem, as they name it, in the centre of a circle. This could be "low mood" or "anxiety," for example. Then create a spectrum with the four ecosystemic layers from 1–3 (or 1–6 or 1–10), meaning that the child can explore with you how each layer contributes to the problem (Figure 11.5).

Therapeutic time involves monitoring psychological progress, and the child ecosystem measure (CEM) allows you to track change over time, ideally moving towards lower levels of the presenting problem. Working with time reminds us that no single session completes a process because change unfolds at the speed of their family and social relationships. The child's growth, the family's adaptation, the system's flexibility ... all of these evolve gradually and invisibly. Our role is to mark progress, however subtle, and to ensure that each layer of time supports the others rather than competes with them.

A session might begin in the body, travel through a family memory, touch a classroom conflict, and end in a reflection about growing up. Ecosystemic thinking reminds us that behaviour is circular because one action triggers another until the loop either stabilises or escalates. We needn't hold in mind every layer of the ecosystem and every dimension of time. But our advice is to be open to the four ecosystemic layers and the four dimensions of time, allowing the child to lead you in the direction that best suits their needs.

Conclusion

The beginning of ecosystemic counselling is, of course, not a set of compartments but a way of thinking. According to a number of early theorists and the counselling tradition, the child's problem is explained by emotion, behaviour, or self-image. Other traditions argue that the child's problem derives from family feuds or history. And yet others focus on the role of society in socialising the child into the problem. Our approach takes each view seriously and reclaims these fragmented viewpoints to create a bigger picture.

When we attend to the child's inner life, we are already touching the family patterns that formed it. When we work with family patterns, we are already sensing the wider systems that sustain or challenge them. And when we widen the lens to the social world or the passage of time, we are still in contact with the small, living moments of feeling that give therapy its depth. The ecosystemic model of children and young people's counselling is, therefore, the counsellor's ongoing act of translation between different scales of human life (see Figure 11.6).

In fitting this picture together, we begin with our therapeutic presence. The counsellor listens deeply to what the child says and to where each experience belongs in their systems. We believe that a gesture may speak of family allegiance, a silence may carry the weight of a discriminatory culture, and a glance at the clock may tell of time running too fast. We treat each detail as a doorway towards understanding and supporting the child's development. Working ecosystemically teaches humility about our therapeutic influence. We do not see ourselves as changing children, as such. We are, however, fully aware of the power we hold in influencing a change in trajectory, which begs the question about how we use this power to promote individual wellbeing and a broader culture of inclusion and social justice.

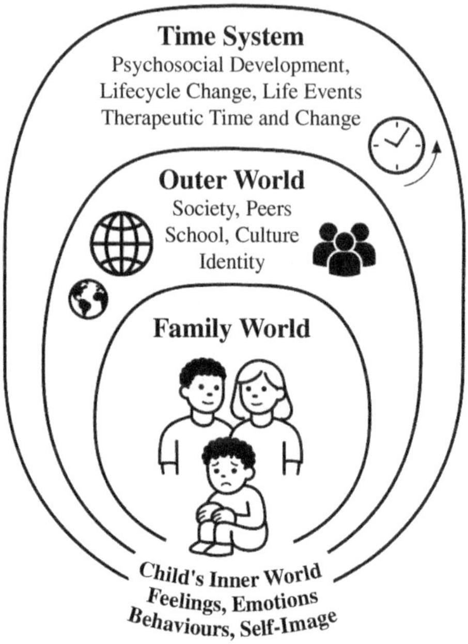

Figure 11.6 The ecosystemic model with children and young people.

Rather than sitting on our chairs, distancing ourselves from our clients under the cloak of our "expert neutrality," we involve ourselves with curiosity, and we participate in changes that are already trying to happen. We are mindful that, even when working with the child alone in the room, a shift in one part of the system often releases movement elsewhere. A child who feels valued by the therapist creates a new self-image and new social habits, which reverberate across the family, bringing the possibility for a new narrative about "us" (the family) and "them" (the other agencies and individuals that constitute the outer system). A child who gains confidence and starts to do well academically can reconcile the family system with the school system and promote integration. The counsellor's skill lies in noticing where the system is ready to move and offering just enough support for that motion to take hold.

The ecosystemic perspective, therefore, offers not only a method but a philosophy of change. It reminds us that systems, like living organisms, move towards balance when conditions allow. Our responsibility is to co-create those conditions, which are safety, curiosity, reflection, and dialogue. From there, change takes its own course, and the child grows, the family adapts, and the world imperceptibly shifts a little around them. And the ecosystemic counsellor, having witnessed this broader change between the client and their environment, understands that healing is not a single act but an unfolding relationship between all the systems that sustain the child's life.

Chapter 11: Summary

Key Ideas

- A child's difficulties are shaped not only by inner life and family patterns but by the wider social worlds and historical moment in which they are growing up. Identity is co-created in classrooms, peer groups, communities, and cultures over time.
- Culture and social narratives influence what emotions are welcomed, silenced, or turned into bodily distress. Emotional expression is always socially patterned.
- Time is an active dimension of change. Developmental stages, family life cycle transitions, historical legacies, and the flow of therapy itself all shape how problems emerge and transform.

Practice Implications

- Map the child's social world concretely. Drawings, figures, stories, and role-play help make patterns of inclusion, exclusion, and power visible so behaviour can be understood relationally.
- Work with process as much as content. Notice tone, posture, hesitations, and relational dynamics in the room as live expressions of the child's social positioning.
- Bring time into the room through tools like timelines, family transition maps, and genograms. These help children recognise

patterns of change, loss, and growth across their lives and generations.

- Attend to therapeutic time. Prepare for beginnings, middles, and endings; use rituals and measures to consolidate learning and support the child in integrating change into their wider systems.

Reflective Prompts

- When a child presents with "behaviour" or "anxiety," how do you explore the outer world that gives that experience meaning?
- Which aspects of identity and power are easiest for you to notice – and which do you tend to overlook?
- How comfortable are you working with time explicitly, linking present distress to developmental, family, and historical transitions?
- In your practice, how do you mark therapeutic endings so change can travel beyond the counselling room?

Bibliography

Ainsworth, M.D.S., Blehar, M.C., Waters, E. et al. (1978). *Patterns of Attachment: A Psychological Study of the Strange Situation*. Lawrence Erlbaum.

Bateson, G. (1972). *Steps to an Ecology of Mind*. Chandler.

Beck, J.S. (2011). *Cognitive Behavior Therapy: Basics and Beyond*, 2e. Guilford Press.

Bronfenbrenner, U. (1979). *The Ecology of Human Development: Experiments by Nature and Design*. Harvard University Press.

Carter, B. and McGoldrick, M. (1989). *The Changing Family Life Cycle: A Framework for Family Therapy*, 2e. Allyn & Bacon.

Epston, D. and White, M. (1990). *Narrative means to Therapeutic Ends*. Norton.

Erikson, E.H. (1963). *Childhood and Society*, 2e. Norton.

Freud, S. (1917/1957). *Introductory Lectures on Psycho-analysis*. Hogarth Press.

Gendlin, E.T. (1962). *Experiencing and the Creation of Meaning*. Free Press.

Gendlin, E.T. (1996). *Focusing-oriented Psychotherapy: A Manual of the Experiential Method*. Guilford Press.

Haley, J. (1976). *Problem-solving Therapy*. Jossey-Bass.

Hoffman, L. (1981). *Foundations of Family Therapy: A Conceptual Framework for Systems Change*. Basic Books.
Lambert, M.J. and Ogles, B.M. (2004). The efficacy and effectiveness of psychotherapy. In: *Bergin and Garfield's Handbook of Psychotherapy and Behavior Change*, 5e (ed. M.J. Lambert), 139–193. Wiley.
Minuchin, S. (1974). *Families and Family Therapy*. Harvard University Press.
Rogers, C.R. (1951). *Client-centered Therapy: Its Current Practice, Implications and Theory*. Houghton Mifflin.
Watzlawick, P., Beavin, J.H., and Jackson, D.D. (1967). *Pragmatics of Human Communication*. Norton.
White, M. (2007). *Maps of Narrative Practice*. Norton.
Yalom, I.D. (2002). *The Gift of Therapy*. HarperCollins.

Chapter 12
Bringing the Ecosystemic Model to Life
By Abbie Franklin

My name is Abbie Franklin, and I'm a children and young people's counsellor. I trained in the ecosystemic approach, and the authors have asked me to write a concluding chapter, discussing my work with young people's sexual orientation. I want to show how the ecosystemic model fits with identity counselling. Whilst this is a single case study about sexual orientation, my counselling process can help young people with any aspect of social identity. The aim in this chapter is to illustrate how inner experience, family relationships, peer relationships, and the wider social context intersect in identity development, and how ecosystemic counselling helps young people make sense of themselves within those overlapping worlds.

Identity is one's sense of self, defined by a range of social roles and by physical and psychological characteristics. Being able to make sense of our identity and fully engage with it, along with a sense of continuity, can foster positive wellbeing. During Erikson's developmental stage of identity, occurring during adolescence, individuals are trying to find where they fit in their wider social system, aligning their inner world with their outer world. Erikson would argue that difficulty in this stage can lead to social isolation and can have negative implications in adulthood, especially due to a lack of a sense of self.

When a young person enters the counselling room, they are experiencing a process of becoming themselves. One identity aspect can involve figuring out one's sexual orientation. This is a Social Grace that is discovered throughout time. How adolescents experience questions of sexual orientation within their inner world is influenced by family beliefs and the attitudes in the outside world. Particularly thinking about young people who identify with nonheterosexual identities, discrimination and stigma arise from the outer system. Minority stress theory says that young people are trying to figure out where they belong, who they belong with, and stigmatising messages from their environment create levels of chronic stress. This often leads to the concealment of homosexuality, preventing them from self-expression and from receiving support from the LGBTQIA+ community. For those unfamiliar with this acronym, it stands for Lesbian, Gay, Bisexual, Transgender, Queer (or Questioning), Intersex, and Asexual, with the plus sign (+) representing additional sexual orientations and gender identities not specifically listed.

As an ecosystemic counsellor with children and young people, one way in which I work alongside clients is supporting them to make sense of their identity across their systems. I want to take you through a session I had with Tom, aged 14, who self-referred to school counselling due to struggling with feelings around his sexual orientation. As Tom and I explored what had brought him to counselling, I widened our focus to consider how these feelings were shaped across the different systems in his life:

Counsellor: I wondered if we could explore your identity in different systems and contexts across your life.

I provided Tom with the CEM, shown in Chapter 11. I asked him to consider how each system influences his feelings about his sexual orientation. Exploring Tom's inner system first was not because this is the first level, more that I followed Tom's natural conversation – which began in the body:

Tom:	Whenever relationships come into conversation, I get this sinking feeling in my stomach and start feeling really sick. I feel really exposed like everyone is looking at me, and I feel really uncomfortable in myself.
Counsellor:	Where does the uncomfortable feeling sit in your body?
Tom:	Mostly in my stomach, but also I guess I get really fidgety, and my legs just want to move me out of the situation. I don't feel comfortable or relaxed until I am out of the conversation.

Tom is exploring his inner world by tuning into bodily sensations when he is worried about discussing relationships. Asking him to locate the feeling in the body helps him connect more deeply with the way mind and body are connected. For Tom, discrimination and stigma are not merely a matter of principles; they reside in the body and make the body respond to situations in a way that reinforces the stigma's self-perpetuating cycle. Feeling sick, Tom is also painfully aware of how this exposes him and withdraws even further.

I use active listening to stay with the inner system. Usually, the client organically speaks about other systems, especially in cases such as this one, where the other systems are directly involved in the problem. My job is, therefore, to move with Tom's exploration, ensuring the space between us remains safe, free from judgement, and open enough to allow even the most uncomfortable conversations to happen – if the client so wishes. As our conversation moves forward, Tom transitions into reflecting on his family system:

Tom:	I have always felt like the abnormal one in my family. My siblings are straight and have it all figured out with their partners, and I am just out here not really knowing who I am. I worry that when I get older, my parents will start asking loads of questions about why

I have never been in a relationship. How can I tell them I am gay? That's not what they wanted for me in life.

Tom's family script about sexual orientation appears to be heteronormative, with relationships other than those between men and women being uncommon. "Uncommon," in Tom's meaning-making process, translates directly into "not normal," and "not normal" into "unacceptable." From a CMM perspective, it seems that, for Tom, remaining authentic and embracing his true self feels incompatible with maintaining a positive relationship with his family. This traps him in a strange loop with no way out, where each attempt to be himself confirms the fear of rejection, and that fear then reinforces the belief that he must hide who he is. Tom's meaning making is deeply embedded within the cultural and social pressures that he and his family have been subjected to, which currently reverberate through their interactions. Tom might be conflicted between cultural values from the LGBTQIA+ community and other supporting groups, which he would feel spontaneously aligned with, and, on the other hand, deeply ingrained perceptions about what it means to be a good son, putting family first and respecting parents in a heteronormative, traditional way.

As a result, Tom might feel weak and cowardly for not being able to embrace his true identity, feeling tortured about the idea of "coming out." He perceives that being gay could inflict a painful wound on his parents and bring disgrace to the family. With this complexity in mind, I decided to gently bring this up with Tom:

Counsellor: It sounds like you feel quite different to the "standard" in your immediate family. And this is mixed with feelings of not being sure whether they will accept you for who you are.

Tom: Yes, you're right. As you say, I am realising that maybe it is not about my family disliking gay people, it's just that heterosexuality is all they have known. I actually don't know anyone else who is gay or bisexual in my family.

Tom is making sense of his family script, where it has come from, and how it could be changed through his homosexuality, ultimately shifting the way he views himself. My role here is to explore with Tom the meaning of the script, how helpful or unhelpful it may be, and his role in this script, whether static or changing. Judgement in the family explains why Tom has a sickness in his stomach – it's the body's alarm signal for hiding from a discriminatory family belief. This is a typical situation where counsellors may trap themselves within a binary dilemma, where our desire to remove the stigma from our client might (perhaps unconsciously) translate into judgement towards the family. Ecosystemic counselling encourages professionals to break the vicious blame-game cycle in which one member or the other is scapegoated. Instead of using our authority as experts to redefine who is to blame (e.g. not Tom but his parents), we regain our stance of curiosity, acknowledging how the family is significant in how identity is expressed or oppressed but also that the family members may be victims of the same oppressive discourse. We, therefore, connect the family story to the wider social stigma, highlighting tension between the family itself and the broader cultural environment. No family is an island, and, moving forward into discussing Tom's outer system, we help him to process the wider social context embedded in his anxiety:

Tom: My friends are the only people I am "out" to. But I can't help but feel like I don't fit in with them. I don't think they get it. It almost feels like they are stepping on eggshells with me, and don't want to say the wrong thing. Since telling them, it has definitely created an uncomfortable dynamic, which I hate.

Counsellor: It sounds like you're navigating a tricky situation with conflicting feelings. If your friends were here in this room and heard what you just said, what do you think they would say and feel?

Tom: Hmmm, that's an interesting question. I think they would say that they don't want me to feel like that and don't actually see me any differently – in a good way. I just feel so worried about talking about it all the time.

This is an example of using circular questions to explore Tom's outer system. At the same time, from a person-centred position of unconditional acceptance, we support the client to be more deeply in touch with his own feelings. The fusion of empathy and circular questions encourages the client to become a compassionate outside-observer of his own world. Other people's feelings and thoughts, family dynamics and social interactions, and the counsellor's felt responses, each of these new territories is made available by circular questioning. Instead of seeking the client's agreement or correcting thoughts or feelings, circular questions invite the client to look in new directions and think systemically. The effect on Tom is that he is starting to make sense of how his inner world intertwines with his outer system – how his feelings about sexual orientation are intimately connected with the four layers of his ecosystem.

As discussed in previous chapters, there are multiple ways in which the child's behaviour and bodily responses display these mutual influences. Children who feel constantly sick despite not having medical issues are often unaware of how sickness signals something social. Helping counselling clients think about identity in relation to family and the body is an effective way to reduce anxiety, low mood, or presenting issues more generally. In Tom's case, ecosystemic counselling in the context of his sexual orientation can lead to identity integration and empower him. Being able to recognise how his sickness is literally a visceral response to social restrictions about being gay, Tom said in his next session that he managed to "come out" to his mum. We celebrated this moment together and reflected on the experience. Tom felt confident in his identity. While the therapeutic goal wasn't to support Tom to come out to anyone specifically, counselling strengthened his identity, and this allowed him to share with others. This case study demonstrates the power of talking about sexual orientation directly and making sense of identity across different ecosystems.

Tom's situation illustrates that identity counselling with children and young people can be approached in a structured yet flexible way. Although every young person's journey is unique, the ecosystemic approach offers a set of guiding steps that help counsellors remain curious and collaborative. I have spoken about sexual orientation, but these steps can be applied to any identity work. Let's review the steps below.

1. Begin Where the Young Person Begins
   Ecosystemic counselling always follows the client's lead. Some young people will start with their feelings, others with their family, their friendships, or their worries about school and society. The first step is, therefore, to listen carefully and notice which system the young person naturally brings forward. In Tom's case, the work began with bodily sensations – the sinking feeling in his stomach and the urge to escape difficult conversations. Starting where the client starts communicates respect and builds safety.
2. Map the Systems Together
   Although we convey acceptance and respect towards our clients and we embrace their perspective on their human situation, as ecosystemic counsellors, we do not end where the client ends. We believe that a stance of curiosity is necessary to cross the borders of our client's immediate experience to venture into the uncharted territory of what this experience means and stands for. And, in this journey of curiosity, we take our client with us, sharing the responsibility of meaning making in an ongoing process of shifting leadership, where we both get to be the expert at some point. For instance, using a tool such as the CEM enables the young person to visualise the different parts of their world and how they are interconnected. Or, through the Daisy model, discussed in Chapter 6, we look at who is absent from the room but extremely influential in the client's emotions and values.

   The counsellor and client explore the inner system (thoughts, feelings, and body), the family system, the peer system, and the wider cultural and social systems. Mapping helps children begin to see how experiences in one system connect with another, and their early confusion about their problem often turns into understanding.

3. Attend to Body Awareness
   Identity struggles frequently show themselves first in the body. Anxiety, shame, and fear are carried physically, long before they can be put into words. Helping young people to notice and name bodily responses is, therefore, a central part of change. By asking Tom where his discomfort sat in his body, the counselling made his experience visible and meaningful rather than mysterious and overwhelming. Body awareness grounds the work and allows emotional experiences to be processed safely. It also constitutes the first step towards a reframing of the problem. When Tom attends counselling for the first time, his sickness is something undesirable, an enemy residing within his own body. Exploring the embodied problem through dialogue and meaningful co-construction meant that Tom saw his sickness differently, being curious about the message it carries. In some ways, his process resembles what we have seen in the movie "The Sixth Sense." When the child, guided by me as his therapist, stops running away from ghosts, he becomes interested in what they have to say (except this time the counsellor is alive, of course!).
4. Use Person-Centred Presence and Curiosity
   Throughout the process, the counsellor offers empathy, unconditional positive regard, and authenticity. These person-centred qualities create the relational conditions in which identity can be explored without fear of judgement. For many young people questioning their sexual orientation, or any aspect of identity, counselling may be the first place they feel fully heard. Change begins when the young person experiences themselves as accepted exactly as they are. Curiosity adds an ecosystemic awareness to empathy, accepting the child's perspective while supporting them to adopt multiple viewpoints.
5. Explore Family Scripts and Relationship Patterns
   Family beliefs and expectations play a powerful role in shaping identity. Ecosystemic counselling invites young people to examine these scripts with curiosity rather than blame. Questions about what has been said or unsaid in the family, what is considered "normal," and how these messages have developed

over time help young people understand that family views are learned rather than fixed truths. In Tom's work, recognising his family's heteronormative assumptions allowed him to reinterpret their attitudes and reduce his sense of personal defectiveness. That led him to take a different approach, allowing change to occur in family relationships. Not all families will respond openly to a young person's identity, and, as such, ecosystemic counselling tracks relationship patterns over time, supporting clients with family dynamics.

6. Consider the Wider Social Context
   No identity develops in isolation. Cultural norms, media messages, school environments, and community attitudes all influence how safe a young person feels to be themselves. By discussing the impact of stigma, counsellors help young people locate their difficulties within a broader social picture. This shift from "something is wrong with me" to "I am responding to pressures around me" is often deeply relieving. Tom viewed his friends as walking on eggshells, when it was his own discomfort and anxiety rather than their judgement that accounted for his difficult feelings. Exploring peer dynamics enables clients like Tom to express themselves and engage more openly with friends.
7. Use Narrative Approaches to Reauthor Identity
   As understanding grows, the counsellor supports the young person to tell new stories about themselves. Narrative questions invite alternative meanings: Who sees you differently? What would your friends say about you? When have you felt most like yourself? Through these conversations, problem-saturated stories are gradually deconstructed, understood, and "reauthored." Telling previously unheard or unvoiced stories supports the client's self to become richer and more open to hope and change. Tom moved from a narrative of being "abnormal" to a narrative of being a young person discovering his authentic self. Once this narrative shifted, it was surprisingly easier to be openly gay.
8. Integrate Learning Across Systems
   Finally, the work focuses on helping the young person integrate these new understandings into everyday life. This may involve

trying out conversations with family members, seeking support from peers, or practising ways of caring for the body when anxiety arises. Change is consolidated when insights from the counselling room begin to influence real-world relationships and experiences. Integration requires us to hold the four ecosystems in mind but not to spend equal time in each. Some young people will pursue the required change by focusing on the body, others by exploring social narratives. The ecosystems needn't be discussed in every counselling conversation, but their mutual influence is always present – and progress on one level creates progress in the others.

Concluding Thoughts

Working with identity in children and young people requires sensitivity, creativity, and an appreciation of the many worlds they inhabit. The ecosystemic approach offers a way of holding all these worlds together – inner experience, family relationships, peer connections, and social context – without reducing the young person to any single part. Tom's journey shows that when young people are helped to make sense of themselves across these interconnected systems, they often become more confident, more integrated, and more able to live authentically. The goal of ecosystemic counselling is not to direct identity choices but to create the conditions in which children and young people can safely discover and inhabit who they truly are.

In many respects, our ecosystemic view of counselling aligns with Rogers' values of unconditional acceptance and authenticity. We believe them to be crucial in establishing the therapeutic alliance and the creation of a safe space for clients. However, we also believe that, while our acceptance is unconditional, our approach to their stories is curious and reflexive. We remain curious to understand how those stories reflect the genuine feelings and emotions of our clients; whether such stories free our clients' true selves or trap them in conflicting cages of incompatible beliefs. Our reflexivity is about recognising that we enter the room with our own stories, emotions, embodied perceptions and memories, and we join them in a meaningful dance of co-construction. As a result, ecosystemic counselling is an invitation for counsellors to promote anti-oppressive practice, guided by a deep awareness of our own Social Graces and the ever-changing context in which both our clients and we live. Every client's story deserves to be told, and listened to, and sometimes the counselling room is the only place where such stories can be held safely enough for a young person to begin understanding who they are.

Bibliography

Beck, A.T. (1976). *Cognitive Therapy and the Emotional Disorders*. International Universities Press.

Bronfenbrenner, U. (1979). *The Ecology of Human Development: Experiments by Nature and Design*. Harvard University Press.

Burnham, J. (2012). Developments in social GGRRAAACCEEESSS: visible–invisible and voiced–unvoiced. In: *Culture and Reflexivity in Systemic Psychotherapy* (ed. I-B. Krause), 139–160. Karnac.

Cronen, V.E. and Pearce, W.B. (1985). Toward an explanation of how the Milan method works: an invitation to a systemic epistemology and the evolution of family systems. *Family Process* 24 (1): 13–28.

Erikson, E.H. (1968). *Identity: Youth and Crisis*. Norton.

Gendlin, E.T. (1978). *Focusing*. Everest House.

McGoldrick, M., Carter, B., and Garcia-Preto, N. (2016). *The Expanded Family Life Cycle: Individual, Family, and Social Perspectives*, 5e. Pearson.

Meyer, I.H. (2003). Prejudice, social stress, and mental health in lesbian, gay, and bisexual populations: conceptual issues and research evidence. *Psychological Bulletin* 129 (5): 674–697.

Minuchin, S. (1974). *Families and Family Therapy*. Harvard University Press.

Pearce, W.B. (2007). *Making Social Worlds: A Communication Perspective*. Blackwell.

Rogers, C.R. (1951). *Client-centred Therapy: Its Current Practice, Implications and Theory*. Houghton Mifflin.

Rogers, C.R. (1961). *On becoming a Person*. Houghton Mifflin.

von Foerster, H. (1995). *Cybernetics of Cybernetics*, 2e. Future Systems.

Wampold, B.E. and Imel, Z.E. (2015). *The Great Psychotherapy Debate: The Evidence for What makes Psychotherapy Work*, 2e. Routledge.

White, M. and Epston, D. (1990). *Narrative means to Therapeutic Ends*. Norton.

Afterword

This book has invited counsellors to listen beyond a child's symptoms. Anxiety and depression are powerful emotions that distract attention from the family and social relationships in which they make sense. Each unmanageable feeling or negative intrusive thought expresses culture and relationships through the child's developing body. Without a wide enough lens, childhood problems start to look like deficits. Young people are storied as destructive, selfish, and even attention-seeking – and deficit language hides the systems that surround them. We encourage you to see children's wellbeing as signals within an ecosystem. Much like a word that has no meaning outside a social context, neither does an angry feeling have a meaning outside a family or social norm.

The ecosystemic framework moves from individual fault to a contextual understanding. Moving from a view of childhood disorder and of individual mental health, we find that counselling problems look clearer. While every problem can be described as a fault in the child's regulation system, it seems more explanatory to view the child's regulation as part of family and cultural processes. When a child feels uncontrollable rage, helping them regulate by providing throwable sand or rippable paper lessens the overwhelm. But seeing the rage as a signal of unmet attachment needs or a protest against social exclusion changes how we respond. Regulation still matters, but it is no longer the endpoint. Emotions become the doorway through which we begin to understand what the child's system is trying to communicate. We hear the child's behaviour as a message about relationships that exist beyond the therapy room. When we widen the lens in this way, the counsellor's task shifts. We are not only helping a child calm down; we are helping them make sense of the emotional environments they are living in. Rage, withdrawal, anxiety, or numbness are forms of language. They speak to us about the pressures placed upon a young person as they grow. Seen ecosystemically, the child is not the problem; the child is the place where the problem becomes visible.

The most common therapy approaches already describe each idea in this book. However, they tend to explain alternative theories from disconnected islands. Person-centred and cognitive behavioural therapies, for example, spotlight the child's inner world: Systemic therapy, by contrast, explains that children's problems arise from families; Ecological theories locate presenting issues within society and culture, and childhood development theories position wellbeing as time-bound. Our work has been to extract the therapeutic principles from these ways of working, forming them into a single approach. This is a way of holding complexity without learning each island's counselling language. Readers from different therapy schools are encouraged to recognise their practice within this framework and to let the borders between different models relax. No single approach needs to be abandoned; rather, each can be understood as describing one part of a larger human system.

When these perspectives are held together, theory is no longer disjointed but cooperative, offering a fuller picture of the child in context. Ecosystemic counselling invites readers to look beyond familiar explanations and to trust that children's emotions make sense contextually. It supports a practice that connects inner life with family, culture, and development over time. Seen ecosystemically, counselling contributes to children growing up with a confident sense of themselves and a stronger capacity to navigate the social worlds they are growing into. We hope this book will enrich your therapy practice and contribute to your positive impact on the children and young people with whom you work.

Claire, Elisa, Ferdinando, Matt, and Rick

Index